VISUAL QUICKSTART GUIDE

MACROMEDIA CAPTIVATE

FOR WINDOWS

Tom Green

 Peachpit Press

Visual QuickStart Guide
Macromedia Captivate for Windows
Tom Green

Peachpit Press
1249 Eighth Street
Berkeley, CA 94710
510/524-2178
800/283-9444
510/524-2221 (fax)

Find us on the World Wide Web at: http://www.peachpit.com
To report errors, please send a note to errata@peachpit.com
Published by Peachpit Press in association with Macromedia Press
Peachpit Press is a division of Pearson Education

Macromedia Press Editor: Angela C. Kozlowski
Development Editor: Susan Hobbs
Technical Editor: Rob Williams
Production Coordinator: Simmy Cover
Copyeditor: Emily K. Wolman
Compositors: Jerry Ballew, Christi Payne
Indexer: Ron Strauss
Cover design: The Visual Group

ISBN 0-321-29417-3

9 8 7 6 5 4 3 2 1
Printed and bound in the United States of America

Dedication

This book is dedicated to Keltie, my wife and life partner for the past 30 years, who, finally, has a book dedicated to her.

Acknowledgements

Books of this genre aren't written in smoke-filled garrets by suffering artists. There is a whole team of people behind every author that helps the book move from neural synapses and neurons to the printed page.

First on the list is Linda Harrison, my original editor at New Riders. A tougher editor you would not want to meet, but having worked with her for two years I quickly learned my craft from a master. Along the way, I have gained a dear friend and mentor, which is more than I could have expected when we first met.

Thanks also go to Angela Kozlowski, my Peachpit/Macromedia Press editor. Her wicked sense of humor, attention to detail, and understanding when things were at their roughest are deeply appreciated and also moved this book to a place where I originally thought I could take it.

Susan Hobbs, my development editor, and I have worked together on a previous book. In many respects, Susan taught me how to write these books and there isn't a word on any page of this book, or anything else I write for that matter, where I didn't feel her somehow looking over my shoulder.

Many thanks are also due to Rob Williams, my technical editor. Rob is a former student of mine who is destined for an amazing career in the New Media field. It is always fascinating when the student becomes the teacher and the teacher becomes the student. Thanks, Rob.

There are three people at Macromedia who should also be mentioned. Magnus Nirell, Macromedia's R&D Manager, patiently explained many of the more esoteric features of the application and stoically suffered through a few of my temper tantrums during the Captivate beta. Silke Fleisher, the Captivate Product Manager, introduced me to eLearning and the eLearning process. And I can't forget Suzanne Smith, the Captivate technical writer who helped when I got "stuck" trying to explain some of the more technical aspects of the application. I would also be remiss in not acknowledging the guidance, insight, and exposure to the RoboDemo community provided by Steven Shipe and Larry Walther who, it seems were RoboDemo users from Day One.

Though I went solo on this project, I want to thank former my coauthors, two of the infamous "Three Lost Souls" from the other two books we wrote together. Jordan Chilcott and Chris Flick were always there when I needed to "vent." Thanks guys!

TABLE OF CONTENTS

INTRODUCTION

I am a teacher. More specifically, I have the title of Professor, Interactive Multimedia through Humber College's School of Media Studies and Information Technologies" in Toronto. It is a fancy title, but I have never regarded myself as anything more than a simple teacher.

I am also a writer. With this, my fourth book dealing with a Macromedia technology, plus a slew of articles and tutorials for Community MX and The MX Developers Journal as well as my web site at http://www.tomontheweb.ca, I have rediscovered how much I enjoy the writer's craft and how it can be applied to my role as a teacher. Which brings me to this Captivate book.

I write about Macromedia web technologies and have discovered that sometimes it is better to demonstrate a technique rather than write about it. Although there are a number of solutions available, there always seemed to be something missing or a rather steep "learning curve."

Two years ago, when I was a judge for the EMMA Foundation awards, a company named Ehelp submitted an entry with the odd name of RoboDemo. It wasn't in my judging category, but I was given a quick run through of the product by one of my fellow judges and I couldn't help but think, "This is

continues on next page

one seriously neat product." I then proceeded to focus my efforts on writing a couple of books dealing the Macromedia Studio MX and Studio MX 2004 products. While I was writing those books, Macromedia announced it had acquired the RoboDemo product, and in late 2004, turned it inside out and rearranged its molecules as Captivate.

Over the course of the years 2003 and 2004, Humbert College dean William Hanna and I engaged in a conversation around distance education and eLearning. From an institutional point of view, there was very little room for a college to grow in the traditional sense. There were no parking lots that could be sacrificed for new buildings to accommodate an increased student population. We had purchased a Macromedia product called BreezeLive that creates a virtual interactive classroom. From my perspective, I felt the only piece missing was the ability to easily add screen captures and movies to BreezeLive presentations.

At the same time, a number of my New Media colleagues were starting to receive inquiries about adding demonstrations, quizzes, and so on to their Flash or HTML Internet or intranet sites. ELearning was also starting to take hold among corporate trainers and educators in both the private and public sectors, and the individuals charged with that task were looking for a solution that was easy to master, feature rich, and easy to implement.

This brings me back to my office where I am about to start writing about Captivate—yet another Macromedia product. If you are a RoboDemo user, you are about to discover that the application has fundamentally changed for the better. If you are new to the product, you will discover that Captivate meets those three criteria at the end of the previous paragraph—easy to master, feature rich, and easy to implement.

What's in it for You?

Although this book can't hope to be Captivate: From A to Z, it is designed to be a handy reference guide if you are familiar with Captivate or RoboDemo. If you aren't, this book will help you develop the skills to use the application to its full potential.

The book is broken into three sections.

The first two chapters comprise the first section and introduce you to the application and how to create a Captivate movie. The first chapter starts with a general overview of the application and the interface. You are shown where various menus are located and, most important of all, the purpose each of the various screens and windows you encounter when you open the application for the first time.

The next chapter essentially pushes you into the proverbial "deep end" of the pool and shows you how to create and edit a Captivate movie. Here you are introduced to the Capture window and many of the powerful features found in the window. After the capture is created, you are shown how the Edit and Storyboard views in Captivate are used to edit your movie. Along the way you discover how to create and use a Captivate template, set the Captivate preferences, and add playback controls to a movie. You also discover how to add audio to the movie or a slide as well as how to manipulate the captured onscreen movement of the mouse in your movie.

Chapters 3 to 8 form the second section of the book. Each chapter in this section is a detailed exploration of the various tools you use when working with Captivate. As you progress through these chapters you learn how to work with slides, the new Captivate timeline, captions, audio, and how to add audio and Rich Media to your Captivate presentation.

The final section, Chapters 9 to 13, show you how content can be brought into Captivate. Chapter 9, for example, reviews how to create buttons and playback controllers in Macromedia Fireworks MX 2004 for use in Captivate. Being a Macromedia product, Captivate also has the capability to "connect" to Flash MX 2004 or Flash MX Professional 2004. Chapter 10 reviews this process.

Chapter 11 deals with the heart and soul of Captivate—eLearning. This chapter shows you how to use the very powerful eLearning features of Captivate ranging from creating true/false quizzes to connecting the results with an eLearning system.

The final two chapters deal with the complexity and the end game of the process. Chapter 12 shows you how to use the MenuBuilder feature of Captivate to link to Captivate movies. In this manner an entire course, consisting of a number of modules, can be broken into a series of small manageable Captivate movies. The last chapter shows you how to get your final product onto the web, onto CD, into a Macromedia Breeze presentation, and even how to FTP the presentation to a web site... all from within Captivate.

As you move through this book, you discover the power of this application. More importantly, you also discover that the amount of fun you can have with this application should be illegal.

WHAT'S IN IT FOR YOU?

THE CAPTIVATE WORK ENVIRONMENT

Before you start creating Captivate movies and adding them to Flash MX 2004 presentations, your Web site, or other media, it's useful to familiarize yourself with your working environment. This way, you can quickly identify many of the tools, panels, menus, and other features of the application.

When you open a Captivate movie, you are placed immediately into the Captivate authoring environment. This environment is divided into two distinct panels:

◆ The *Storyboard View panel* enables you to perform a variety of tasks or edit an existing movie.

◆ The *Edit View panel* enables you to select various slides in the movie and perform specific tasks upon each selected slide.

This chapter's quick tour of the Captivate authoring environment will familiarize you with the location and use of many of the interface features.

✔ Tip

■ If you are opening Captivate projects created in older versions of RoboDemo—V5 or lower—the .ncp and .rd file extensions have changed to .cp (a Captivate file) or .cpt (a Captivate template). If you open an older file in Captivate, the .ncp extension changes to the newer .cp extension.

The Captivate Metaphor

Remember those flipbooks you had when you were a child? Each page contained a piece of an animation. You would flip through the pages, and the objects on the page would appear to move.

This is exactly how Captivate works. Each slide of a Captivate movie contains content. When the computer flips through each slide, the content appears to move. This is why, as you move through this book, you will discover how important slides are in the Captivate authoring process.

The Captivate Workflow

Captivate projects don't start with you firing up Captivate, capturing a bunch of stuff, and then editing the results in Captivate. Instead, think about the purpose of the capture, what needs to be captured, what assets need to be added to or created for the capture, and how the final product will be delivered. Captivate was designed to help you through this process.

The purpose of the capture is critical. There are three capture modes in Captivate (**Figure 1.1**), and each is designed to meet the unique needs of a capture's purpose:

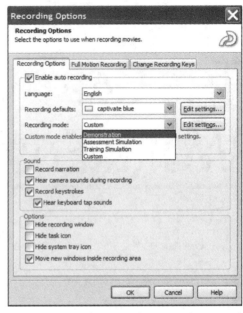

Figure 1.1: The capture mode determines the tone and the approach to the entire development process.

♦ **Demonstration** In many respects, you can think of this mode as being noninteractive. The viewer watches the movie and learns how to complete a task. When you use the Demonstration mode, Captivate automatically adds the captions and inserts the highlight boxes where you click the mouse, and will also track mouse movement.

♦ **Simulation** This type of movie requires user involvement and usually tells the viewer, "OK, now you try it." This mode adds click boxes automatically where you click the mouse, captions indicating success or failure, and even captions with hints. What this mode does *not* do, however, is record the movement of the mouse.

♦ **Training** Training is the most complex mode of all. Though similar in many ways to the Simulation mode—success and hint captions, no mouse-movement recording—it also requires both the trainer and the user to participate in the process. This is the mode in which questions are asked, and the user must answer them either though mouse clicks or text entry. It is also the mode in which you can send those responses to a Learning Management System (LMS) to be "graded."

After the capture is created, Captivate returns you to the Captivate work environment. This is where you can add sound, text, questions, video, and other content to each slide captured. You can also change the timing of each element on a slide and determine how it appears on the slide using special effects. In fact, if you have experience with Macromedia Flash MX 2004, you can even edit the slides in that application to take full advantage of its features.

You don't have to use Captivate to create content. If, for example, you use the tools in the MX Studio 2004—Fireworks MX, Freehand MX, and Flash MX 2004—you can create slide content ranging from movie controllers to Flash Video in those applications and easily add it to your Captivate presentation. In fact, you can create images, buttons, and other interface elements in most imaging and drawing software. Add to that the capability to import PowerPoint slides directly into Captivate, and you quickly realize there is a serious amount of power under Captivate's hood.

Finally, you need to determine the media to be used for the final movie. Captivate enables you to create content CDs, the Web, kiosks, users' computers, Breeze, Microsoft Word, and even email.

THE CAPTIVATE WORKFLOW

Understanding the Captivate View Panels

The Captivate work environment is divided into three major view panels. They are the Start, Storyboard and View panels. This is a rather handy way of approaching your workflow because each panel contains only those tasks, relevant to the panel. For instance, the Start panel is only used to open new or existing projects. The Edit panel, where you will spend the bulk of your development time, is where individual slides can change. This would include the addition of such items as sound, object timing and the addition or deletion of captions.

The Start panel

When you launch Captivate, the first panel you will see is the Start panel (**Figure 1.2**), which is commonly referred to as the Start page. This is your entry into the movie-creation and editing process, and enables you to choose a number of tasks ranging from creating a new movie to adding a number of features to individual slides of an existing movie.

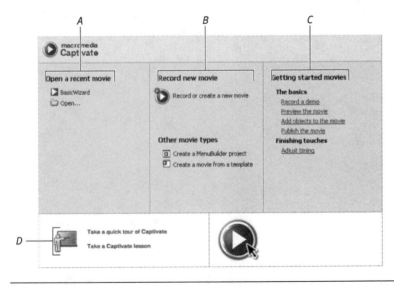

Figure 1.2 Captivate's Start panel lets you get right to work. You can choose to open a movie you have been working on or another Captivate file (A). Also, you can record a new movie (B), create a MenuBuilder project, or use a template to create a new movie (B). Finally, you can work your way through a series of tutorials (C) or directly access the Captivate area of the Macromedia site (D).

The Start page is modeled on the Start pages that are common to many Macromedia applications. This is where you can decide to create a new movie, open an existing movie, open a template, or launch MenuBuilder. On the left side of the panel is a listing of the recent movies that have been created. Click a movie in this section to open it. In the center of the Start page, you can choose to create a new movie, create a new MenuBuilder project, or open a template you've created.

The right side of the page contains links to a series of tutorials that were added when you installed Captivate. The lower left corner enables you to explore the new features of Captivate, while the lower right corner is reserved for announcements from Macromedia. This functions in exactly the same manner as the other Macromedia applications and is a "one-click" method of obtaining product updates and so on.

The Storyboard View panel

When you open a movie, you will most likely find yourself in the Storyboard View panel. This panel replaces the Frames View panel of RoboDemo and is available only when you open a movie. Each slide of the movie is presented in Thumbnail view, which is invaluable in giving you an idea of how your movie flows. It is also quite robust.

Here are just a few of the tasks you can accomplish in the Storyboard View panel:

◆ Double-click a slide to open the slide in the Edit panel.

◆ Right-click a slide to open the context menu and change the slide's properties.

◆ Select multiple slides by holding down either the Shift or Control key and clicking the thumbnails.

continues on next page

UNDERSTANDING THE CAPTIVATE VIEW PANELS

- Press Control-A or select Edit > Select All Slides to select all of the slides in the panel.

- Drag selected slides to new locations in the movie.

On the left side of the Storyboard View panel are a number of Slide tasks ranging from adding audio to a slide to changing a slide's properties. At the bottom of this area is the Movie Information section at the bottom of the Tasks panel, which displays basic information like the size of the movie and how many slides are in it (**Figure 1.3**).

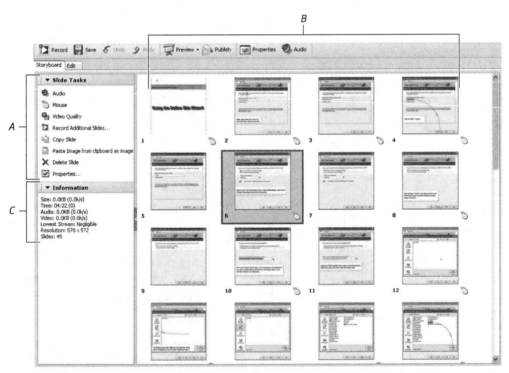

Figure 1.3 The Storyboard View panel is quite robust. You can perform a number of tasks (A), from adding audio to a slide to changing a slide's properties. The slides are visible in Thumbnail view (B), and the Movie Information (C) provides you with information including the size of the movie to how many slides are in it.

The Edit View panel

The final panel is the Edit View panel. You will soon discover that you will be spending most of your time here, for this is where you edit or modify slides by adding images, captions, and interactivity to your movie.

Double-clicking a slide in the Storyboard View panel or clicking the Edit tab opens this panel. At the top of the Edit View panel is the new Timeline feature of Captivate. The Timeline enables you to control the timing and duration of a number of objects in the slide. On the right side of the panel is the Advanced toolbar. The left side displays the Filmstrip, which shows all of the slides of a movie even when you are editing a single slide (**Figure 1.4**).

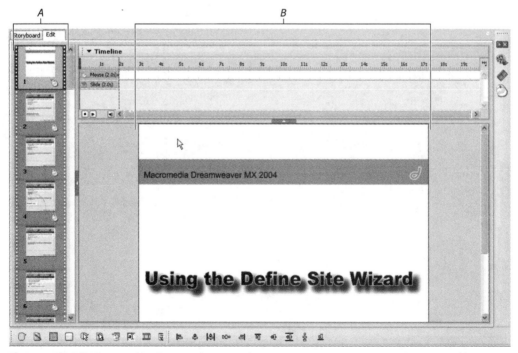

Figure 1.4 The Edit View panel is where you do your work in Captivate. Selecting a frame in the Filmstrip (A) opens the contents of the frame (B), which you can edit.

UNDERSTANDING THE CAPTIVATE VIEW PANELS

Holy Smokes! Where Did RoboDemo Go?

Captivate is RoboDemo 6. Macromedia purchased EHelp, the company that developed RoboDemo, and, essentially, kept the interface and functionality of the RoboDemo application. In many respects, it was eHelp's RoboDemo with a Macromedia logo stuck on it. This revision of the app brings the interface and functionality into line with the rest of the Macromedia products. If you're a RoboDemo user, many of the changes you will notice were designed to give the application the look and feel of a Macromedia product. The first change is the replacement of the Project View panel with the typical Macromedia Start page. Other changes to the application include the following:

◆ To export, either choose Publish or Import/Export from the File menu. The Export dialog box is a thing of the past.

◆ Frames are no longer referred to as *frames*. They are known as *slides*.

◆ Captivate includes a Timeline for editing the duration and properties of objects in a slide.

◆ There's automatic switching between normal and full motion recording. For example, if you drag a slider during recording, Captivate will switch to full motion recording automatically when you drag. Release the mouse, and Captivate returns you to normal mode.

◆ You can record audio and your screen recording simultaneously.

◆ The Edit and View panels have been replaced with Storyboard View and Edit View panels, respectively.

◆ Macromedia Breeze has been added to Captivate's Export options to enable the direct import of your movies to Breeze or BreezeLive.

◆ The Flash module has been withdrawn. Now you can edit your movie directly in Flash by using the Import/Export item in the File menu.

◆ There are now three automatic recording modes: Demo, Simulation, and Training.

◆ You can attach audio to any object in the slide.

◆ Captivate uses the Product Activation feature introduced in the Macromedia MX 2004 products.

◆ The import of PowerPoint shows into Captivate was improved.

All of these new features and more are explained in greater detail throughout this book.

Customizing Your Work Environment

You can customize the Captivate work environment to suit how you work.

You can change the size of the thumbnails if you find it hard to see some of the detail in them. You can also click the Splitter Bar to close the Tasks panel. The Splitter Bar is a great way of buying screen real estate when you need it because the application default is to have the thumbnails constantly visible. Another space saver is turning off the Main toolbar at the top of the Captivate window by selecting View > Main Toolbar. If you need even more room, press the F11 key to maximize the Captivate window (it will fill the screen). Press F11 again to return to the normal window.

There are also a couple of other features you can turn on or off, depending on how you work:

◆ You can turn off the captions in the Main toolbar and have only the icons visible by selecting View > Captions on Toolbar.

◆ If you don't need to be reminded constantly of where your movie is located, you can turn off the status bar at the bottom of the Captivate window by selecting View > Status Bar.

◆ If you don't need to see your movie information or slide tasks in the Storyboard View panel, click the down arrow to close that area. Clicking Slide Tasks or Movie Information will also close the Slide Tasks and Movie Information areas.

◆ If there are toolbars in the Edit View panel that you rarely use, turn them off by selecting the View menu. Open toolbars have check marks beside them.

Using the Captivate Filmstrip

The Filmstrip, available in the Edit View panel, is an important feature of the application. Apart from presenting you with a global slide-by-slide overview of your movie (**Figure 1.5**), the thumbnails are visible while you edit an individual slide.

Another interesting feature of the Filmstrip is that it doesn't always have to sit on the left side of your screen. If you select View > Filmstrip orientation, you can have the Filmstrip move to the top, the bottom, or the right side of your screen. This is handy if you are used to having panels in other locations in your workspace.

Being able to see each slide gives you an overview of the presentation's flow. Still, there will be occasions in which you'll need to move slides to other positions in the movie. In this case, simply drag a slide to the new location in the Filmstrip and release the mouse. As you drag the mouse, the slides in the Filmstrip will slide down to indicate where you can place the frame you're dragging, and the number of the dragging slide will also change (**Figure 1.6**).

✔ Tip

- You are not restricted to moving single slides. To select multiple slides, press the Shift or Control key and click the slides (for example, slides 2, 5, 9, and 14), which you can then move as a group. If you want to move a group of ordered slides (for example, slides 2, 3, and 4), press and hold the Shift key, and then click the slides to be moved to select them.

Another space-saving trick is the ability to reduce the size of the thumbnails in the Filmstrip. You have three choices—Small, Medium, and Large—available through

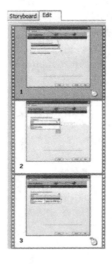

Figure 1.5 The Edit View panel's Filmstrip enables you to open slides without changing to the Storyboard View panel.

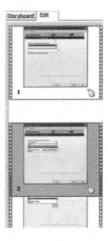

Figure 1.6 You can reorder slides in the Filmstrip by dragging a slide to a new location.

Figure 1.7 If you need room on your screen, you can resize the thumbnails.

View > Thumbnail size. The smallest size reduces the width of the thumbnail area to reveal more of the selected slide. It also shows you more slides in the small view (**Figure 1.7**). If the Filmstrip isn't needed, turn it off by clicking the Splitter Bar.

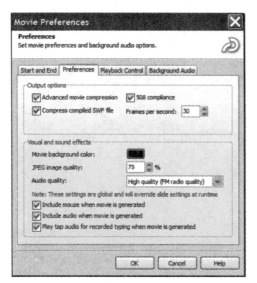

Figure 1.8 The Movie Preferences are applied only to the movie that is open.

Using the Captivate Movie Preferences

Captivate's movie preferences are a bit different from those of many Windows applications you may use. In Captivate, the preferences are applied only to the currently opened movie, not the application. For example, suppose you decide to change the background of all of the slides in your movie from white to black. You do this by selecting Movie > Preferences and selecting Black in the Movie background area (**Figure 1.8**). In a lot of applications, this will result in all slides created having a black background. Yet in Captivate, that black background is applied only to the currently open movie. You can also make a stop at the Preferences dialog box before you publish the movie. With the Publish dialog box open, click the Preferences button to launch the Preferences dialog box.

Working with the Captivate Toolbars

Captivate contains a number of toolbars that give you convenient one-click access to a number of features that you may—or may not— use all that often. You can also choose which toolbars are visible and their locations in the application window. Captivate contains four primary toolbars:

◆ Main

◆ Advanced

◆ Objects

◆ Alignment

The Main toolbar

The Main toolbar (**Figure 1.9**), which is visible by default, provides one-click access to a number of global features:

◆ **Record** Click to begin recording additional slides for the currently open movie.

◆ **Save** Click to save the selected movie.

◆ **Undo** Click to undo the last slide action.

◆ **Redo** Click to redo the last slide action.

◆ **Preview** Click to compile the selected movie as a Flash SWF file and view the movie.

◆ **Publish** Click to export the movie in a variety of formats ranging from a Flash SWF to a Linux Projector.

◆ **Properties** Click to view the properties for the currently selected slides.

◆ **Audio** Click to open the Record Audio window.

Figure 1.9 The Main toolbar provides one-click access to a number of global features and tasks.

Figure 1.10 The Advanced toolbar provides one click access to such slide features as the addition of a playback controller to the movie to the editing of mouse click sounds and movement.

The following two icons appear on the Main toolbar when you click the Edit tab:

◆ **Back arrow** Click to go backward one slide.

◆ **Forward arrow** Click to go forward one slide.

✔ Tip

■ These tools all have equivalent menu items (to which they provide one-click access).

The Advanced toolbar

The Advanced toolbar (**Figure 1.10**) enables you to perform a number of tasks such as backing up a movie to a folder and setting the mouse properties in a movie. Its features are as follows:

◆ **Movie Controls** Click to turn on or off the movie controls during movie playback.

◆ **Movie preferences** Click to open the Movie Preferences window.

◆ **Movie Start and End** Click to open the Movie Start and End dialog box.

◆ **Mouse Pointer Properties** Click to choose from several mouse properties, including the icon used for the mouse pointer.

WORKING WITH THE CAPTIVATE TOOLBARS

The Objects toolbar

The Objects toolbar (**Figure 1.11**) provides access to a number of the more common objects that you can add to the slides of a Captivate presentation:

Figure 1.11 The Object toolbar enables you to add objects like captions and animations to a movie frame.

◆ **Caption** Click to open the New Caption dialog box.

◆ **Image** Click to locate an image used in the slide.

◆ **Highlight Box** Click to open the New Highlight Box dialog box.

◆ **Button** Click to open the New Button dialog box.

◆ **Rollover Caption** Click to add a caption that will appear on a rollover.

◆ **Rollover Image** Click to locate the image that will appear on a rollover.

◆ **Click Box** Click to open the New Click Box dialog box.

◆ **Text Entry** Click to add a text entry box for a slide.

◆ **Animation** Click to locate an animation that you can insert into a slide.

◆ **Text Animation** Click to create an animated text object.

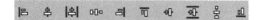

Figure 1.12 The Alignment toolbar.

The Alignment toolbar

You can align objects in a slide either individually or together. Captivate uses an anchor object such as the center of a slide to determine the alignment of the selected objects. If you are familiar with Flash MX 2004, Fireworks MX 2004, or Freehand MX, you've seen the icons in the Alignment toolbar (**Figure 1.12**):

- ◆ **Left Alignment** Click to align the left edges of the selected objects.

- ◆ **Center Align** (Horizontal) Click to align the centers of all the objects to the horizontal center of the anchor object.

- ◆ **Center in window** (Horizontal) Click to space the selected objects in the center of the slide.

- ◆ **Space Equally** (Horizontal) Click to align the objects across the horizontal center of the slide and space them equally from each other.

- ◆ **Align Right** Click to align the right edges of the selected objects.

- ◆ **Align Tops** Click to align the top edges of the selected objects.

- ◆ **Center Align** (Vertical) Click to align the centers of all the objects to the vertical center of the anchor object.

- ◆ **Center Vertically** Click to center the selected objects in the slide vertically.

- ◆ **Space Equally** (Vertical) Click to align the objects across the vertical center of the slide and space them equally from each other.

- ◆ **Align Bottoms** Click to align the bottoms of the selected objects.

Summary

This chapter began the journey through the Captivate work environment by starting where all Captivate projects start: with a plan.

First, you learned that there are three types of captures that you can create, and each mode has unique features and purposes. Content for Captivate slides can come from a variety of sources, and Captivate movies aren't limited to Web delivery. The addition of Breeze, for example, makes your movies available to users without your needing to know how to design a Web page.

Then the chapter examined the Start page, which is new to Captivate, and the features of the Storyboard View and Edit View panels. Being the replacement for RoboDemo, those of you who are RoboDemo users can expect some major changes, such as the inclusion of the Timeline and a terminology change: frames are now called slides.

We all have our preferred way of working with applications, so this chapter showed how to customize your Captivate workspace and how to "buy" screen space through the Filmstrip and the Captivate preferences. Finally, the chapter finished exploring the Captivate work environment by reviewing the application's major toolbars.

Having looked at the big picture, it is time to get to work and create a Captivate movie, which is the subject of the next chapter.

CREATING

CAPTIVATE MOVIES

Creating Captivate movies involves much more than simply doing a screen capture and adding stuff here and there. Whether it is demonstrating a software technique, a product demonstration, quiz, or tutorial, the key to success is that old business adage: Plan your work, work your plan.Although Captivate is an extremely powerful software tool with a myriad of applications, never forget there will be a human watching the presentation. In this case, the message that the movie conveys is far more important than the technology. Though you can add audio, animation, and other interactive media to your movie, always keep in mind that these features should add to the viewer's experience. The least successful presentations are those where the developer says, "Aren't I clever?"This chapter focuses on the movie creation process. This process starts with planning—in many respects, the most time-consuming aspect of creating a Captivate movie. You'll learn how to record a movie, manage movies you have created, and create and use a Captivate template.Creating a movie in Captivate is both uncomplicated and fast. Still, there is a workflow that follows these general steps:

continues on next page

1. Plan your movie using storyboards, scripts, and any other organizational material such as written notes or project planning software.

   Storyboards are especially useful because they can show the frame-by-frame progression of a movie, including audio, animations, mouse movements, and so on that will appear in the frame. Story boards range from hand drawings on paper to PowerPoint presentations, for example, that lay out the content in the slide and its purpose.

2. Determine the playback media.

   Captivate movies can be played back from CDs, from hard drives, and through the Web. In each case, the final playback media will have a major role in determining the assets and recording of the movie.

3. Gather your assets.

   You can add images, sounds, animations, and even other Captivate movies to your movie. Make sure these assets are readily available to you.

4. Open Captivate, set the recording options, and, if needed, set the movie preferences.

5. Record your movie.

   The flexibility of Captivate enables you to record a movie from scratch, utilize slides and animations from previously recorded movies, and even reorder the slides you have just recorded.

6. Add the captions, images, sounds, and other assets called for in the storyboard.

7. Generate and preview the movie.

8. Save the movie as a Flash SWF file and export it in the format best suited to the media being used for playback.

Planning the Captivate Movie

The first rule of planning any interactive media project is this: "Focus on the user. Don't focus on the technology."

You are not the audience for the presentation. When planning a Captivate movie, the first step in the process is not to open the application but to ask yourself the following questions:

◆ Who is the audience?

A movie designed for primary-school children will look and feel a lot different from one designed for software engineers.

◆ What does the audience need to learn from the movie?

These are the learning objectives, and the fewer—two or three—the better. What is the audience's skill level regarding the content of the presentation?

A presentation designed for people who have never used software will be a lot more basic than one designed for power users. Knowing the audience's skills will also give you a good idea of the project's scope and complexity.

After you have determined the project's scope and understand the audience, you can then move into planning the movie's content. This is where the importance of a storyboard or script can't be understated.

Using storyboards and scripts

Storyboards use rough sketches to plan the progression of the movie. These can range in detail from a series of pencil sketches on a sheet of blank paper to full-color drawings created in drawing or imaging applications like Macromedia Freehand MX and Fireworks MX 2004. If you will be using lots of screen shots in your movie with few captions or minimal text, a storyboard would work well.

Traditionally, scripts are created using word processing software. Scripts enable you to describe, in depth, the contents of each screen and to present the movie in a logical, sequenced order. If your movie will contain numerous captions, text, voiceover audio, and so on, you should create a script.

Fireworks MX 2004 is Macromedia's Web imaging application. Apart from creating GIF animations that can simulate each frame of a recording, you can use this application to optimize images used in Captivate. Further, the use of a symbols library in Fireworks enables you to reuse such items as logos text without the inevitable file size increase. Unlike RoboDemo, Captivate does include a Storyboard View panel. The purpose of this area is not to let you plan your movie, but to rearrange the slides in the movie prior to its being published.

Storyboards and Macromedia Studio MX 2004

If you own Macromedia Studio MX 2004, you have three very powerful storyboard creation tools at your disposal—Freehand MX, Flash MX Professional 2004, and Fireworks MX 2004.

Freehand MX is a vector-drawing tool. One of the application's features is the ability to create multipage documents. Also, you can use master pages—which can hold commonly used elements such as logos and headings—and apply them to any or all of the pages in your document. For example, the new Connector tool enables you to create flowcharts showing the branching in quizzes, and the new Action tool lets you to add basic Flash actions to a storyboard destined for the Web. You can also print out the storyboards and use them as client deliverables.

Flash MX Professional 2004, though aimed squarely at the Web coder, also contains a powerful storyboarding tool—the Slide Presentation. This feature allows even non-Flash users to quickly prepare an interactive presentation that can then be presented to the client for approval.

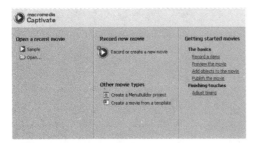

Figure 2.1 The Captivate Start page.

Figure 2.2 The New Movie dialog box enables you to choose the movie types from recording an application to creating a blank movie.

Recording Your Movie

Recording a movie in Captivate follows this general workflow:

1. Start the recording process.

2. Set the recording options, the full motion recording options, and the recording keys.

3. Record the movie.

To set up a new movie:

1. Launch Captivate and, from the Start menu, click Record or create a new movie (**Figure 2.1**) to open the New movie options dialog box.

2. Determine what type of capture you will be undertaking by choosing an option in the Record new movie area of the dialog box (**Figure 2.2**):

   ▲ **Application** Choose to record everything you will be demonstrating in an application. The application must be open, and you will capture all movement within the application window.

   ▲ **Custom size** Choose to record the actions in a specific area of the screen.

   ▲ **Full screen** Choose to capture the entire screen. This is particularly useful if your movie moves between several open applications.

   Two other movie types are available:

   ▲ **Blank movie** Choose to create a blank slide. It is useful if you will be copying slides from other Captivate movies and pasting them into this one.

   ▲ **Image movie** Choose to create a slide show.

continues on next page

3. Click OK to open the Recording window (**Figure 2.3**).

✔ Tip

- You can't record a movie without Captivate being open. When you create a new recording, the Recording window will open, but you must then navigate to the application in which you will be recording the movie.

To add new slides to an existing movie:

1. Open the Captivate movie to which the slides will be added and open the application in which you'll do the recording.

2. *Do one of the following:*

In the Storyboard View panel, either click the Record button on the Main toolbar or select Record Additional Slides from the Slide Tasks option (**Figure 2.4**) to open the Recording window.

Or

In the Edit View panel, click the Record button on the Main toolbar to open the Recording window.

3. Select whether the new slides should be appended automatically to the end of the movie or added in at a specific place.

4. Click OK to open the Recording window.

Figure 2.3 The Captivate recording window and controls.

Figure 2.4 Click Record Additional Slides in the Slide Tasks to open a new recording window.

Figure 2.5 Click the Options button to open the Recording Options dialog box.

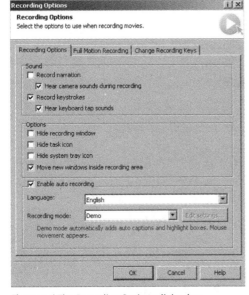

Figure 2.6 The Recording Options dialog box.

To set the recording options:

The first step in recording a Captivate movie is determining what sounds will be used, whether autorecording is on or off and deciding which interface elements will be visible during the recording. These are contained in the Captivate recording options. The interesting thing about these options is that you can set them before you record. You can apply them only to new frames added to the movie.

- ◆ *Do one of the following*:

    In the Recording window (**Figure 2.5**), click the Options button to open the Recording Options dialog box

    Or

    Open a Captivate movie, then select Options > Recording Options to open the Recording Options dialog box (**Figure 2.6**) and then select your options.

✔ Tip

- ■ You can apply the Recording Options globally without selecting a new movie or an existing movie. Select Options > Recording Options in either the Storyboard View or Edit View panel.

Setting Recording Options

The Recording Options dialog box is divided into three distinct areas: Recording Options, Full Motion Recording, and Change Recording Keys.

Selecting the Recording Options tab reveals the following recording options:

◆ **Record narration** Select to record any narration that may be done during the capture.

◆ **Hear "camera" sounds during recording** Select to hear a camera shutter-release sound when the recording starts. This is especially useful if you are using autorecording. The sound is only an aural clue that the recording process has started; it won't be audible in the finished product.

◆ **Record keystrokes** Select to record any key presses or text input as you record the movie.

◆ **Hear keyboard "tap" sounds** Select to hear an aural clue that you are using the keyboard during the recording. These sounds will not appear in the finished movie.

◆ **Hide recording window** Select to hide the red bounding box in the Recording window and to remove the Captivate icon from the taskbar. This is especially useful for full screen recording or movies that incorporate the use of the taskbar.

◆ **Hide task icon** Select to remove the Captivate icon from the taskbar.

◆ **Hide system tray icon** Select to hide the system tray during recording.

Figure 2.7 Custom recording options enable you to determine how a variety of elements will be added to your movie.

◆ **Move new windows inside recording area** Select to have any windows that may open during recording moved automatically inside the recording area. This is quite a useful feature when you're recording applications that require the user to see a number of windows or dialog boxes.

◆ **Enable auto recording** Select to capture screen shots automatically each time the mouse is clicked, your application moves to the front, or you press a key on your keyboard. This option is enabled by default.

◆ **Language** Choose one of 13 languages for captions and tool tips.

◆ **Recording mode** Four recording modes are available:

▲ **Demo** Select to include captions and highlights automatically to the auto-recorded movie.

▲ **Simulation** Select to include automatically click boxes with success and failure captions to the auto-recorded movie.

▲ **Training** Select to include rollover captions and click boxes during the autorecording process.

▲ **Custom** Select to determine which elements are added to the autorecording. Click the Edit Settings button to open the Custom Recording Options dialog box (**Figure 2.7**). After you make your choices, click OK.

✔ Tip

■ Other actions that will start an auto-recording are clicking a capture key, opening a menu or dialog box, clicking a toolbar button or a button in a dialog box, and as dragging and dropping.

Setting Full Motion Recording options

Full motion recording is an automatic process in Captivate. It enables you to smoothly capture drag-and-drop actions, to capture mouse movement in the capture area, and to adjust the video quality of the capture.

The Full Motion Recording tab contains the following options (**Figure 2.8**):

◆ **Automatically use full motion capture for drag-and-drop actions** Select to capture dragging objects from one area or the capture screen to another.

◆ **Show mouse in full motion capture mode** Select to include mouse movement in the movie.

◆ **Record at higher capture rate for smoother movie** Select to disable any hardware acceleration during playback. The result of this is not a sped-up playback. Rather, it actually releases system resources that sometimes result in a choppy capture or jerky onscreen movements at playback. Selecting this option will cause your screen to flicker momentarily when you begin and end the recording as the acceleration is turned off and then turned back on.

◆ **Video quality** Enter a value that will determine the smoothness of the playback. As is typical with all digital media, the better the quality of the onscreen material, the larger the file size.

◆ **Working folder** Click the Browse button to open the Browse for folder dialog box. Navigate to the folder to be used as the final location of movie and click OK.

◆ **SWF conversion** Select the color depth of the SWF file. Selecting 16 Bit color results in a reduced color palette and a smaller file size. Selecting 32 Bit increases the color palette significantly and also results in a larger file size.

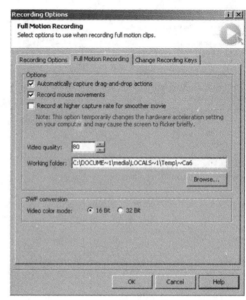

Figure 2.8 Full motion recording options enable you to choose which events initiate a full motion recording.

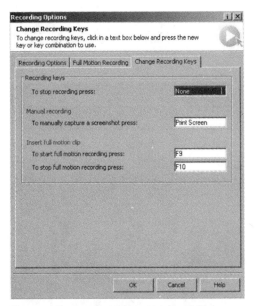

Figure 2.9 You can determine which keys initiate a recording when Captivate is open.

Setting Change Recording Keys options

Your final choice is to determine the keystrokes that initiate and end a recording. You can set these keys by selecting the Change Recording Keys tab and making choices in the Change Recording Keys dialog box (**Figure 2.9**).

Your choices are as follows:

◆ **To stop recording press** The default is End. If you want to change it, select the choice and press a new key or key combination.

◆ **To manually capture a screen shot press** The default is Print Screen.

◆ **To start full motion recording press** Press F9 after the recording starts to initiate this action.

◆ **To stop full motion recording press** Press F10 to stop a full motion recording.

✔ Tip

■ In previous versions of this application, full motion recording was a separate operation. In Captivate, selecting the options will trigger full motion recording during the capture.

To set the capture area manually:

You aren't limited to the area defined by the red capture box when you start the recording process. You can change the size of the recording area. Here's how:

1. Select File > "Record or create a new movie" if you are working with a previously recorded movie, or click "Record or create a new movie" on the Start page.
   The New Movie Options dialog box opens.

continues on next page

RECORDING YOUR MOVIE

2. Select Application and click OK.

The Recording window opens.

3. From the "Record specific window" pop-down list, select the application in which you'll be recording (**Figure 2.10**).

The application window to be recorded opens.

4. Drag a resize handle (the eight squares on the edges of the capture box) inward to shrink the bounding box or outward to grow the bounding box (**Figure 2.11**).

5. Click and drag the red line, not a handle, to move the bounding box to another screen location.

✔ Tips

- If you make a mistake, click the Cancel button in the Recording Controls to return to the Captivate interface.

- Clicking the "Snap red recording are to fit selected window" button will expand the red recording box to the dimension of the open window and thus defeat the purpose of this exercise.

- If the window to be recorded is larger than the recording area, select the window from the list in the "Optionally, select a window you'd like to record" pop down and click the "Snap window to fit inside the red recording area" button.

- If your movie is destined for Web playback, consider these suggested capture screen sizes for efficient playback:
  28.8 kbps modem: 640 × 480
  33.6 kbps modem: 800 × 600
  56 kbps modem: 800 × 600
  DSL, cable, T1: 1024 × 768

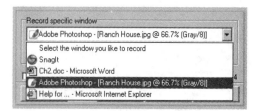

Figure 2.10 You can record specific windows in currently open applications.

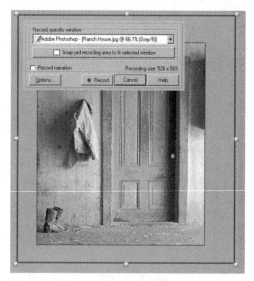

Figure 2.11 Clicking and dragging a handle in the capture area resizes the capture area.

Figure 2.12 Click the Preview button on the Main toolbar to preview the movie just captured.

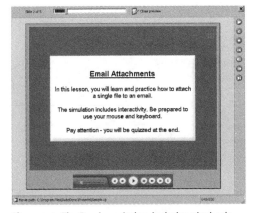

Figure 2.13 The Preview window includes playback controls.

✔ Tip

- Use the Preview feature to review any changes you will make to your slides. The playback matches that of the final file, meaning this is the place to identify problems and address them. You can also use the playback control in the window to pause the movie and move between slides.

To record a movie:

1. If necessary, adjust the recording area or move the recording area bounding box to its final position.

2. Click the Record button.

3. Perform your actions within the bounding box.

4. Press the End key to stop recording.

   You will be returned to the Storyboard View panel, where your new movie will be available as a series of thumbnails.

✔ Tip

- If you want to pause the recording process, press the Pause/Break key on your keyboard. To resume recording, press the Pause/Break key again.

To preview your capture:

1. Open the Storyboard View or Edit View panel.

2. Click the Preview button (**Figure 2.12**) on the Main toolbar.

   The resulting pop-down menu contains the following options:

   - ▲ **Movie** Choose to preview the entire movie.

   - ▲ **From this slide** Choose to have the movie play from the selected slide to the end of the movie.

   - ▲ **Next 5 Slides** Choose to play a small six-slide segment of the movie.

   - ▲ **In Web Bowser** Choose to compile the movie and play it back in your browser.

   After you make your choice, a "Generating progress" dialog box opens. Once the movie has been compiled, the Preview window opens and the movie starts to play.

3. To return to the Storyboard View or Edit View panel, click the "Close preview" button (**Figure 2.13**).

RECORDING YOUR MOVIE

Creating and Using Captivate Project Templates

You can save movies as templates. The advantage to templates is they introduce consistency to your design efforts and are reusable.

As in other applications, such as page layout or multimedia applications, templates also contain commonly used items such as logos. In Captivate, these items could include corporate identification, a common opening and closing frame, and even a common movie size. The advantage to you is a reduction in production time and a consistent look and feel that meets the corporate design standard.

To create a project template:

1. Record and save a Captivate movie.

2. Select File > Save as Template (**Figure 2.14**) to open the Save As dialog box.

3. Enter a name for the project template.

4. Click Save.

✔ Tip

■ Captivate templates have the .cpt extension, and all templates are saved to the Templates folder located in the Captivate application folder.

To edit a project template:

1. Open Captivate and select File > Edit Template (**Figure 2.15**). The Open window opens, displaying the templates in the Templates folder.

2. Double-click the template you want to open.

3. Make your changes to the template and, when finished, select File > Save.

4. When the file has been saved, select File > Close.

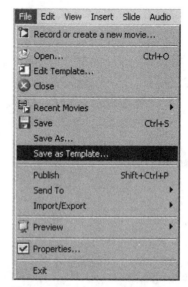

Figure 2.14 You can save movies as templates.

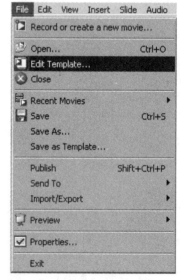

Figure 2.15 You can also edit templates.

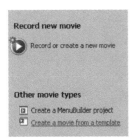

Figure 2.16 You can record a new movie from a template right from the Start page.

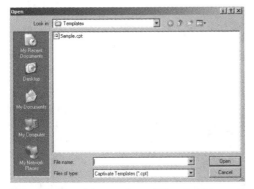

Figure 2.17 Templates use the .cpt file extension.

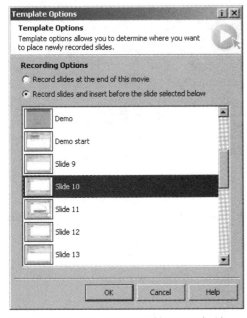

Figure 2.18 Template options enable you to decide where new slides will be placed.

To use a template to create a new movie:

1. Open Captivate and click "Create a movie from a template" in the Other Movie Types area of the Start screen (**Figure 2.16**).

   The Open dialog box appears, displaying the list of templates in the Captivate folder on your hard drive (**Figure 2.17**).

   The Template Options dialog box opens (**Figure 2.18**).

   ▲ **Record slides at the end of this movie** Select if the template contains slides that are always played first.

   ▲ **Record slides and insert before the slide selected below** Select if the slides are to be added throughout the template. If you select a slide in the list of thumbnails, the capture will be placed between the selected slide and the one under it.

   Click OK to close the Template options dialog box. When the dialog box closes the recording window opens.

2. Click the Record button to start recording.

3. Press the End key to stop recording.

   The new frames appear in the Storyboard View panel in the location you set in step 3.

Captivate Movie Properties

In Captivate, the movie properties don't have a lot to do with the physical size of the movie or streaming options. Rather, they're the general movie information—such as the author's name, email address, and Web address—that is readily accessible during movie playback.

To set the movie properties:

1. Select File > Properties to open the Movie Properties dialog box (**Figure 2.19**).

   ▲ **Movie Name** Enter a name for the movie.

   ▲ **Author** Enter the name of the movie's author or authors.

   ▲ **Company** Enter the company name.

   ▲ **E-mail** Enter an email address.

   ▲ **Web site** Enter the company's Web address.

   ▲ **Copyright** Enter any required copyright information.

   ▲ **Description** Enter a short description of the movie's contents.

2. Click OK.

   When the movie has been exported, a series of playback controls is added to the movie's interface.

3. Click the Information button on the controls.

   The movie properties appear in a separate window (**Figure 2.20**).

✔ Tip

■ Before you enter the movie properties, you should consult with your client. Companies tend to have Web sites and email addresses they use for customer contact or other purposes. Also, it is common courtesy to ask if you can enter your name in the author area.

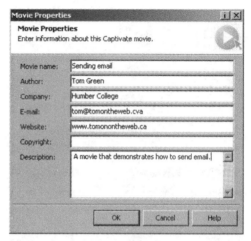

Figure 2.19 The Movie Properties dialog box.

Figure 2.20 The movie properties appear when the movie is played.

CAPTIVATE MOVIE PROPERTIES

Resizing Captivate Movies

There will be occasions where you will capture a movie and then discover that its dimensions need to be changed. Luckily, you can do this without rerecording the movie.

To resize a movie:

1. Open a movie in Captivate and select Movie > Resize Movie.

   The Movie Resize dialog box opens (**Figure 2.21**).

2. Make your size adjustments and then click OK.

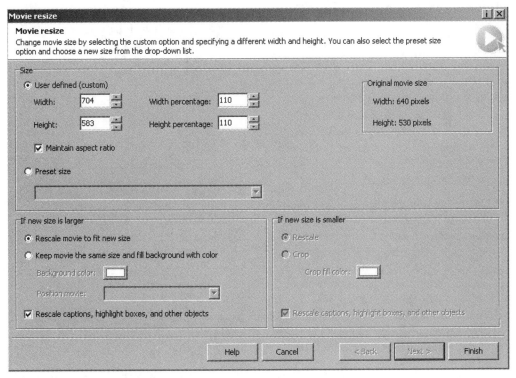

Figure 2.21 The Movie resize dialog box.

Resizing Your Movie

The Movie Resize dialog box gives you a lot of valuable information and asks some rather important questions. It is divided into four areas:

- **Size** Enter the new dimensions of the movie.

- **Original movie size** Displays the length and width of the movie about to be resized. You can't modify this information.

- **If new size is larger** Indicate what happens if you increase the size of the movie.

- **If new size is smaller** Indicate what happens if you decrease the size of the movie.

Following is the information required for each of the input areas:

- **User defined (custom)** Enter a new width and height or change the percentage values. Changing the width will also change the percentage, so you need to enter either a pixel value or a percentage value, not both.

- **Maintain aspect ratio** Select to maintain the relationship of the movie's dimensions to each other and to avoid distortion. For example, a digital video has a 4:3 aspect ratio. Increasing the size of a 200 × 150 video to 400 × 300 will not introduce distortion, yet increasing it to 211 × 153 will, because 211 is not divisible by four and 153 is not divisible by three. A good rule of thumb is to never deselect this when resizing a movie.

- **Preset size** This pop-down menu gives you one-click access to a number of presets (**Figure 2.22**), which range in size from fitting on a Pocket PC screen to a full screen Breeze slide.

After the size is set, the movie becomes either physically larger or physically smaller. If the movie is made larger:

- **Rescale movie to fit new size** Select to rescale the movie's physical dimensions. To avoid distorting the content, be sure to select Rescale captions, highlight boxes and other objects at the bottom of this area.

- **Keep movie the same size and fill background with color** Select when the accrual movie has to stay the same size but the background area it sits on has to be larger. This is an odd but extremely useful option.

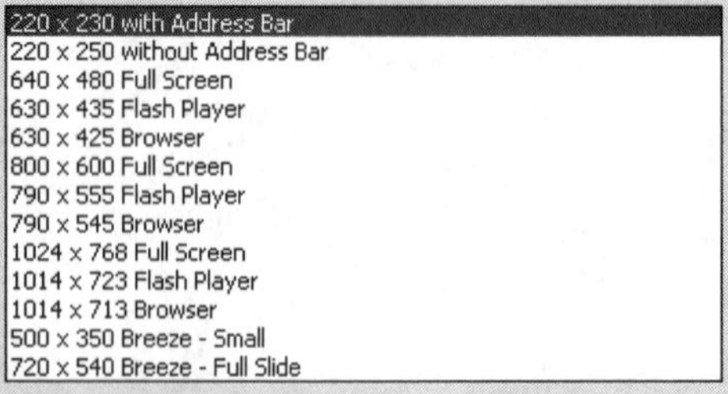

220 x 230 with Address Bar
220 x 250 without Address Bar
640 x 480 Full Screen
630 x 435 Flash Player
630 x 425 Browser
800 x 600 Full Screen
790 x 555 Flash Player
790 x 545 Browser
1024 x 768 Full Screen
1014 x 723 Flash Player
1014 x 713 Browser
500 x 350 Breeze - Small
720 x 540 Breeze - Full Slide

Figure 2.22 You can resize movies to a number of preset sizes.

Resizing Your Movie *continued*

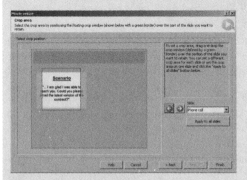

Figure 2.23 You can resize movies by cropping them.

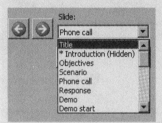

Figure 2.24 You can crop individual slides.

If the movie is made smaller:

◆ **Rescale** Select to rescale the movie's physical dimensions. To avoid distorting the content, be sure to select Rescale captions, highlight boxes and other objects at the bottom of this area.

◆ **Crop** Select to crop the movie to its new size. If there is any background space, you can select the color using the Crop fill color box. After selecting Crop, click the Next button to open the Crop Area dialog box. You have two choices: crop the entire movie to the new size or crop individual frames to the new size.

▲ To crop the movie to a new size, click the Next button to open the Crop dialog box (**Figure 2.23**). Drag the Crop window to its new location and click the "Apply to all slides" button.

▲ To crop individual slides, use either the left or right green arrow buttons to move up or down in the slide order. You can also select the slides from the pop-down list (**Figure 2.24**). Drag the Crop window to its new position over the area to be retained. Repeat this process for each slide to be cropped. When you're done, click the Finish button.

Adding Background Audio to Your Movie

You can create background audio for your movie. When you add a background audio track, the sound will play while the slides of your movie are shown. Background audio can be music, sound effects, or virtually any kind of sound you can import or record. Just keep in mind that Captivate can read only a WAV and MP3 files. You'll have to convert AIFF, WMA, and other audio formats to one of these two prior to placing them into your Captivate movie.

You can also use background audio together with individual slide audio for a truly professional effect. This is accomplished by lowering the volume of a background audio track when a slide with audio assigned plays. For example, you can import a music file and have it play while the movie plays. When the movie reaches a slide where there is a voice-over narration, the background music track's volume will be lowered while the narration plays. Audio, if used properly, makes the viewer's experience with your work a positive one. The problem with audio, though, is the inevitable tradeoff a developer must make between quality and size. The better the sound quality, the higher the file size, and vice versa.

Captivate can help you with this tradeoff, because it enables you to control the way a sound is recorded based upon your input and output needs.

There are two methods of recording background audio in Captivate:

◆ Record a voiceover narration using a microphone.

◆ Create the audio using another recording, which connects directly to your computer. When recording, the sound will be captured as a WAV file that is subsequently converted to an MP3 file.

Figure 2.25 A number of prerecorded audio files are installed with Captivate and can be added to your movie through the Import Audio dialog box.

Captivate also contains a handy little feature that enables you to write the voiceover narration script used for each slide.

This section covers only how to capture a voiceover narration. Other ways to use audio will be discussed in Chapter 6.

To import background audio into a Captivate movie:

1. Open a Captivate movie and select Movie > Preferences.

2. When the Movie Preferences dialog box opens, select the Background Audio tab.

3. Click the Import button.

   The Import Audio dialog box opens (**Figure 2.25**).

4. Select the file and click Open.

   The Import Audio dialog box closes, and you are returned to the Background Audio dialog box.

5. To preview your sound file, click the Play button.

6. In the Fade In and Fade Out areas of the Background Area dialog box, which become active when a file is imported, use the arrows or input fade in and fade out values.

7. Select "Lower background audio volume on slides with additional audio" to reduce automatically the background audio volume on slides that have individual audio files—such as voiceover narration—assigned.

8. Select "Loop audio" to have the background audio file play over and over again.

9. Select "Stop at end of movie" to have the background audio stop when the movie ends.

continues on next page

10. When you are finished, click OK to close the dialog box and add the background audio to your movie.

✔ Tips

■ Captivate ships with a number of pre-recorded background sound loops and files in the MP3 format. You can find them in your Program Files\Macromedia\Captivate\Gallery\Sound folder.

■ The fade values apply when the movie starts and when the movie finishes. They are not related to the duration of a slide.

To record a background audio file:

1. Connect your microphone to your computer and open a Captivate movie.

2. Open the Background Audio preferences and click the "Record new" button to open the Record Audio dialog box.

3. Click the Options button.
The Audio Options dialog box opens.

4. Select Microphone as your input source.

5. Click the "Calibrate input" button in the Audio Options.
The "Calibrate microphone" dialog box opens (**Figure 2.26**).

6. Speak into the microphone.
The Recording Level meter on the right side of the dialog box changes color, and you will be informed whether the input level is acceptable. Click OK to return to the Audio Options dialog box.

7. Select your audio quality from the Audio Quality pop-down menu and click OK to return to the Record Audio dialog box.

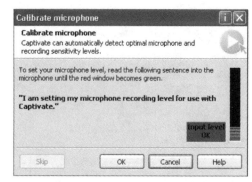

Figure 2.26 The Calibrate microphone dialog box.

Figure 2.27 The Record Audio dialog box.

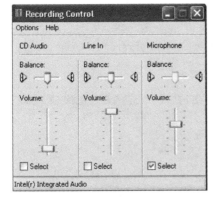

Figure 2.28 Calibrate a microphone using the computer's Recording Control options. Don't use Captivate.

8. Click the Record button and speak into the microphone.

A VU meter appears in the Record Audio dialog box (**Figure 2.27**).

9. When you finish recording, click the Stop button (the button with the square on it).

The file is converted to an MP3 file and appears in the Record Audio dialog box. You'll see that the file is ready and its duration.

10. If you want to delete the audio file, click the "Remove audio" button (the button with the red X).

11. Click OK to return to the Background Audio dialog box.

12. Select your options and click OK to close the dialog box.

✔ Tips

- Be sure that the microphone is active in your computer's Recording Control options.

- The "Calibrate microphone" dialog box is inaccurately named. It doesn't calibrate a edx microphone, it detects a microphone and the resulting audio levels. If your recording level is too high, reduce the volume control in the Microphone section of your computer's Recording Control options (**Figure 2.28**). You won't be able to do it in Captivate.

- Keep an eye on the VU meter as you record. If it moves too far to the left, turns red, and stays there, you are speaking too loudly. In this case, stop the recording and start over.

ADDING BACKGROUND AUDIO TO YOUR MOVIE

To write a script used for narration:

1. In the Edit View panel, double-click the slide to which the script will apply.

   The Slide Properties dialog box opens.

2. Click the Slide Notes button and enter the text for the script in the Slide notes dialog box (**Figure 2.29**).

3. Click OK to accept the note and close the dialog box.

4. Click OK to close the Slide Properties dialog box.

5. Click the Audio button on the Main toolbar to open the Audio Properties dialog box.

6. Select View Script.

   The note appears in the dialog box (**Figure 2.30**).

7. Click the Record button and read the script.

✔ Tip

- You can use more than just notes as scripts. You can also use caption text. This is especially important in situations where accessibility for the visually impaired is a key issue. By narrating a caption, the soundtrack is embedded into the final file. This makes Flash, which is a generally inaccessible product to screen readers, accessible.

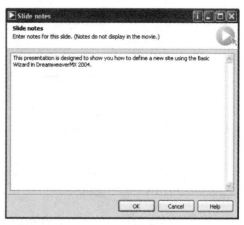

Figure 2.29 Enter the slide's narration script into the Slide notes dialog box.

Figure 2.30 Selecting View Script in the Audio Properties opens the script, in which you can write a caption or note.

Bitrate

The data flow into a computer. A bit is the computer's raw material, with a value of either a 1 or a 0. If the bitrate is 10 kbps (kilobits per second), the processor is handling 10,000 bits every second. If you use the Internet, you are already familiar with this term: The fastest dial-up modems can send 56,000 bits of information per second (56 kbps) to your computer.

Some Sound Terminology

When working with sound in Captivate, it helps to understand what much of the terminology used actually means.

WAV The default sound file format on the PC.

MP3 A compression format for sound. The official name is Moving Pictures Expert Group Level-2 Layer-3 Audio. These files are very small because, in very basic terms, they "throw away" sounds that are inaudible to humans.

kHz Kilohertz. A hertz is the frequency of one sound wave; a kilohertz is 1000 sound waves per second. An 11 kHz sound is less accurate than a 44 kHz sound.

8 bit/16 bit The number of samples, measured from peak to peak, in a sound wave. An 8-bit sound wave is broken into 256 samples; a 16-bit sound wave is broken into 66,000 samples. The more samples there are per wave, the higher the file size and the better the sound quality.

Mono/Stereo One sound channel or two sound channels. A stereo sound has a file size twice that of its mono counterpart.

Setting a Movie's Mouse Options

When a movie is playing, the mouse is usually moving around the screen if mouse movement has been captured. As the mouse moves, the cursor, called a *pointer* in Captivate, changes depending on the action being undertaken. You can modify how the mouse moves as well its speed, its sound, its visibility, and even the color used when something is clicked. You can even change the path of the mouse from one slide to the next and the shape of the mouse's path from curved to straight and vice versa.

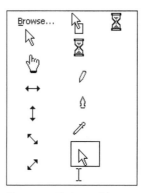

Figure 2.31 Project pointers enable you to customize the pointer used in the movie.

To change the mouse pointer:

1. In Storyboard view, click Mouse in the "Slide tasks" area to open the Mouse Options pop-down menu.

2. Select either Project Pointers or Current Theme Pointers.

   You can use the Project pointers (**Figure 2.31**) to change the pointer used in the slide.

   The Current Theme pointers (**Figure 2.32**) are the ones that your computer uses.

3. When the pop-up menu of pointers appears, select a pointer by clicking it.

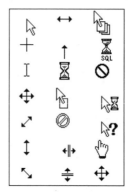

Figure 2.32 Current Theme pointers are based upon those used in the operating system.

✔ Tips

■ The Current Theme pointer is directly related to the Windows theme set in your computer's Display control panel. Even though a theme can be changed, end users don't need to have the same themes on their computers for the movie to work. The pointers used will be exported with the project.

■ If the selected slide has no mouse actions associated with it, a new default mouse movement will be added to the slide.

■ You aren't limited to just the pointers shown in the Project Pointers pop-down menu. If you click Browse in the Project Pointers pop-down, you will be taken to the Cursors folder in your computer's Windows folder. From here you can choose from all of the cursors that your system uses.

■ If you are in the Edit View panel, you can access the pointers by selecting Slide > Mouse.

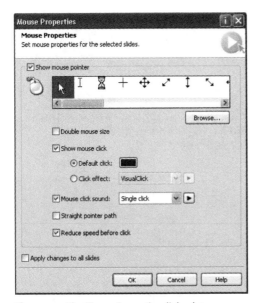

Figure 2.33 The Mouse Properties dialog box.

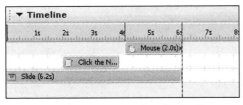

Figure 2.34 Adjust mouse speed on the timeline.

To change the mouse pointer's size:

1. Select a slide in the Edit View panel.

2. Click the Mouse button on the Advanced toolbar.

    The Mouse Properties dialog box opens (**Figure 2.33**).

3. Select Double Mouse Size and click OK.

4. To change back to the normal size mouse, deselect Double Size Mouse.

✔ Tip

■ You can change the size of the cursor in the Storyboard View panel by selecting Properties from the Mouse context menu in the Slide Tasks area.

To change how quickly the mouse moves:

1. In either the Storyboard View or Edit View panel, double-click a slide containing an icon showing the presence of a captured mouse movement.

2. Open the timeline at the top of the Edit View panel. by clicking the down arrow beside the word *Timeline*.

    The mouse object is indicated on the timeline (**Figure 2.34**), and the length the mouse is visible is indicated by the duration, in brackets, and the length of the mouse span on the timeline. Also, placing the pointer on the mouse span will result in a tool tip that shows the start time of the mouse movement and the duration of the movement.

3. Click and drag the right side of the mouse object to the right to decrease the mouse speed or to the left to increase the mouse speed.

continues on next page

SETTING A MOVIE'S MOUSE OPTIONS

✔ Tips

- The click-and-drag to the right or to the left actually makes sense. If you drag the right edge of the mouse object to the right, you are increasing the mouse object's duration in the slide. The effect is to have the same movement distance over a longer time, which means the mouse is effectively slowed down. Moving to the left has the opposite effect: The same movement in a shorter time period means the mouse speed is increased.

- Double-clicking the mouse object in the timeline opens the Mouse Properties dialog box.

To change the mouse's visual effect:

You can change the color used in the movie to indicate a mouse click, or you can use a Flash SWF file to change the visual effect of a clicking an object in your movie. There are two that are added when you install Captivate on your computer. Here's how to change the mouse click color and the mouse click effect:

1. Open the Mouse Properties dialog box.

2. To change the color of a mouse click, select "Default click" in the "Show mouse click" area.

3. Click the color chip to open the Color Picker, select a new color and click OK. The new color appears as the default.

4. To change the mouse click effect, select "Click effect" and select one of the two options from the pop-down menu (**Figure 2.35**). Click the Play button (it has an arrow) to see the effect chosen in the preview area.

5. Click OK.

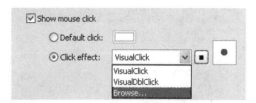

Figure 2.35 The mouse click effect is a small Flash SWF file. Click the Play button to preview your selected effect.

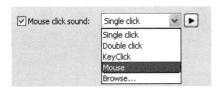

Figure 2.36 You can apply sound to mouse clicks.

Setting Keyboard Sounds

It isn't only mouse click sounds that can give an aural clue to the user that something is changing. Keystrokes can also be given a "tap" sound. Here's how:

1. Open a Captivate movie.

2. Select Movie > Preferences and select the Preferences tab.

3. Select "Play tap audio for recorded typing when movie is generated."

4. Click OK.

✔ Tips

■ You can have either a click color or a click effect. Selecting one will deselect the other.

■ You can create your own click effect in Flash. In this case, create the SWF file, place it in the Visual clicks folder (Captivate\Gallery\Mouse\Visual Clicks) and select it using the Browse button in the Visual Clicks pop-down menu.

■ You can apply click colors and visual clicks to the entire movie, not just a slide. Select "Apply changes to all slides" in the Mouse Properties dialog box to apply your selection globally.

To change the mouse click sound:

1. In either the Storyboard or Edit View panels open the Mouse Properties dialog box.

2. Select Mouse click sound and select a sound from the pop-down menu (**Figure 2.36**).

3. Click the Play button to preview the sound.

✔ Tips

■ Mouse clicks are an invaluable audible clue to the user that something has happened. If the action you are performing requires either a single or a double click, you can add the mouse sound that matches the action. You can even turn off the sound.

■ If you don't want to have a mouse sound, deselect Mouse click sound.

■ If you have a library of mouse click sounds, you can add their WAV or MP3 versions to Captivate\Gallery\Mouse\Click Sounds and access them by clicking the Browse button in the Click Sounds pop-down menu.

To change the mouse movement direction and location:

1. In the Edit View panel, select a slide containing a mouse movement.

2. Roll your mouse to the endpoint of the animation.

   Your cursor changes to a grabber-hand cursor.

3. Click and drag the pointer to a new location on the screen.

4. Drag the pointer to the opposite side of the start point to change the direction of the mouse movement.

✔ Tip

■ Slides containing mouse movements have a mouse icon in the lower right corner of the slide's thumbnail, and the path of the mouse on the slide is indicated by a blue line with arrows showing the direction on the movement.

To change the mouse path to a curved or straight line:

1. In the Edit View panel, open a slide.

2. Click a slide with a mouse icon in the Filmstrip.

3. When the slide opens in the Edit View panel, click the mouse icon to open the pop-down menu.

4. Select Straight Pointer Path (**Figure 2.37**). The curved path changes to a straight path.

✔ Tip

■ To change back to a curved path, deselect the Straight Pointer Path option.

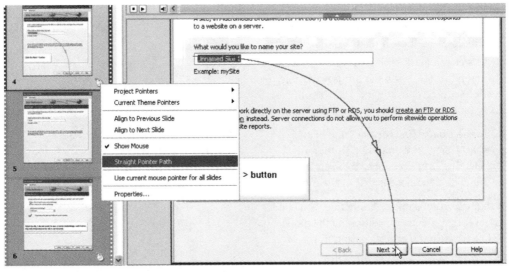

Figure 2.37 You can straighten a curved mouse path.

The "peek-a-boo" mouse pointer

Captivate's ability to relocate mouse animation on the screen is a great feature. What if you don't need the mouse to be visible in a slide? How do you align a changed mouse movement to avoid having the mouse disappear and "magically" reappear at another screen location as you move to the previous or next slide?

There will be occasions where a moving pointer is unnecessary. For example, you may record a movie and discover the narration is more important than watching the pointer move. In this situation, you can hide the pointer in a particular slide—or in the entire movie.

To hide the pointer:

1. In the Edit View panel, open a slide with mouse movement.

2. Open the Mouse Properties dialog box and deselect Show Mouse Pointer.

   The check mark beside the Show Mouse menu item tells you the mouse is visible. Deselect the check mark, and the mouse is gone in that frame.

3. In the Mouse Properties dialog box, deselecting Show mouse pointer and selecting "Apply changes to all slides" will hide the mouse for the entire movie.

If you reposition a mouse animation, you will discover that manually positioning the mouse to line up with the exact location in the previous or next slide is virtually impossible.

To align your pointer:

1. Right-click the pointer to open the context menu.

2. Depending upon your need, select Align to Previous Frame or Align to Next Frame (**Figure 2.38**).

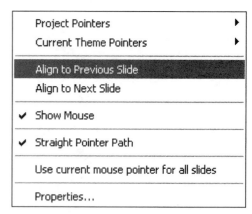

Figure 2.38 Changes in a mouse path can be reflected in the frames on either side of the mouse path.

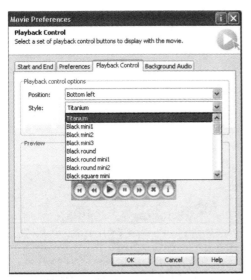

Figure 2.39 Choose playback controls for completed movies in the Playback Control dialog box.

Adding, Changing, and Creating Custom Movie Playback Controls

When a movie plays, the user will control the movie using buttons such as Play or Pause. Playback controls are especially useful in movies where you provide step-by-step instructions or the user needs to review sections of the movie prior to a quiz.

Captivate enables you to provide your viewers with a regular playback controller or one that you create. This controller always "floats" above the movie. You can also choose which controls appear in the controller.

To select the playback controls used in a movie:

1. Open a movie and, in either the Storyboard View or Edit View panel, select Movie > Preferences.

   The Movie Preferences dialog box opens.

2. Select the Playback Control tab.

   The Playback Controls dialog box opens (**Figure 2.39**).

3. Choose the controller position from the pop-down menu.

4. Select your style from the pop-down list.

   To preview the styles in the list, click one; it will appear in the preview area of the dialog box.

5. If "progrees bar" is not grayed out, you can choose to add a progress bar.

6. Click OK.

✔ Tip

■ The progress bar option is tied directly to the style you may choose. If the selected style does not include a progress bar, this option will be grayed out.

To create a custom playback controller:

1. Create all of the buttons, including their states, in a graphics program such as Macromedia Fireworks MX 2004 or Freehand MX.

2. Save all of the buttons as BMP images using the naming conventions presented in the sidebar "Building Your Own Buttons."

3. Create a single image that contains all of the buttons in their final position.

   This composite image will be used when the playback controls are previewed.

4. Place all of the images in the Captivate Playback Controls folder (Program Files\Macromedia\Captivate\Gallery\Playback Controls).

5. Add the controller to your movie.

✔ Tips

■ You can make areas of your control transparent by changing the name from style-playbuttonup.bmp to style-play-*trans*buttonup.bmp (in other words, add *trans* before the word *button*). The transparent color will be obtained from the top left pixel; any other pixels of the same color will appear transparent.

■ Controls you create don't always have to use a horizontal orientation. You can make your controls appear vertically by using the word *vertical* in the name of your playback control (for example, style*vertical*-playbuttonup.bmp).

Choosing a Playback Control Style

The list of styles that are available when Captivate is installed is quite extensive. Keep in mind the word *style* not only refers to the visual style of the controls, but also to the style of the buttons used. Some of the styles contain several buttons, while others contain as few as three. Pay close attention to the preview area of the dialog box when choosing your styles to ensure that you have the both the proper number of control elements and that the style complements the design of the movie.

If you choose to create a full screen movie, it is important that you choose a style that contains a Close button. This will allow your viewers to leave the movie and perform other computing tasks.

Also, all control styles added to a movie contain an Info button. Users who click this will see the information you entered when you set the movie properties, including author, company name, URL, and Web address.

If you are adding playback controls, be aware of their locations on the screen, and plan to leave those areas blank. What you don't need is to have your controls covering elements of the movie.

Building Your Own Buttons

If you are a New Media designer, you are quite used to creating custom controls and adding the code that makes them function. Captivate makes your life easier because it writes the code for you. The major difference between your normal approach to building buttons and Captivate's approach is that buttons in Captivate have only Up and Down states; there is no Over state.

If you create your own buttons, follow these guidelines:

◆ All buttons must have the same width and height.

◆ Playback controls can have only the following buttons:
  ▲ Play
  ▲ Back
  ▲ Forward
  ▲ Pause
  ▲ Exit
  ▲ Rewind

◆ All buttons must use the following naming convention: *ControlStyleName-ButtonNameButtonState.extension*. For example, assume we create a style named VQSBlue. A rewind button for this style would have two files associated with it: VQSBlue-rewindbuttonup. bmp and VQSBlue-rewindbutton-down.bmp. The composite image for this controller, which would appear in the oreview area of the Playback Control dialog box, would be named VQSBlue-preview.bmp.

To preview a movie:

1. Open the movie in Captivate, or open the Storyboard View or Edit View panel.

2. Select File > Preview or click the Preview button on the Main toolbar.

3. Select how the movie will be previewed by selecting an option from the pop-down menu.

   Your choices are to preview the entire movie, preview certain slides of the movie, or have the movie preview in a browser.

   The movie compiles and then opens in the preview window. Use the playback controls to play the movie.

4. Click the Close Preview button to exit the preview.

✔ Tip

■ You don't have to use the playback controls to move through the movie preview. You can use the Slide Number slider at the top of the preview window as a jog controller. Drag the slider, and the movie will skip through the slides.

Creating an Image Movie

There will be occasions where images are far more effective than an interactive screen capture. A typical scenario for this is when a client wishes to include a series of product shots for the user to view or a series of images used for eLearning purposes that include click boxes, captions, and text input. The solution here is an Image movie.

Though Macromedia is positioning this feature as a form of slide show, seeing an Image movie in this rather myopic way would be a mistake. The images in an Image movie are embedded into the background of each slide. This means they can't be moved around on the slide or otherwise manipulated. If you need this flexibility, plan to import each image manually into a separate slide.

Still, the ability to quickly create a movie from a series of images and then adding the interactive elements or eLearning features is well worth exploring.

To create an Image movie:

1. Open Captivate and select "Record or create a new movie" on the Start screen.

    The New movie options dialog box opens (**Figure 2.40**).

2. Select Image movie from the "Create other movie type" section of the dialog box.

3. Click OK.

    The Image movie dialog box opens (**Figure 2.41**).

4. If you are creating a movie requiring a custom screen dimension, select "User defined (custom)."

5. Enter the screen dimensions into the text input area, or use the up and down arrows beside the Width and Height input boxes to increase or decrease the screen dimensions in one-pixel increments.

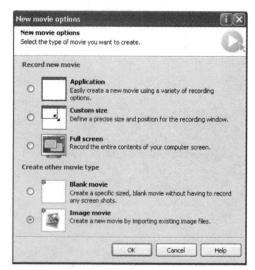

Figure 2.40 Creating an Image movie.

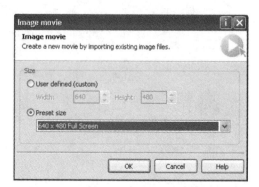

Figure 2.41 The Image movie dialog box enables you to set a custom size or choose from a number of preset sizes.

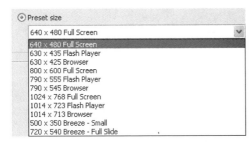

Figure 2.42 The Image movie presets are quite varied.

Figure 2.43 If you need to crop or resize images before they appear in an Image movie, you can do this in the Import Image dialog box.

Figure 2.44 An Image movie shown in the Storyboard View panel.

6. When you're finished, click OK.

7. Select Preset Size and select a slide size from the list in the pop-down menu (**Figure 2.42**).

8. Click OK. The Storyboard View panel and the Open dialog box will both open.

9. Navigate, in the "Open" dialog box to the folder containing the images to be used in the Image movie.

10. Hold down the Shift key, select the images to be used in the Image movie, and click OK.

11. If some of the selected images are too large for the screen, the Import Image dialog box may open (**Figure 2.43**), asking how you want to deal with this situation. In this case, determine whether images will be cropped or scaled, and click the appropriate button. If there are a number of images that need to be cropped or scaled, select "Apply to all images" and then make your choice.

The images are imported, and each imported image appears on a separate slide in the Filmstrip of the Edit View panel or as a series of slides in the Storyboard View panel (**Figure 2.44**).

✔ Tip

■ Though using the Crop or Rescale buttons in the Import Image dialog box can be a real time-saver, you have absolutely no control over the final size. If this a major issue, consider using the batch-processing features of an imaging application such as Fireworks MX 2004 or Photoshop prior to importing the images into the Image movie.

Creating a Blank Captivate Movie

Creating a blank movie may, at first, seem a bit odd. The purpose of a movie is to fill a screen with content that can be seen, can be read, or that moves. It isn't to create a blank page.

Yet in fact, a blank movie is a valuable feature. For example, Captivate doesn't allow you to create styles that can be applied throughout the movie. A blank movie does just that: You create the blank movie—which is a single, empty slide—and then add formatted content from click boxes to the slide. From there, you can add extra slides to the movie and copy and paste the movie elements into the new slides.

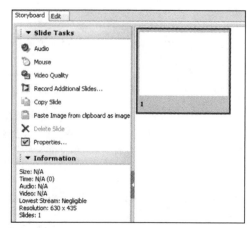

Figure 2.45 Blank movies have an important role in the movie creation process.

To create a blank movie:

1. Open Captivate and select "Record or create a new movie" on the Start screen.

   The New Movie Options dialog box opens.

2. Select Blank Movie from the "Create other movie type" section of the dialog box.

   Click OK to open the Blank Movie dialog box.

   Determine your screen size and click OK.

   The Blank Movie dialog box closes, and a single blank slide is visible in either the Storyboard View or Edit View panel (**Figure 2.45**).

Summary

This chapter stressed the importance of "Planning your work and working your plan." As you discovered the many features in the Recording Options and Movie Preferences dialog boxes allow you to execute your plan.

I covered a number of general subjects as well. They included setting the recording area and modifying and resizing a movie that has been recorded. This is important to know because the physical size of a movie, especially if it is being delivered for web playback, will have a direct effect upon the user's experience.

Sound is a major media element in Captivate and narrations are a major aspect of the development process. I discussed how to add a background sound track to your movie, how to record a narration and how captions can also be used as scripts for voice-over narrations.

Your movies will also contain mouse movement and I showed how you can speed up or slow down these movements, change their path, remove them and how to align them with each other as you move from slide-to-slide.

Allowing the user to control the flow and pace of a movie is another key element of interactivity. I demonstrated how to apply playback controls to a movie and change their position on the screen. I finished the chapter by showing you how to create a Captivate slide show by creating an Image Movie and how to create a Blank Movie that can serve as a sort of style sheet for your entire movie.

Now that you understand the broad features of Captivate—the movie—the next chapter narrows the focus and concentrates on what you can do with the slides that compose the Captivate movie.

SUMMARY

USING SLIDES TO BUILD A MOVIE

3

The raw material of a Captivate movie is the slide. A movie is nothing more than a series of individual slides that play sequentially, at a rate of about one slide every two seconds. In Captivate, a slide can be anything from a static screen shot to one containing fully animated mouse movement with sounds and captions.

Practically everything you do in this application involves working at the slide level. In fact, the main interfaces—the Storyboard View and Edit View panels—are devoted to working with the content of individual slides in your movie.

Adding Slides to Your Movie

In the previous chapter, you learned how to record a movie. Recording is an inexact process and, inevitably, there will come a time when you discover you have either omitted a step or have to insert new slides into the movie. Instead of rerecording the movie, you can record the new sequence of slides and insert them into the existing movie.

The various types of slides available to you include:

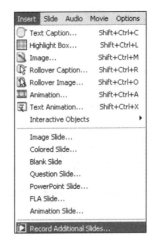

Figure 3.1 Slides are inserted using a menu.

◆ **Image slides** Composed of a BMP, GIF, or JPG image.

◆ **Colored slides** Contain a colored background that you create.

◆ **Blank slides** Empty slides to which you add content, ranging from logos to text. They are ideal for separating sections of a movie.

◆ **Question slides** Used to create quizzes based upon the presentation.

◆ **PowerPoint slides** Contain an entire PowerPoint presentation.

◆ **FLA slides** Designed to hold Flash content.

◆ **Animation slides** Contain animations such as Flash SWF files, animated GIFs, and AVI movies.

To record new slides:

1. Open a movie and, in either the Storyboard View or Edit View panel, select Insert > Record Additional Slides (**Figure 3.1**). The Record Additional Slides dialog box opens.

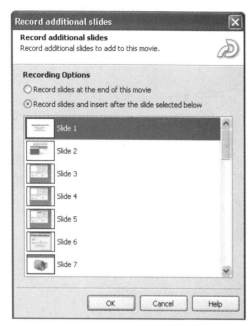

Figure 3.2 You choose where the additional slides will be placed after they are recorded.

Figure 3.3 You can import slides into a movie from another Captivate movie.

2. Choose "Record Slides at the end of this movie" to add the new slides after the last slide of the movie, or choose "Record slides and insert after the slide selected below" to select a slide from the thumbnails and have the new recoding added after the selected slide.

3. Click OK.

The Recording window opens.

4. Finish recording by pressing the End key.

The new slides are inserted into your movie at the location indicated in step 2 (**Figure 3.2**).

To import new slides from one movie to another:

1. Open the target movie into which the slides are to be imported.

2. Select File > Import/Export > "Import Slides/Objects from other Captivate Projects" (**Figure 3.3**).

continues on next page

ADDING SLIDES TO YOUR MOVIE

3. Select the file from which the slides are to be imported and click the Open button.

You are presented with the thumbnails of all of the slides in the selected movie (**Figure 3.4**) as well as several options.

4. To select an individual slide, select Slide Only or Slide and Objects from the Import drop-down below the desired slide.

To select multiple slides, navigate through the dialog box by moving the slider and selecting the slides you want to import in the Import drop-down.

To select all of the slides, click the Select All Button.

To deselect all of the slides selected, click the Clear All button.

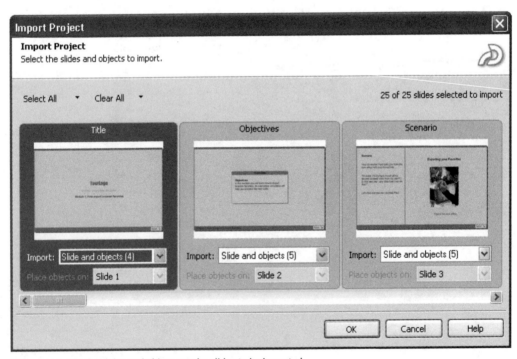

Figure 3.4 Select the slides and objects on the slides to be imported.

ADDING SLIDES TO YOUR MOVIE

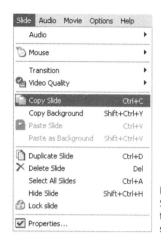

Figure 3.5 Use the Slide context menu to copy and paste slides into a movie.

To import just the objects in a slide, elect objects only from the Import drop-down. The Objects Destination pop-down list, which contains all of the slides in the target movie, becomes available. Select the slide in the target movie into which the objects will be loaded.

5. When you have completed importing slides and/or objects into the target movie, click OK.

The imported slides appear at the end of the movie.

6. Open the Slide View panel and move the imported slides to their desired locations in the target movie.

To use Copy and Paste to add new slides:

1. Open a movie and, in either the Storyboard View or Edit View panel, select the slide or slides to be copied.

2. Press Control-C, right-click the slide, and select Copy Slide from the context menu or select Edit > Copy Slide (**Figure 3.5**).

3. Open the movie where the new slides will be located.

4. Right-click the target slide where the copied slides are to be pasted and select Paste Slide from the context menu.

✔ Tip

■ In step 2, be careful with the copy method you choose in the context menu. Selecting "Copy Slide to clipboard as a bitmap" will flatten the slide and turn it into an image. You will lose all interactivity.

You can select multiple slides for copying by pressing the Shift or Control button and clicking the desired slides. If you want to copy all of the slides of a movie, press Control-A or select Edit > Select All Slides.

ADDING SLIDES TO YOUR MOVIE

To add blank slides to a movie:

1. In the Storyboard View or Edit View panel, select the slide before the location where the slide is to be inserted.

2. Select Insert > Blank Slide (**Figure 3.6**). A new blank slide is inserted into the movie.

To insert a colored slide:

1. In the Slide View panel, select the slide before the location where the colored slide is to be inserted.

2. Select Insert > Colored Slide. The color picker opens.

3. Select your color and click OK. The new slide is inserted into the movie (**Figure 3.7**). If you are adding the slide in the Storyboard View panel, clicking OK opens the new slide in the Edit View panel.

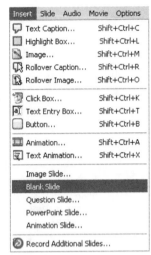

Figure 3.6 Blank slides are ideal for adding personalization to a movie.

Figure 3.7 A colored slide is inserted into a movie.

To delete a slide from your movie:

1. Select the slide (or slides) to be deleted in either the Storyboard View or Edit View panel.

2. Press the Delete key.

   An alert opens asking you if you really want to do this.

3. Click Yes.

To rearrange the slide order in a movie:

1. Open a Captivate movie in the Storyboard view.

2. Select the slide or slides to be moved.

3. Drag the selection to its new location and release the mouse.

✔ Tip

- If the slide being moved contains a mouse movement (there is a mouse icon in the bottom right corner of the thumbnail), consider aligning the movement with the previous slide or the next slide. Do this by clicking the mouse icon and selecting a mouse alignment option from the pop-down menu.

A Word About Blank Slides

At first glance it might seem a bit odd to be inserting empty slides into the movie. Yet blank slides are, in many respects, a canvas upon which you can add content. This content could be an image, a logo, a credits screen, or anything else that can be placed in a slide.

Use blank slides to divide sections of your movie. For example, you may have a software demonstration that is immediately followed by a quiz or demonstration of some of the software's advanced features. A blank slide enables you to transition smoothly between the two sections and give the user a visual clue that things are about to change.

A colored slide, in Captivate, is nothing more than a blank slide with a colored background.

Features of the New Image Box Dialog Box

There are a lot of features in the New image box dialog box. On the Image tab, you'll find the following:

- **Transparency** Either enter a value or use the arrows to add transparency to an image. The higher the value, the more transparent the image.

- **Transparent background** Select for images such as round buttons or other irregularly shaped images that sit on a solid background color. Be careful with this one: Objects with drop shadows may have artifacts surrounding the shadow when this option is selected.

- **Image scrolling** Though the image preview may have Horizontal and Vertical sliders, roll the cursor over the image and, when it turns to a four-pointed cursor, click and drag to move the image inside the preview area.

- **Reset to original size** Select to revert a scaled or distorted image to its original dimensions.

- **Change image** Click to switch the current image with another.

- **Apply properties to all "image boxes" in the movie** Select to apply all of your choices to every image in the movie. Be very careful with this one.

The following features appear on the Options tab:

- **Display time** Either enter a value or use the arrows to set how long an image will appear on a slide (**Figure 3.8**). You don't have to return here to increase or decrease the time—you can change it on the timeline.

Figure 3.8 You can set the various timing options for the image in this dialog box.

Figure 3.9 Audio can be added to images.

◆ **Appear after** Enter how much time elapses before the image appears on the slide. Again, you can change this value on the timeline.

◆ **Display for rest of movie** Select to have the image appear until the movie ends. This feature is useful for logo placement and design elements that are in consistent positions throughout the movie. Be careful with this one.

◆ **Effect** Choose how the image displays when the slide starts to play. Options are "Fade in and out," "Fade in only," "Fade out only," and "No transition."

◆ **In** Enter a time value or use the sliders to determine the duration of a fade-in. You cannot change this value on the timeline.

◆ **Out** Enter a time value or use the sliders to determine the duration of a fade-out. You cannot change this value on the timeline.

The following features appear on the Audio Options tab:

◆ **Play** Click to preview any audio associated with the image (**Figure 3.9**).

◆ **Stop** Click to stop the audio playback.

◆ **Remove audio button** Click to remove the audio track from the image.

◆ **Edit** Click to perform some basic audio-editing tasks on the audio file associated with the image.

◆ **Record new** Click to open the Record Audio window.

◆ **Import** Click to open the Import Audio dialog box.

continues on next page

- ◆ **Audio Library** Click to select any of the audio currently used in the movie. This one is a Captivate gem.

- ◆ **Fade in** Enter a time value or use the slider to have the sound fade in over the time you enter. You cannot change this on the timeline.

- ◆ **Fade out** Enter a time value or use the slider to have the sound fade out over the time you enter. You cannot change this on the timeline.

✔ Tips

- ■ You can apply the options in the New image box dialog box even after you've placed an image in a slide. Double-clicking an image in a slide launches the Image dialog box.

- ■ You don't have to use the menu to insert an image. Simply click the image button on the Objects toolbar, and the Open dialog box appears.

Inserting Images into Slides

Images ranging from logos to photographs are key elements in a presentation. Captivate enables you to add these elements to your movies. For example, you could create an image in Fireworks containing words, drawings, photos, and special imaging effects to use as the title screen for your movie. You can also add elements such as your company logo to every slide.

You can use images in Captivate in one of two ways: as an image slide or as content.

An image slide is constructed around an image. You place a selected image into the background of the slide and then place content—such as captions, logos, and animations—over it. Images placed in an image slide can't be manipulated or moved around in the slide. This sort of slide is ideal for providing or introducing transitions between sections of your movie.

Images used as content can be moved to other locations in the slide, resized, have opacity applied to them upon import, used as a watermark, and can even be set to fade in and out during playback.

Images in Captivate can be either line art or continuous tone. Graphics such as logos would be an example of line art, and a photograph would be an example of a continuous tone image. You can import these images into Captivate in one of four formats:

- ◆ **GIF** This format has a very limited color palette—usually 216 Web-safe colors—and would be inappropriate for photographs.

continues on next page

- **BMP** This is the Windows bitmap image standard. It has had a rather rocky history and is better suited to line art containing fewer than 256 colors than to photographs.

- **JPG** This format has become the standard for images viewed on a computer screen. Use this for photos.

- **PNG** Portable Network Graphics format which is the default format used by Fireworks.

To create an image slide:

1. Select the slide directly behind where you want to insert the image slide.

2. Select Insert > Image Slide.

   The Open dialog box opens (**Figure 3.10**).

3. Navigate to the folder containing your images and select one.

   When you select an image, the thumbnail appears on the right side of the dialog box.

4. Click the Open button.

   A new slide containing the image is added to your movie (**Figure 3.11**).

There will be occasions where the image's dimensions are larger than those of the slide in which they will be placed. For example, if the image is 800 × 600 and the slide is 640 × 480, Captivate will open the Import Image dialog box (**Figure 3.12**) before creating the slide. You have three choices:

- **Crop** Select to center the image in the slide and trim off any part of the image outside of the slide's dimensions.

- **Rescale** Select to have the application scale the image proportionately to fit the slide.

- **Cancel** Click if neither option appeals to you.

Figure 3.10 The Open dialog box shows the images in the folder.

Figure 3.11 The Image Slide is created.

Figure 3.12 You can scale or crop oversize images before import.

Figure 3.13 The New image box dialog box lets you make a number of decisions.

Figure 3.14 Drag a handle to scale an image.

Although I am a big advocate of letting the software do the work, in this instance this might not be the best solution. If you have a number of oversize images, use the batch/automate features of Fireworks MX 2004 or Photoshop CS to resize them. This way, you control the size of the image instead of accepting what Captivate hands you.

To add an image to a slide:

1. In the Edit View panel, click the desired slide in the Filmstrip.

2. Select Insert > Image or press Shift-Control-M.

   The Open dialog box opens.

3. Navigate to the folder containing the image and select it.

4. Click Open.

   The New image box dialog box opens (**Figure 3.13**).

5. Use the tabs to set options for the image:
   - ▲ **Image** Add transparency to the image, navigate around the image, or replace the image.
   - ▲ **Options** Set the timing options and transitions for the image.
   - ▲ **Audio** Add music, sound effects, or narration to the image.

6. When you are finished making your changes, click OK.

   The image appears on the slide.

To scale a placed image:

1. Click the image once in the Edit View panel.

   Handles appear (**Figure 3.14**).

2. Click and drag a corner handle to scale the image proportionally.

INSERTING IMAGES INTO SLIDES

To change the quality of a JPG image:

1. Open a movie.

2. Select Movie > Preferences.

3. Click the Preferences tab and either enter a value or use the arrows to increase or decrease the quality of a JPG image (**Figure 3.15**).

✔ Tip

■ Changing the JPG quality changes the image quality for all images in the movie. This is a rather dangerous control, because decreasing image quality essentially recompresses all of the images in the movie. Due to the fact that JPG compression is *lossy*—image information is lost on compression—you run the risk of degrading your images. For example, images with too much compression have colors that suddenly look flat, or "banding" is introduced into gradients or areas of subtle color change.

To adjust image transparency:

1. In Storyboard view, double-click the slide containing the image to be changed.
   The slide opens in the Edit View panel.

2. Double-click the image to be changed.
   The Image Properties dialog box opens.

3. Use the Transparency arrows to select the transparency amount to be applied to the image (**Figure 3.16**).
   You will see the change in the dialog box's Preview window.

4. Click OK.

✔ Tip

■ A common use for transparency in a Captivate movie is to fade an image enough so it is barely visible and can function as a watermark. You can then use your company logo on each slide of the movie.

Figure 3.15 The quality of a JPG image can be set using a slider.

Figure 3.16 Adding opacity to an image.

Creating Animation Slides

So far you have seen how to add new slides and images to your Captivate movie. You can also create animation slides, which allow you to add animations ranging from Flash to video to your movie. These slides can then function as introductions to the movie or as sections in which new information may be presented or a new topic introduced.

The animation formats that can be imported are SWF, AVI and animated GIF. In the case of the last two, the files are converted to the Flash SWF format upon import.

When importing animations into Captivate, be aware that, especially in the case of AVI and SWF files, Captivate movies play at a standard frame rate of 20 frames per second. The issue here is timing. If the Flash movie is authored at 12 frames per second (the Flash MX 2004 default) and played back at 20 frames per second, things could happen a lot faster. You also should be aware that Captivate supports only Flash Player 6 or lower.

Finally, the duration of the animation slide will equal the duration of the content placed into it. For example, if a 30-second AVI file is placed in an animation slide, the animation slide will be visible for 30 seconds. When the animation is finished, the next slide in the sequence will play.

✔ Tip

- If you want an animation to be on screen for a shorter amount of time, select the animation slide in the Storyboard View panel and click the Properties button on the Main toolbar. This opens the Slide Properties dialog box, where you can change the timing. If you are in Edit view, you can either click the Properties button on the Main toolbar, or right-click the animation and select Properties from the context menu.

To add an animation slide to your movie:

1. Open a movie and select either the Storyboard View or Edit View panel.

2. Select Insert > Animation Slide (**Figure 3.17**).

   The Open dialog box appears.

3. Navigate to the folder where the animation to be inserted is located.

   Captivate goes to Program Files/ Macromedia/Captivate/Gallery/ SWF Animation by default.

4. Either double-click the file or select the file and click the Open button.

   If you have chosen an animated GIF or AVI file, a progress bar showing the conversion to the SWF format appears. When it finishes, the new slide containing the animation opens and starts playing in the Edit View panel. The thumbnail also appears in the Storyboard View panel and in the Filmstrip of the Edit View panel (**Figure 3.18**).

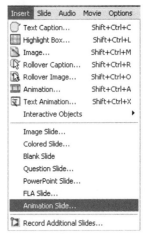

Figure 3.17 Animation Slides can be added to your movie.

Figure 3.18 Add animation slides through a menu selection.

✔ Tips

■ If you are creating content in Flash MX 2004, for inclusion in Captivate be aware that Captivate will accept files that are compatible with the Flash Player 6 or lower only.

■ You can always tell where your animation slides are located in your movie: The thumbnail icon for the slide contains a Flash SWF icon.

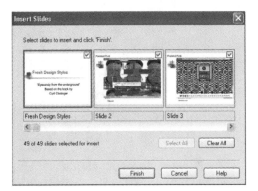

Figure 3.19 PowerPoint slides can be imported into a Captivate movie.

Figure 3.20 Extracting slides from a PowerPoint Presentation.

Using PowerPoint Presentations

If there can be said to be a corporate presentation standard, it would be Microsoft's PowerPoint. Used by everyone from grade-school students to the captains of industry, the odds are you will eventually be asked if a PowerPoint presentation can be used in your Captivate movie. The answer is yes. In fact, you can use the entire presentation or individual slides from the presentation in your Captivate movie.

The advantage to you, the developer, is you now have access to content that already exists. This is a potentially huge productivity boost, because you don't have to re-create or repurpose the content for use in your movie.

In previous version of PowerPoint, you could import only a PowerPoint file—with the .ppt extension—into the movie. Captivate expands this so now you can import both PPT and PPS (PowerPoint slide show) files into your movie.

To import a PowerPoint presentation:

1. With a movie open, select either the Slide View or Edit View panel.

2. Select Insert > PowerPoint Slide to open the Insert PowerPoint Slides dialog box (**Figure 3.19**).

3. Click the Browse button to navigate to the folder containing the PPT or PPS file.

4. Select where the imported slide(s) should be placed in the Captivate movie and click OK.

   You will see a dialog box—"Extracting thumbnail images"—that shows a progress bar tracking the process of converting the PowerPoint Slide to a series of thumbnail images (**Figure 3.20**).

continues on next page

After the progress bar is complete, the Insert Slides dialog box opens (**Figure 3.21**). This dialog box contains a thumbnail representation of each slide in the PowerPoint presentation.

5. Click the check box in the upper right corner of each slide you want to import.

6. Click again to deselect it (**Figure 3.22**). Click the Finish button to import the selected slides into your movie.

The Importing PowerPoint Presentation dialog box opens. When the import is finished, the box closes and the selected slides are added to your movie (**Figure 3.23**).

✔ Tip

■ The default behavior for importing PowerPoint slides is to import all of the slides in the presentation. This explains why the Select All button in the Import Slides dialog box is grayed out. If you want to import only certain slides, click the Clear All button to deselect all of the slides.

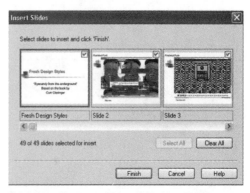

Figure 3.21 The Insert Slides dialog box enables you to select the slides from the PowerPoint presentation to be inserted into the movie.

Figure 3.22 Clicking the check box tells captivate which slides will be imported into the movie.

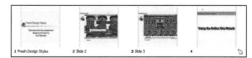

Figure 3.23 The imported PowerPoint slides are added to the movie.

Figure 3.24 FLA files can be imported directly into Animation slides.

Adding Flash Movies to Slides

If PowerPoint is the corporate presentation standard, Flash is the Web animation standard. It has become so ubiquitous on the Web that well over 90 percent of those who use the Web have the Flash 6 or Flash 7 plug-in installed on their computers. As well, many corporations and other users are also using Flash for such things as kiosks and handheld devices such as Pocket PCs.

Captivate enables you to import Flash content directly into a single slide of your movie. If you are a Flash developer or work with one, you can also import the entire FLA file (the file from which the Flash SWF is compiled) into a slide.

To add a Flash movie to a slide:

1. Open a Captivate movie and select Insert > Animation Slide.

2. Navigate to the folder containing the FLA file to be used, select the file, and click the Open button.

   The SWF file is created, and a slide containing the FLA file is added to your movie (**Figure 3.24**).

✔ Tip

- The Flash file used in Figure 3.24 is a small streaming-video file done in Flash. It is there to demonstrate that you don't have to limit yourself to animated Flash content in Captivate. Streaming video, audio, and interactive Flash movies can be added if they are to your movie.

To edit a Flash slide in Captivate:

1. Select the Flash slide in the Edit View panel.

2. Double-click the animation.

   The Animation dialog box appears, telling you that Captivate will remain open while you edit the Flash file (**Figure 3.25**).

3. Click OK.

   Flash launches.

4. Make your changes, save the file, and close it.

   The changes are incorporated into a new SWF file, which replaces the one in the Flash slide.

Figure 3.25 Double-clicking an imported FLA file will launch Flash.

Adding Full Motion Slides

There will be occasions where a slide-based approach to a capture is not suitable to the scope of the project. For example, you may wish to demonstrate how to apply a Live-Effect to an object in Fireworks MX 2004 or how to add a new site in Dreamweaver MX 2004. In this case, a full motion slide is the best solution.

Full motion slides are captured as AVI movies, converted to the SWF format, and then placed in a slide of the movie. The advantage to you is these captures are much smoother and display more detailed motion than the normal slide-based approach. This is because full motion recordings are captured at a higher frame rate—20 frames per second—than the usual capture method.

Whether to use the full motion feature rather than regular recording is a personal decision. Yet there are two important differences that should help drive the decision:

◆ Full motion recordings are as is: They can't be enhanced with captions, audio, or other features that can be added to regular slides.

◆ Full motion recordings result in a higher file size. A regular capture contains two frames for every second of playback; full motion recordings contain 20 frames per second of playback.

To add a full motion slide to a new movie:

1. Open Captivate and select "Record new movie" on the Start page or select File > Record or create a new movie.

2. Select your capture area size and click OK. The Recording window opens.

3. Click the Options button and select the Change Recording Keys tab.

    The Recording Keys window opens. Note the start and stop keys used in the Insert Full Motion Clip area; the defaults are F9 to start recording and F10 to stop recording (**Figure 3.26**).

4. Click OK to return to the Recording window.

5. Make any necessary adjustments to the size and position of the bounding box, and click the Record button.

6. Press the F9 key to start the full motion recording.

7. Complete your task and press the F10 key to stop recording.

8. Press the End key.

    You are returned to the Storyboard View panel. The recording, with a video camera icon, appears in the in thumbnails (**Figure 3.27**).

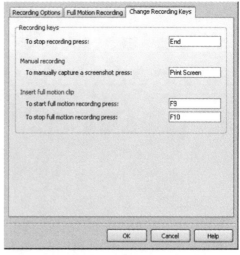

Figure 3.26 You can change the full motion recording keys in the Recording Keys dialog box.

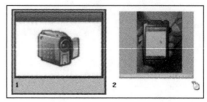

Figure 3.27 The icon for a slide containing a full motion recording uses a video camera.

To add a full motion slide to an existing movie:

1. In either the Storyboard View or Edit View panel, select Insert > Record Additional Slides.

   The Recording window opens.

2. Select where the additional slides should be placed in the movie and click OK.

3. Make any necessary adjustments to the size of the bounding box and click the Record button.

4. Press the F9 key to start the full motion recording.

5. Complete your task and press the F10 key to stop recording.

6. Press the End key.

   You are returned to the Storyboard View panel. The recoding, with a video camera icon, appears in the in the thumbnails.

ADDING FULL MOTION SLIDES

Editing Movie Slides

After recording slides, there are a number of editing tasks you can perform on them:

◆ Duplicate slides

◆ Reorder slides

◆ Set the timing for slides

◆ Add slide labels

◆ Add slide notes

◆ Delete slides

◆ Hide slides

◆ Lock and unlock slides

To duplicate a slide:

1. Open a movie and select either the Edit View or Slide View tab.

2. Right-click the slide and select Duplicate Slide from the pop-down menu.

✔ Tip

■ You don't have to use a menu to duplicate a slide; you can select the slide and press Control-D.

To reorder slides:

◆ If you are in Storyboard view, click the slide to be moved and drag it to the new location.

◆ If you are in Edit view, in the Filmstrip, click the slide to be moved and drag it to its new location.

Figure 3.28 You can change the timing of individual slides.

Figure 3.29 Slide timing can be changed on the Timeline.

To set the timing for slides:

1. In the Storyboard View or Edit View panel, select the slide whose timing is to be changed.

2. Select Slide > Properties.
   The Slide Properties dialog box opens.

3. Enter the time the slide is to be displayed in the Display Time box (**Figure 3.28**).

4. Click OK.

To use the timeline to change slide timing:

1. Double-click a slide to open the slide in the Edit View panel.

2. If the timeline is not open, click the Splitter tab at the top of the Edit View panel to open the timeline.

3. Roll the cursor to the end of the span for the slide object.
   The cursor changes to the split cursor (**Figure 3.29**) when it is over the dotted line, indicating the end of the slide's duration.

4. Drag the dotted line inward to the left to reduce the timing or outward to the right to increase the timing.

5. Release the mouse.
   The new timing is now applied.

✔ Tip

■ You can't reduce the timing of a slide to one that is less than the object on the slide with the longest duration. For example, Figure 3.29 contains a mouse action (and resulting mouse object on the timeline) that occurs over one second. Therefore, you can't reduce the slide's duration to less than one second.

To add a slide label:

1. Open a movie and select either the Storyboard View or Edit View panel.

2. Right-click a slide and select Properties. The Slide Properties dialog box opens.

3. Enter the label text in the Slide Settings area (**Figure 3.30**) and click OK.

   The text entered appears in the slide's thumbnail in both the Storyboard View panel (**Figure 3.31**) and the Edit View panel.

Figure 3.30 You can add labels to slides.

✔ Tips

■ You can also open the Slide Settings dialog box opened by selecting the slide and clicking the Properties button on the Main toolbar.

■ Use labels as short descriptions of the slide. It's much easier to reorder slides by name or description than by slide number.

Figure 3.31 A labeled slide.

To add a slide note:

1. Select a slide and open the Slide Properties dialog box.

2. Click the Notes button.
   The Slide Notes dialog box opens.

3. Enter your text (**Figure 3.32**) and then click OK.

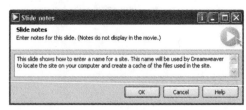

Figure 3.32 You can use slide notes for a variety of purposes.

✔ Tips

■ Use slide notes as a form of speaker notes if the presentation is to be published as a Word document. You can also use slide notes to contain the text for voiceover narrations. Additionally, if you are in a production environment, attaching a note to a slide is great way of communicating with other team members who are working on the file.

■ To tell if a note is attached to a slide, open the Slide Properties dialog box. The Notes button will use bold text.

■ To remove a note, select the text in the note and delete it.

Figure 3.33 Hidden slides are grayed out.

To delete a slide:

1. Right-click the slide to be deleted in either the Storyboard View or Edit View panel.

2. Select Delete Slide from the pop-down menu.

A confirmation dialog box appears, asking you, "Are you sure you want to delete the slide?"

3. Click Yes.

✔ Tips

■ Selecting the slide and pressing the Delete key is another way to delete a slide.

■ You can delete multiple slides in a row by holding down the Shift key, clicking the slides to be deleted, and pressing the Delete key. If the slides to be deleted are not contiguous—for example, slides 5, 9, and 23—hold down the Control key while you click the slides to be deleted.

To hide a slide:

1. Right-click the slide to be hidden.

2. Select Hide Slide from the pop-down menu. Alternatively, you can select Slide > Hide Slide or press Control-Shift-H.

The hidden slides will be grayed out (**Figure 3.33**).

✔ Tip

■ You don't have to hide just one slide. If the slides are in a group, marquee them with the mouse, right-click one of the selected slides, and select Hide Slide. If the slides are not beside each other, Control-click the slides and then open the context pop-down menu.

EDITING MOVIE SLIDES

Hiding slides enables you to add customization without having to make separate movies. If you created a movie that uses individual slides for customization purposes, you can hide the slides that don't pertain to that group. For instance, suppose you developed a movie to show the users in a company how to create PowerPoint slides. The Marketing, Financial and Administration staffs will see the presentation. The first three slides of the movie welcome the areas to the presentation. The Marketing group will see their slide, but the slides aimed at Finance and Administration are hidden and won't be visible on playback.

Figure 3.34 A locked slide has a small padlock in the slide's thumbnail.

To lock a slide:

1. Right-click the slide to be locked.

2. Select Lock Slide from the pop-down menu.

   The locked slide will have a small padlock icon in the bottom right corner of the slide's thumbnail (**Figure 3.34**).

✔ Tip

■ Lock your slides if the movie is being reviewed and you don't want the reviewer to make changes to the slides.

To unlock a slide:

1. Right-click a slide containing a lock icon to open the context menu.

2. Select "Unlock slide."

✔ Tip

■ Clicking the lock icon on the slide's thumbnail will also unlock the slide.

THE CAPTIVATE TIMELINE AND OBJECTS

The key to working with any sort of New Media presentation is understanding the importance of time. We can, for example, have objects appear in a slide for durations ranging from one-tenth of a second to infinity. One of the frustrations encountered when working with Captivate's predecessor—RoboDemo—was an inability to control time. Slide timing was dependent upon the duration of the objects on a slide. As well, controlling when those objects appeared was a convoluted process at best.

The introduction of the timeline in Captivate puts the control of time back in the hands of the developer. Best of all, this control is graphical. Everything on the slide—from audio to mouse movement—is visible, not only can each element be moved forward or backward on the timeline, but the amount of time it is visible or plays can be changed easily.

The timeline also introduces the concept of objects to Captivate. Any thing on the timeline is now referred to as an "object." Thus, audio files appearing on a timeline are "audio objects," mouse movements are "mouse objects," and so on.

continues on next page

The other place where "objects" appear is in the Edit View panel. When a slide is captured, it isn't fixed in place and unable to be edited or manipulated. It can be enhanced through the use of objects. Objects in Captivate are, essentially, extra items that can be added to the slides in your presentation. The list of the objects both created from within Captivate and from external applications is surprisingly quite extensive. You can add the following objects to a Captivate slide:

- Animations such as AVI files and Flash files

- Buttons

- Captions

- Click boxes

- Highlight boxes

- Images created or edited in a variety of drawing applications, such as Fireworks MX 2004 or Freehand MX

- Rollover captions

- Rollover images

- Text entry boxes

- Audio files

This chapter reviews how to use the timeline and how to add or otherwise manipulate objects, in general.

The Captivate Timeline

If you are a Flash MX 2004 or Director MX user, have edited video or audio, or worked with other applications that have a time-based focus, you are quite used to working with a timeline. In simple terms, a timeline gives you a graphical overview of the time used by each object on a slide. Moving objects on the timeline affect when they appear on the slide, and lengthening or shortening their size on the timeline affects how long they remain visible. This is exactly the way the Captivate timeline operates.

To open and close the timeline:

1. Open a Captivate movie and open a slide in the Edit View panel.

2. Click the Splitter at the top of the Edit View panel (**Figure 4.1**).

The Captivate timeline opens.

3. Click the Splitter again to close the timeline.

Splitter button

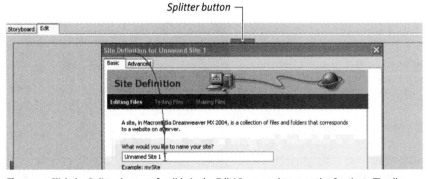

Figure 4.1 Click the Splitter button of a slide in the Edit View panel to open the Captivate Timeline.

Touring the Captivate timeline

Though it may look a little complicated, at first glance, the Captivate timeline (**Figure 4.2**) is actually quite intuitive. Each object in a slide is contained in its own layer. The length of the strip indicates the duration of the object; objects with longer strips are visible for longer than objects with shorter strips.

Rolling the mouse over an object on the timeline displays a tool tip that shows the start and end time of the object and, in the case of a caption, the caption text.

There will be occasions where you want an object to appear at a particular point in time. You can do this using the playhead. You can also drag the playhead across the timeline. This technique, called *scrubbing*, lets you test a slide to ensure everything on the slide is where it is supposed to be and appear when it is supposed to appear.

The object type of each element on the slide is indicated by an icon. Mouse objects have mouse icons, captions have caption icons, sounds show the waveform, and so on.

The order of appearance is determined by the object's location in the timeline. Objects on the left side of the timeline appear before objects on the right side. You can move objects, in their layer, to right or the left, but you can't move them up or down to other layers in the timeline. You can only move the layer.

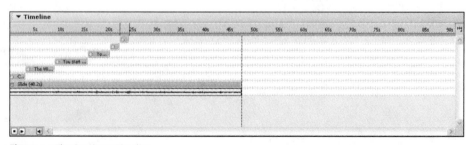

Figure 4.2 The Captivate Timeline.

Figure 4.3 The timeline can be collapsed or opened by clicking the arrow beside the word "Timeline."

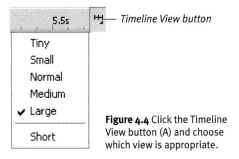

Timeline View button

Figure 4.4 Click the Timeline View button (A) and choose which view is appropriate.

Also, you can delete objects from the timeline which also removes the object's layer from the timeline.

For precise positioning on the timeline, you can expand or contract the timeline view.

Selecting an object on the timeline also selects it in the Edit View panel.

To collapse or open the timeline view:

1. With the timeline open, click the down arrow beside the word *Timeline* at the top of the timeline. The timeline closes (**Figure 4.3**).

2. Click the arrow again to expand the timeline.

✔ Tip

- Use the collapse or expand feature when you are working on a slide in the Edit View panel. Collapsing the timeline gives you extra screen real estate and reduces screen clutter.

To expand or contract the timeline view:

1. With the timeline open, click the Timeline View button once.
   The "Timeline view options" menu (**Figure 4.4**) opens.

2. Make selections using the following options:
   - ▲ Select Tiny to shorten the timeline view to increments of 5 seconds.
   - ▲ Select Small to increase the view to 1-second increments.
   - ▲ Select Normal (the default) to add increments of one-tenth of a second to the timeline.
   - ▲ Select Medium to view the timeline in half-second increments.

continues on next page

THE CAPTIVATE TIMELINE

▲ Select Large to view the timeline in one-tenth-of-a-second increments.

▲ Select Short to compress the height of the layers in the timeline. This is useful if there are a lot of objects contained in the slide.

Once you make your choice, the timeline changes to the view selected.

To move objects on the timeline:

1. Select the object on the timeline.

   The cursor changes to a grabber hand when it is over the object.

2. Drag the object to the right or the left.

3. Release the mouse.

In **Figure 4.5**, you can see the value of being able to drag objects on the timeline and place them in different locations. The "step" pattern indicates the appearance of the objects as the slide plays. The object that is the bottom step will have played and disappeared before the object in the next step.

To change the duration of a slide:

1. Open a slide in the Edit view and open the timeline.

2. If necessary, scroll to the end of the timeline or change the slide view to Tiny or Small.

   The dotted line indicates the end of the slide.

3. Roll the cursor over the right edge of the slide object on the timeline.

   Your cursor will change to a split cursor (**Figure 4.6**).

4. Click and drag the split cursor to the right to decrease the slide duration or to the left to increase the slide duration.

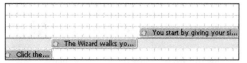

Figure 4.5 Objects are placed in their own layer and can be moved to the right or left on the timeline. They can't be moved to other layers in the same timeline.

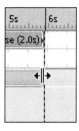

Figure 4.6 You can change the duration of a slide on the timeline when you see the split cursor.

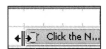

Figure 4.7 You can change the duration of an object by dragging an edge inward or outward on the timeline.

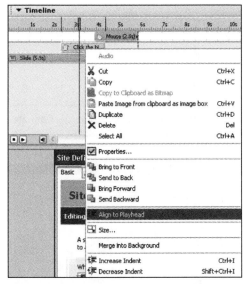

Figure 4.8 You can align objects on the timeline to the position of the playhead.

✔ Tip

- You can also set a slide's duration in the Slide Properties dialog box. Double-click the slide in the Storyboard or Edit View panel to open the Slide Properties dialog box, and then change the duration in the Display Time area.

To change the duration of an object:

1. Open a slide in the Edit View panel and open the timeline.

2. Roll the cursor over the left side or the right side of an object on the timeline.

    Your cursor changes to a split cursor (**Figure 4.7**).

3. If your split cursor is on the right side of the object, click and drag the split cursor to the right to increase the object's duration or to the left to decrease duration. If your split cursor is on the left side of the object, click and drag the split cursor to the right to decrease the object's duration or to the left to increase the duration.

✔ Tips

- You can manually change an object's duration in the object's Properties dialog box.

- You can't increase or decrease the duration of audio objects on the timeline.

To align objects to the playhead:

1. Drag the playback head to the 2-second mark on the timeline.

2. Right-click the object to be moved.

    The context menu opens.

3. Select Align to Playhead (**Figure 4.8**).

    The selected object will snap to the right side of the playhead on the timeline.

THE CAPTIVATE TIMELINE

Object Basics

In the previous chapter you discovered how to add an image to a slide. What if you want to use that same image in another Captivate movie? What if you want to have a caption appear when the user rolls a mouse over the image, or to use the same image in a number of different slides in your movie? What if you don't need the object to float in the slide but want to add it to the slide as a background?

These four operations are the basics of working with Captivate objects.

To import objects between movies:

1. Open the movie to which you want to add the objects.

2. Select File > Import/Export > "Import Slides/Objects from other Captivate projects."

   The Import Captivate Project dialog box opens (**Figure 4.9**).

3. From the list of movies, select the movie containing the objects you want to add to the currently open movie, and then click Open.

   The Import Project dialog box changes to show you all of the slides in the movie you just selected.

4. Click the Clear All button to clear any selections that have been made.

5. Select the slide or slides containing the object or objects you may need.

6. Select objects only from the Import pop-down menu.

   The number of objects in that slide is indicated by the number between the brackets (**Figure 4.10**).

Figure 4.9 Objects can be imported from one Captivate movie to another using the Import Captivate dialog box.

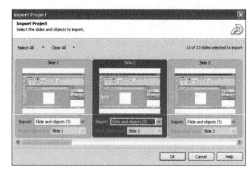

Figure 4.10. You can choose to import the slide or the objects in the slide into a Captivate movie.

OBJECT BASICS

Figure 4.11 Objects on a slide can be duplicated.

7. Select the target slide from the list in the pop-down menu of the open movie where the objects are destined.

8. Click the OK button.

A progress bar opens, displaying the progress of the import. It closes when the objects have been added to the Target Slide of the open movie.

✔ Tip

■ Slides containing no objects available for import will have "No objects on slide" directly below the Import pop-down, and none of the Object Import options will be available.

To duplicate an object:

1. Open a movie in the Storyboard View panel.

2. Double-click the slide containing the object to open the Edit View panel.

3. Right-click the object and select Duplicate from the context menu (**Figure 4.11**).

A copy of the object is created and placed within the slide. The duplicated object is fully editable without affecting the original object.

To merge objects into a slide:

1. Double-click a slide in the Storyboard View panel, or double-click its thumbnail in the Edit View panel.

The slide opens in the Edit View panel.

2. Right-click the object to open the context menu.

3. Select Merge into Background from the pop-down menu.

You will be warned this operation cannot be undone.

4. Click Yes to complete the merge or click No to stop the merge process.

OBJECT BASICS

To add audio to slide objects:

1. Double-click a slide in the Storyboard View panel or its thumbnail in the Edit View panel.

   The slide opens in the Edit View panel.

2. Double-click the object to open the object's Properties dialog box. You can also right-click the object and select Properties from the context menu, or select the object on the slide and click the Properties button on the Main toolbar.

3. Click the Audio tab to open the audio properties for the object.

4. If you are using a microphone to capture the audio, click the Record New button to open the Record Audio dialog box. When finished recording, click the Stop button and click OK in the dialog box to return to the object's audio options. (For full details regarding recording audio, see Chapter 2, "Creating Captivate Movies.")

5. If you are importing a prerecorded sound, click the Import button in the Audio Options dialog box. When the Open dialog box appears, navigate to the folder containing the audio file and double-click the file to add it to the object.

6. Click OK to close the audio options and to add the sound to the object.

Keeping It Tidy

If you would like to add all of the objects from the source movie but don't want to spread them across multiple slides of the target movie, here is a little trick:

1. Add a blank slide to the start or the end of the target movie.

2. Select Import/Export > "Objects from other Captivate Projects."

3. Select the source movie, and when the Import Slides dialog box displays the source movie's slides, click the Clear All button.

4. Click the arrow beside the Select All button. A pop-down menu opens.

5. Select Objects from the menu.

6. Scroll through the slides of the source movie and set the object destination to the blank slide added to the target movie.

7. Click OK.

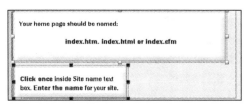

Figure 4.12 When aligning multiple objects with each other, the alignment will be done using the first item selected, which has black handles.

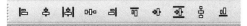

Figure 4.13 The Alignment toolbar.

Aligning Objects

Though you can move objects around on the page easily, aligning them with each other is, in general, an inexact process. This is why it is so important to let the software do the work. In this case, the computer does a better job than a human.

Objects can be aligned horizontally and vertically. Also be aware that, in certain instances, the alignment of the objects is determined by the first object selected. In the case of your selecting multiple objects, the first item selected will have white handles, while the subsequent selections will have black handles (**Figure 4.12**).

Object alignment uses the Alignment toolbar (see Chapter 1, "The Captivate Work Environment"). Two types of alignment are available:

◆ Object alignment where the selected objects align with each other

◆ Slide alignment where the selected objects align either vertically or horizontally with the slide's center

You can also align objects a bit more precisely if you use the grid feature. To view the grid, select View > Show Grid.

To align objects to each other:

1. Shift-click the objects to be aligned with each other.

2. Click the alignment option you need in the Alignment toolbar (**Figure 4.13**).

✔ Tip

■ The buttons on the Alignment toolbar that have one or two thick black bars in their icons align the selected objects to the slide, not to each other.

To align objects to a grid:

1. Open a slide in the Slide View panel and select View > Show Grid.

   The slide's background will be composed of a series of dots (**Figure 4.14**).

2. Drag an object into position. For more precise placement, select the object and select View > Snap to Grid.

✔ Tips

■ You can also align objects "by the numbers." As you drag the mouse around the screen, the horizontal and vertical coordinates of the mouse in the slide appear in the bottom right corner of the Edit View panel.

■ Another way of doing it by the numbers is to use the arrow keys. If you move an object using an arrow key, it moves in one-pixel increments.

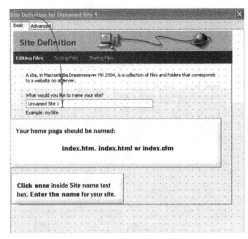

Figure 4.14 You can use the grid for precise placement of objects in a slide.

Changing the Order, Timing, and Size of Objects

If a slide has multiple objects ranging from images to captions, the capability to control when those objects display in the slide is extremely useful. For example, a slide contains mouse movement, an image, and a caption. You may want to have the image appear, followed by the mouse movement, and then have the caption appear last. You also might want to have the caption remain on screen for 5 seconds and the image to shrink to the size of the caption box. You can do all of this on the timeline after you understand how objects in a slide relate to each other.

One issue you will inevitably encounter is a situation where a series of captions, for example, will appear and must all be placed in a precise screen location. If you are familiar with drawing programs such as Adobe Illustrator or Macromedia Freehand MX, you know that objects on a page stack above or behind each other. This is exactly how objects are "stacked" in Captivate. Still, if one larger caption is placed over a smaller caption, you are going to need the capability to edit that caption or object without changing its placement.

Timing refers to how long an object is visible in a slide. This is an extremely useful feature, especially in situations where there may be a voiceover description of a feature on the stage. You don't want the object being described to disappear before the narration finishes. Keep in mind timing changes can be applied only to captions, highlight boxes, text entry boxes, and images. In this case, the timeline is rather limiting. Doing it by the numbers is a lot more precise than dragging.

continues on next page

There will also be occasions where objects may be either too large or too small. In this case, you can resize the objects at the same time. Further, you can resize the selected objects in one of two ways: by the numbers or relative to each other.

To change the display order:

1. In the Edit View panel, double-click a slide containing multiple objects.

2. Right-click any of the objects in the slide and select the new position from the context menu (**Figure 4.15**).

   Your choices are:

   ▲ **Bring to Front** Moves the object to the top of the stack.

   ▲ **Send to Back** Moves the object to the bottom of the stack.

   ▲ **Bring Forward** Moves the object up one level in the stacking order.

   ▲ **Send Backward** Moves the object back one level in the stacking order.

✔ Tip

■ You don't have to right-click an object to change the stacking order. This feature is also available through the Edit menu. You can also change the order by dragging the layers containing the objects to new positions in the timeline.

To change object timing:

1. Open a slide in the Edit View panel.

2. Double-click the object whose timing is to be changed.

   The object's Properties dialog box opens.

3. Click the Options tab.

   The object's timing options opens (**Figure 4.16**).

4. Determine the timing option you want to change, and click the up or down arrows to change the time in one-tenth-of-a-second increments.

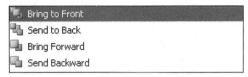

Figure 4.15 You can change the stacking order of objects on a slide using the selected object's context menu.

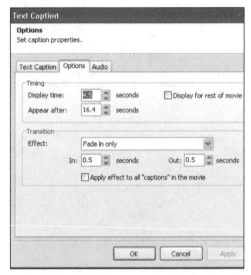

Figure 4.16 Timing can be set "by the numbers" in the object's Options area of its Properties dialog box.

Figure 4.17 Using the Size dialog box, you can resize multiple objects together.

5. Click OK.

The dialog box closes, and the new timing values are applied to the selected object.

✔ Tip

■ You aren't limited to the choices in the timing properties. You can enter your own value into the text input area.

To resize multiple objects:

1. Open a slide in the Edit View panel.

2. Shift-click the objects to be resized.

3. Select Edit > Size, or right-click a selected object and select Size from the context menu.

The Size dialog box opens (**Figure 4.17**).

4. Make your changes and either click Apply to preview the changes or click OK.

Sizing Objects

The dialog box shown in Figure 4.17 offers you many ways to resize objects. You can size the objects to specific values, size them to each other, or affect only the height and width of the object. Be aware that resizing an object containing either text or an image affects only the object—you will not distort the text or the image if you decide to resize an object's height without a similar change in width.

Height choices are:

♦ **No change** The object's height will not change.

♦ **Shrink to smallest** The object's height will shrink to match that of the smallest object in the selection group.

♦ **Grow to largest** The object's height will grow to match that of the largest object in the selection group.

♦ **Custom height** Enter a number to set an exact height—measured in pixels— for all of the selected objects.

Width choices are:

♦ **No change** The object's width will not change.

♦ **Shrink to smallest** The object's width will shrink to match that of the smallest object in the selection group.

♦ **Grow to largest** The object's width will grow to match that of the largest object in the selection group.

♦ **Custom width** Enter a number to set an exact width—measured in pixels— for all of the selected objects.

CHANGING ORDER, TIMING, AND SIZE OF OBJECTS

Creating a Rollover Image

In traditional multimedia, a rollover indicates an image swap or some other event when the mouse is rolled within the boundaries of an object. A classic example is a button in a Web page. This object usually has three images associated with it:

◆ The Up state is the image seen when the mouse isn't over the image.

◆ The Over state is the image seen when the mouse is rolled over the image.

◆ The Down state is the image seen when the mouse is pressed.

Captivate approaches rollovers a bit differently. In Captivate, a rollover is triggered when the mouse rolls over a hot spot. For example, the user rolls the mouse over the hot spot in the slide, and an image appears. When the user rolls the mouse off of the hot spot, the image disappears. This is an extremely valuable feature. For example, you can use rollovers for tool tips. In this case, the user would roll the mouse over a toolbar item, and a small image explaining what the item does would appear.

To add a rollover image:

1. Open the desired slide in the Edit View panel.

2. Select Insert > Rollover Image or click the Rollover Image button on the Object toolbar.

   The Open dialog box appears.

3. Navigate to the image that appears upon the rollover, select it, and click Open.

4. When the New rollover image dialog box appears (**Figure 4.18**), make your selections and click OK.

   The image and hot spot appear in the slide (**Figure 4.19**).

Figure 4.18 The New rollover image dialog box.

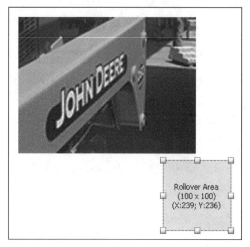

Figure 4.19 The "rollover" image and its hot spot on a slide.

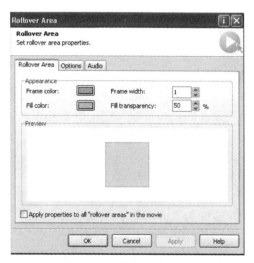

Figure 4.20 Access hot spot settings by double-clicking the hot spot on the slide.

5. Drag the image to its location in the slide, and make any necessary adjustments to the image and the hot spot.

To change the hot spot settings:

1. Open a slide containing a rollover image in the Edit View panel.

2. Double-click the hot spot to open the Rollover Area dialog box (**Figure 4.20**).

3. Change the area's frame color by clicking the Frame Color chip and selecting a color from the color picker.

4. Change the hot spot's fill color by clicking the Fill Color chip and selecting a new color from the color picker.

5. Change the border width by selecting a value from the pop-down menu or entering your own value.

6. Change the hot spot transparency by selecting a value from the pop-down list or entering your own value.

7. Click the Options tab, select a transition and its timing, and decide whether these changes will be applied globally to all hot spots in the movie.

8. Click OK.

9. Drag the hot spot to its location in the slide.

10. Resize the hot spot by selecting it and dragging the handles inward (smaller) or outward (larger).

✔ Tip

■ Previewing a rollover is actually quite simple. Rollovers on a slide are indicated only by the hot spot. Click the hot spot, and the associated image appears on the slide.

CREATING A ROLLOVER IMAGE

Touring the Rollover Image Dialog Box

The Rollover Image dialog box is quite robust and offers you a high degree of flexibility. Your choices are:

◆ **Transparency** Select a value for the image's transparency in the slide. A value of 0 means no transparency. A value of 100 essentially makes the image invisible.

◆ **Transition** Select how the image is handled when it appears in the slide.

◆ **Preview** Displays a preview of the selected image.

◆ **Reset to Original Size** Click to revert back to the original size of the image.

◆ **Change Image** Click to change the image to another image.

◆ **Transparent Background** Click this for odd-shaped images such as round buttons or masked images sitting on a solid background. Be careful with this one. This option has absolutely no effect upon square or rectangular images.

◆ **Apply properties to all Rollover Image items on all slides** Click to apply the settings for the selected image to all rollover images in the movie. Be careful with this one as well.

◆ **Options tab** Determine how and when the image appears on the page.

◆ **Audio tab** Assign an audio effect to the rollover.

Animating Text

There will be occasions where you want to introduce a new section or topic and you need more than a simple fade-in or fade-out transition. This is the purpose of text animations, which enable you to enter some text that the animation then manipulates. For example, enter some text in the Aquarium effect, and a bunch of angel fish will start eating the text when the slide starts playing.

If you are considering using text animations, be aware of the following:

◆ Certain animations use graphics to create the effect. If an animation appears to end suddenly, the only place to lengthen its duration is on the timeline.

◆ Captivate ships with 36 effects ranging from Aquarium to Wizard. You cannot create a custom animated effect for use in your movie.

◆ Don't animate a block of text. These things work best with headlines. A great rule of thumb is, "If you can't say it on a T-shirt, you can't say it in a text animation."

◆ Text animations can't be resized. You get what you are given. The best you can do is place text animations on the slide.

◆ Text animations work best on a separate slide. Add either a blank slide or an animation slide to the movie if you are including a text animation.

◆ Text animations placed on a slide with existing content will not hide anything under them. These small animations use a transparent background.

To add a text animation:

1. Open a Captivate movie and then open the slide to hold the animation in the Edit View panel.

2. Select Insert > Text Animation to open the Text Animation dialog box (**Figure 4.21**). Alternatively you can add a text animation by pressing Control-Shift-X or clicking the Text Animation button on the Object toolbar.

3. Choose the animation effect from the Appearance pop-down menu.

4. Enter the text to be used in the Text input box.

5. Click the Change Font button.
   The Font dialog box opens.

6. Make your changes and click OK.

7. If you want the animation to be somewhat transparent, add a transparency value.
   The values range from 0 (no transparency) to 100 (invisible).

8. Add a delay value to set the time (in seconds) when the text animation appears on the screen.

9. Click the Options tab to set the timing and transition values for the text animation (**Figure 4.22**).

Figure 4.21 The Text Animation dialog box.

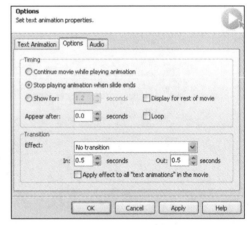

Figure 4.22 Set a text animation's timing and transition values in the Options dialog box.

ANIMATING TEXT

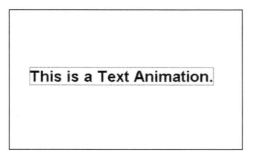

Figure 4.23 A text animation on a slide.

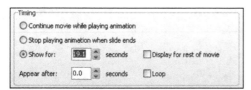

Figure 4.24 You can set the duration of a text animation by the numbers.

10. Click the Audio tab to add an audio effect or file to the text animation.

11. Click OK.

The text animation appears on the slide (**Figure 4.23**).

✔ Tip

■ You can change when a text animation appears by dragging it to a different location on the timeline.

To set the duration of a text animation:

1. Add a text animation to a slide or double-click an existing text animation.

The Text Animation dialog box opens.

2. Click the Options tab.

The Text Animation timing options open.

3. Either enter a time in the Show For entry box or click the up and down arrows to change the value in tenth-of-a-second increments (**Figure 4.24**).

4. Click OK.

Alternatively, you can set the duration of a text animation by following these steps:

1. Open the timeline for a slide containing a text animation.

2. Drag the left or right edge of the text animation object either inward (to increase the duration) or outward (to decrease the duration).

To edit a text animation on the timeline:

1. Open a slide containing a text animation in Edit view and click the timeline Splitter.

   The timeline opens.

2. Double-click the text animation object to open the Text Animation Properties dialog box.

To change the text style for a text animation:

1. Either double-click a text animation in the Edit View panel or double-click a text animation object on the timeline.

   The Text Animation Properties dialog box opens.

2. Click the "Change font" button.

   The Font dialog box opens (**Figure 4.25**).

3. Choose a font, font style, and a point size.

4. Choose a color from the Color pop-down list. If you need more colors, click the Other button to open the Color Picker.

5. Choose a script style from the Script pop-down list (**Figure 4.26**).

6. Click OK to close the Font dialog box and to return to the Text Animation Properties dialog box.

   Your changes appear in the Preview area of the dialog box.

✔ Tips

■ You are not limited to the color choices that appear by default. Selecting Other will open the color picker, from which you can choose a new custom color.

■ The script style refers to the lettering or character styles used in various non-Latin languages.

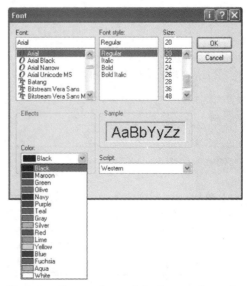

Figure 4.25 You can change the style, type, size, and color of the text used in a text animation.

Figure 4.26 You can also use non-Latin based scripts when choosing a font.

ADDING CAPTIONS

You can have the coolest presentation going. It could contain lots of whizzy stuff, from a thundering sound track and professional animations to detailed imaging. It could also be a complete failure. Why? The focus is on the technology, not the information. That information is contained in the least technical aspect of the presentation—words.

For some odd reason, words tend to be regarded as the "gray stuff that goes around the pictures and the animations." This is a huge error, because words are what we use to interpret the information being presented. They provide the context and access to the information. In Captivate, that context and access is provided by captions.

Captions draw the viewer's attention to areas of a slide or explain the purpose of a tool or icon. Most important, in situations where there is no audio or narration, captions enable you to "speak" to the viewer. As well, you can edit the wording in captions and change the font, font color, point size, and screen location. You can even add your own captions or have the application create them automatically for you.

Adding Captions Automatically

As you are recording a movie, Captivate is generating captions automatically. For example, assume you are recording how to create a new site in Dreamweaver MX 2004. If you select Manage Sites from the Dreamweaver Sites menu during a recording, Captivate will create a caption in a frame with text that reads, "Select 'Manage Sites' from the menu" (**Figure 5.1**).

The actions that create captions automatically include the following:

- Selecting menus
- Selecting menu items
- Clicking buttons
- Entering text into a text input box
- Opening a child window

To add automatic captions:

1. Open the application and open a new movie.

2. Select your recording size and click Next.

3. Click the Options button.
   The Recording Options window opens.

4. Select the Recording Options tab.

5. Select "Enable auto recording" and ensure that the recording mode is set to Demo (**Figure 5.2**).

6. Click the Language arrow to open the pop-down language menu.

7. Select your language preference and click OK.

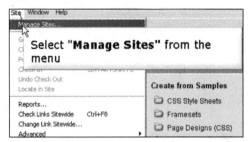

Figure 5.1 Captions are added automatically during the recording process.

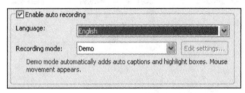

Figure 5.2 Captions are added automatically only in Demo mode by selecting "Automatically insert text captions."

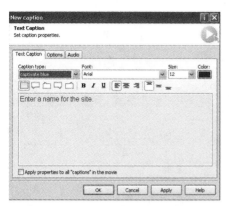

Figure 5.3 Use the New caption dialog box to enter text and determine the caption's properties.

The Recording Modes

Captivate contains four recording modes, each of which is designed for a specific purpose:

◆ **Demo** Select to demonstrate a technique or application feature. Selecting this option adds captions, highlight boxes for mouse clicks, and mouse movement to the recording automatically.

◆ **Simulation** Select if you are asking the user to attempt a technique. Simulation mode creates click boxes and failure captions. It does not record mouse movement.

◆ **Training** Select if the objective is to train an individual in a particular technique and to coach him or her through the process. A Training mode recording includes click boxes with Hint and Failure captions. Mouse movement and regular captions are not created in this mode.

◆ **Custom** Select to choose the objects—such as captions, highlight boxes, and click boxes—you want added to the movie automatically.

✔ Tips

■ Having captions appear in one of nine languages is a wonderful feature. However, it presents a problem with translation, which may not be correct. If you are producing multilingual presentations, be sure to have your client's translator or translation service review the presentation before publishing it on the Web or other media.

■ You can have captions inserted automatically into additional slides you may be recording.

To add captions manually:

1. Open a movie and, in the Edit View panel, open the slide to contain the new caption.

2. Select Insert > Text Caption, press Control-Shift-C, or click the Captions button on the Object toolbar.

   The "New caption" dialog box opens (**Figure 5.3**).

3. Select a caption type from the pop-down list, which offers 31 styles ranging from Transparent to Custom.

4. Select a font from the pop-down list.

5. Select a point size from the Size pop-down list, or enter a size into the text entry box.

6. Select a text color from the color picker.

continues on next page

7. Select a caption style (**Figure 5.4**) from the "Caption type" drop-down list.

8. Select a formatting option: Bold, Italic or Underline. All captions are formatted using Roman or Normal.

9. Select an alignment option (the default is Center).

10. Enter the caption text into the text input area.

11. Select the Options tab.

    The Options dialog box opens (**Figure 5.5**).

12. Select how long the caption will remain on screen and when it will appear using the up and down arrows of the "Display time" and "Appear after" input boxes, respectively. Alternatively, enter values into these input boxes.

13. Select a transition effect from the pop-down list. If you do select an effect, set the transition timing by entering values in the In and Out text input boxes, or use the up and down arrows to change the timing in increments of one-tenth of a second.

14. Select "Apply effect to all captions in the movie" to apply your formatting choices to all captions in the movie.

15. Click the Audio tab to add a sound or voiceover recording to the caption.

16. Click OK.

    The caption appears in the slide (**Figure 5.6**).

Figure 5.4 Caption types are displayed under the style chosen.

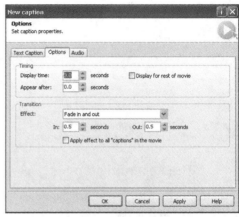

Figure 5.5 Set the timing and the transition, if any, to be used on the caption's Options tab.

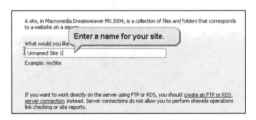

Figure 5.6 A caption on a slide.

ADDING CAPTIONS AUTOMATICALLY

✔ Tips

- To preview the caption styles, select one from the pop-down menu and click the Apply button in the "New caption" dialog box.

- Feel free to use any font you like. Though font embedding is not a feature of this application, there is no risk of font substitution at runtime. This is due to the fact that all captions are converted to bitmaps when the movie is compiled.

- Balloon-style captions are ideal for pointing to an area.

- Transparent captions don't contain a caption type. They are ideal for adding text to pages.

- Select "Display for rest of movie" to have the caption appear on all of the remaining slides. This option is ideal for material common to all slides, such as copyright notices or corporate identification.

- You can also adjust the caption timing in the timeline.

- You can't change the transition timing on the timeline. If you need to change this value, double-click the caption on the screen to open the Captions dialog box.

- Not all formatting choices you make are applied to the captions in the movie. Text, alignment values, and timing values that you enter won't be applied to all captions.

- Narrating a caption is a great feature when it comes to meeting any corporate or institutional accessibility requirements.

To delete a caption:

1. Select the caption to be deleted in the Edit View panel.

2. Press the Delete key, or right-click the caption and select Delete.

   A confirmation dialog box appears (**Figure 5.7**).

3. Click Yes.

Figure 5.7 You will be asked if you want to delete the caption.

Text Is a Design Element

You can change fonts and their weight, color, and alignment. Yet this is no reason to do so indiscriminately. Here are some tips:

◆ Plan the fonts, size, weight, color, and alignment during the planning phase of the project.

◆ If your client has a corporate standard for fonts, use it.

◆ If a font is available as an Oblique, Italic, Bold, or Black version (for example, Arial Black is a bold version of Arial), use that instead of clicking the Italic or Bold buttons.

◆ Never use underlining. Adding emphasis is best done using a bold or italic version of a font or by setting a text color.

◆ Don't change the point size from caption to caption. This is a great way to lose or confuse your viewers.

◆ Just because you have a funky font, that's no reason to use it. Stick with serif (Times, Palatino) or sans serif (Arial, Helvetica) fonts throughout the movie.

◆ Text is readable and legible due, in part, to contrast. Black text against a light background is best. Don't let fads—dark gray text against a medium grey background—drive your design. You are only making life difficult for your viewers if you do this.

◆ A point size between 12 and 16 works best with captions. Fonts have different x-heights, which is why 12-point Arial looks a lot larger than 12 point Helvetica. Use the Apply button to compare various sizes and fonts.

Figure 5.8 You can add rollover captions from the Insert menu.

Creating Rollover Captions

Chapter 4, "The Captivate Timeline and Objects," explained how to create a rollover with an image. You can do the same thing with captions.

Similar to the rollover image, a rollover caption is composed of two elements: a hot spot and a caption. When the mouse rolls over the hot spot, the caption appears on the screen. This is especially useful for drawing the viewer's attention to important areas of the screen or to provide an immediate response to a question. For example, you could assign a series of hot spots to the icons in the Captivate Start page; when the user rolls over the "Record new movie" icon, a caption appears identifying the icon and how to use it.

Not only that, but many applications display a tool tip when the cursor is placed over the object in the interface. You can convert these tool tips to rollover captions during the capture.

Rollover captions are extremely flexible. They are highly customizable—you can modify location, opacity, outline, and color as well as make additional choices in the New Caption dialog box.

To create a rollover caption:

1. Open the target slide in the Edit View panel.

2. Select Insert > Rollover Caption (**Figure 5.8**), press Control-Shift-R, or click the Rollover Caption button on the Object toolbar.

   The New Rollover Caption dialog box opens.

continues on next page

CREATING ROLLOVER CAPTIONS

3. Select a background style for the roll-over caption from the Styles pop-down list. You have 30 choices, ranging from Windows to Custom.

4. Select a font.

5. Select or enter a point size.

6. Select a text color from the color picker.

7. Select a caption style.

8. Enter the caption text.

9. Choose a transition effect.

10. Determine if these properties will be applied to all rollover captions in the movie.

11. Determine if any audio will be added to the caption.

12. Click OK.

   The rollover caption and the hot spot are added to the slide (**Figure 5.9**). The hot spot (the green overlay named "Rollover Area") is where the mouse must be for the caption to appear.

✔ Tip

■ Keep an eye on the Caption style that you choose. Certain caption types don't contain balloons. This is indicated in the Caption Style dialog box. The caption's shape is shown beside the caption type.

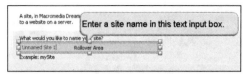

Figure 5.9 The hot spot that triggers a rollover caption is green and named "Rollover Area."

Figure 5.10 You can capture application tool tips as rollover captions in the Custom Recording Options dialog box.

Manipulating Rollover Hot Spots

It is all well and good to create rollover captions but there is a lot more you can do with them than simply have them sit in the same location as the caption. Here are a few ideas:

◆ To change the size of a hot spot, click it and drag one of the handles inward or outward.

◆ For disjointed rollovers (the caption appears in a different area of the slide), drag the hot spot or the caption to a different location in the slide.

◆ To change the look of the hot spot, double-click it to open the Rollover Area dialog box.

◆ If you have a number of hot spots in a slide, determining which hot spot triggers which caption can be confusing. If you click a hot spot, its corresponding caption appear when you click it in the Edit View panel.

To convert application tool tips to rollover captions:

1. Create a new recording and, when the recording window opens, click the Options button.

2. Click the Recording Options tab and set the recording mode to Custom.

3. Click the "Edit settings" button.
   The Custom Recording Options dialog box opens.

4. Select "Covert tooltips to rollover captions" (**Figure 5.10**).

5. Click OK.
   The Custom Recording Options dialog box closes, and you are returned to the Recording Options dialog box.

6. Click OK to return to the recording window.

CREATING ROLLOVER CAPTIONS

Customizing Captions

The five caption styles you see in the Rollover Caption Properties dialog box are what you must create to customize captions. You can create these five styles in an imaging application such as Fireworks MX 2004 or Adobe Photoshop.

Bitmaps created for use as custom captions must be saved as BMP images. Save the files to C:\Program Files\Macromedia\Captivate\Gallery\Captions.

✔ Tip

■ Do not anti-alias the edges of captions.

Naturally, when creating custom captions there are some rules to be followed. These rules are discussed in this section.

Naming conventions for custom captions

The name of each image must

◆ Follow a preset naming convention

◆ Be unique

◆ Appear at the start of each bitmap's filename (**Figure 5.11**)

For example, assume you create a caption named CPgrey. The five bitmaps associated with the caption must be named as follows:

◆ **CPgrey1.bmp** The image with no callout

◆ **CPgrey2.bmp** The image with a callout to the right or upper right

◆ **CPgrey3.bmp** The image with a callout to the left or upper left

◆ **CPgrey4.bmp** The image with a callout to the top or the top right

◆ **CPgrey5.bmp** The image with a callout to the bottom or the bottom left

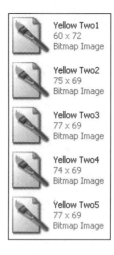

Figure 5.11 All custom captions must contain the same name.

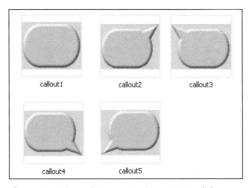

callout1   callout2   callout3

callout4   callout5

Figure 5.12 Place all custom captions on a solid background color.

Colors

Custom captions are, essentially, composed of two color elements in your imaging application. There is the background or canvas color, which has to be a solid color, and the color used in the caption. It is important that you make this distinction when designing custom captions for use in Captivate.

Captions are surrounded by an area of transparency, which means that the canvas or background color of the image will be made transparent. Thus, it is extremely important that the background or canvas color and the caption color be completely different. If they share a common color, that color will also be "knocked out" in the caption. This is due to the fact that the transparency color is determined by the color of the pixel in the upper left corner of the image.

In **Figure 5.12**, the background color is a solid gray (#D8DEE5) and the caption color is green (#D2D98D). When the caption image is rendered, the pixel in the upper left corner containing the value #D8DEE5 will set the color value for the transparency. Thus any pixel in the image that has that value will be rendered transparent. We that value to be found in the caption image, the pixel would be transparent and allow the slide's background to show through.

Text alignment in custom callouts

Depending on the shape of the callout image you have created, the alignment of the text in the callout may not be correct. This can be addressed by setting the left, right, top, and bottom margins of the captions. These margins are measured in pixels.

You can fix text alignment by opening Notepad and entering the text shown in **Figure 5.13**, adjusting the margins by changing the values. You must save this file to the folder containing the custom caption.

Further, the file must contain the same name as the corresponding image and, instead of a .bmp extension, must use an .fcm extension as shown in **Figure 5.14**.

Figure 5.13 Set margins for custom captions in a Notepad document.

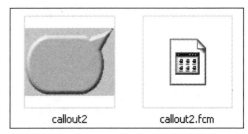

Figure 5.14 The Notepad document must share the same name as the custom captions and use the .fcm extension.

Figure 5.15 You can export captions to Microsoft Word.

Figure 5.16 You will be asked if you want to view the Word document.

Exporting and Importing Captions

From a production point of view, the ability to create captions using word processing software is a huge productivity boost. For example, in certain situations the words on the screen may require approval. A text-based document meets this need. Other examples are the creation of a voiceover narration script using the captions in the presentation and a document that can be submitted for client approval. Further, with a text-based document, you can edit all of the captions in a movie in one place rather than on a slide-by-slide basis.

The format used for this process is the Microsoft Word DOC format. By creating this document, you not only preserve the text in the caption, but also retain (and can change) any formatting applied to the text.

To export captions to Microsoft Word:

1. Open a movie and select File > Import/Export > "Export movie captions" (**Figure 5.15**) to open the Save As dialog box.

2. Enter a name for the caption and click Save.

   The dialog box closes, and a progress bar appears, displaying the status of the export process. When it finishes, you're asked asked if you want to view the captions in Microsoft Word (**Figure 5.16**).

   continues on next page

3. Click Yes to open the document.

Microsoft Word opens, and all of the captions appear in the Word document (**Figure 5.17**).

✔ Tip

- If you have a consistent style for your captions, develop a Microsoft Word style sheet that contains the styles' formatting. When the exported document opens in Microsoft Word, you can then load the style sheet and apply the styles to the captions.

To import Microsoft Word captions into a movie:

1. Open Captivate and select File > Import/Export > "Import Movie captions."

2. Navigate to the folder in which the DOC file containing the edited caption is located, and select the file.

3. Click Open.

Two progress bars appear. The first displays the progress of the import of the text file; the second shows the updating of each slide of the movie. When finished, Captivate displays a dialog box telling you how many captions were imported successfully.

4. Click OK.

Slide ID	Item ID	Text Caption
0	356	Click the **Basic Tab** to open the Wizard.
0	358	The Wizard walks you through the various bits and pieces of information you will need to let Dreamweaver know where your local site is located, its name and its location on the ParaFX server.
0	360	You start by **giving your site a name**. I use tomontheweb so I usually name my site **TOTW**. Before you do this, though, you should have a folder for your site on your computer, a folder named **"Graphics"** should be in that folder along with your **Home Page**.
0	362	Your home page should be named: **index.htm. index.html or index.cfm**
0	8	**Click once** inside Site name text box. **Enter the name** for your site.
4	9425	Enter a site name in this text input box.

Figure 5.17 The Word document enables you to edit and format the captions.

Changing the Order and Timing of Captions

Each slide of a movie can contain numerous captions. Not only can you change the order in which these captions appear, but you can also change how long they remain on the screen.

Changing the display order is important because there will be occasions where you will need to have a caption appear earlier than originally set. For example, you decide the caption that appears fourth in the slide is more important than the one that appears before it. You can easily switch this order.

Display time is also important. Though Captivate calculates the amount of time a caption is visible based on the amount of text in the caption, you may decide to have the caption (or all captions, for that matter) remain on screen for a shorter or longer duration. This calculation is a default setting for the application. To turn it off, select Options > Calculate Caption Timing and deselect the option.

To change the caption order:

1. Open the slide containing the captions in the Edit View panel.

2. Open the timeline and single-click the caption to be moved.

   When you select the caption, the layer turns gray and the selected caption, called an object when it is on the timeline, turns blue (**Figure 5.18**).

continues on next page

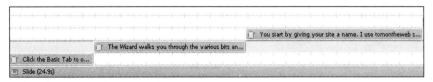

Figure 5.18 You can change caption order on the Timeline.

3. Drag the caption to its new location and release the mouse.

✔ Tip

■ Changing the order of captions is no different from changing the order of objects in a slide (which was explained in Chapter 4). Just keep in mind that the order of appearance is determined by the caption's location on the timeline. If it is at the left, it will display first on playback. If it is at the right, it will display last.

To change the timing of an individual caption:

1. Open the slide containing the caption to be changed in the Edit View panel.

2. Double-click the caption to open the Caption Properties dialog box.

3. Click the arrows in the Display Time area to increment or decrement the display time. You can also enter a new time into this input box.

4. Click OK.

Alternatively, use this method:

1. Open the slide in the Edit View panel and open the timeline.

2. Roll the right edge of the Caption object and, when the cursor changes to the split cursor (**Figure 5.19**), drag the edge to left to shorten the time or to the right to increase the time.

3. Release the mouse.

Figure 5.19 You can change caption duration by dragging the right edge of the caption object to the right or left on the timeline.

ADDING AUDIO

Sound is so ubiquitous we hardly notice it. Yet, like the words in captions, it carries a lot of information. In many respects, audio can be the difference between a positive or negative user experience. Sound can set the mood and reinforce the message you are trying to convey. Done right, the user will learn something from your movie. Do it wrong, and you can be guaranteed the user will eject the CD or leave the presentation in a very short time.

Captivate enables you to add voiceover narrations, music, or sound effects to your movie. You can add audio, in the form of WAV and MP3 files, to movie slides in the same manner that you add images and texts. Though the preferred format is MP3, don't let this guide your efforts: Just as in Flash MX 2004, if you use a WAV file it will be converted to the MP3 format when the movie is compiled.

You can also use Captivate to record voiceover narrations and add them directly to your slides.

continues on next page

When adding audio to your movie, the key issue will be the traditional tradeoff between sound quality and file size. A 16-bit stereo sound recorded at 44 kHz will be immense yet with quality equal to that of a CD purchased at a record store. For example, a 30-second clip recorded using those settings will weigh in at a hefty 5.3 Mb. Convert the sound to mono and the file size drops to 2.6 Mb. Drop the sample rate from 44 kHz to 11 kHz and the file size drops to 600 Kb with a corresponding drop in quality.

Audio is an area in which the needs of the user and your technical needs intersect. If the user has a 56k dial-up connection, you are going to have to keep things small. If the presentation is being played from a CD or kiosk, these issues don't factor into the equation. Even the user's playback equipment will drive your decisions. Most computer systems use rather low-end equipment—the cheap speakers or headphones that were part of the computer package—to play back sound. In this case, stereo is more a luxury than a necessity.

Finally, you can't use Captivate to edit recorded audio. Use a third-party application for that purpose. The best you can do in this application is customize how the sound in a slide or movie is output.

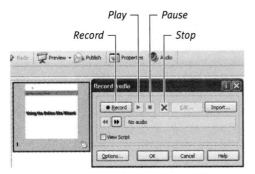

Play — ┌ *Pause*

Record — ┌ *Stop*

Figure 6.1 The Record Audio dialog box enables you to record and play back audio you may create.

The Audio Recording Options

You can record voiceover narrations directly into a movie slide. In fact, Captivate offers a surprisingly robust tool set for this very purpose. As you make your decisions regarding the recording options—this includes target bandwidth and output—always keep the user in mind.

When it comes to audio, the GIGO—Garbage In, Garbage Out—principle comes into play. Use the best microphone you can afford and try to record in an environment where there is very little background noise.

Record audio using the controls at the top of the Record Audio dialog box (**Figure 6.1**):

◆ **Record** Click to start the recording process.

◆ **Play** Click to preview your recorded sound.

◆ **Pause** Click to pause playback.

◆ **Stop** Click to stop recording or playback.

Note that this section assumes you have a microphone connected to your computer and that it is configured properly in your computer's Audio properties. Note also that the Calibrate microphone feature is badly named. The best you can expect from this is to see if your microphone is connected and working.

To set the audio recording options for a voiceover:

1. Open a movie and select the target slide in the Storyboard View panel, or open the target slide in the Edit View panel.

2. Click the Audio button on the Main toolbar to open the Record Audio dialog box.

3. Click the Options button to open the Audio options dialog box (**Figure 6.2**).

4. Select Microphone as the input source and select a quality setting from the "Audio quality" drop-down list. Your choices—CD Quality, "High quality (FM radio quality)," and AM radio quality—determine the size of the sound file.

5. Click the "Calibrate input" button to open the Calibrate microphone dialog box (**Figure 6.3**).

6. Speak into the microphone. Captivate will tell you if the input level is acceptable.

7. Click OK to return to the Audio options dialog box; then click OK again to be returned to the Record Audio dialog box.

8. Click the Record button and start speaking into the microphone.

9. Click the Stop button to stop the recording.

   A progress bar appears, showing the status of the conversion. When it is finished, the file will appear in the dialog box along with its duration.

10. Click the Play button to preview the recording.

Figure 6.2 Set the type of recording and its quality in the Audio options dialog box.

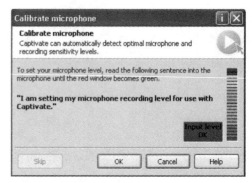

Figure 6.3 "Calibrate microphone" simply checks to see if a microphone is attached to the computer.

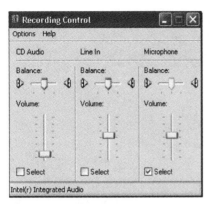

Figure 6.4 Set the microphone properties using your computer's recording controls.

✔ Tips

- To determine which audio quality setting to use, think of the three choices as being a Good, Better, Best scenario. If you are in a development environment where bandwidth is not an issue, use CD quality, which is comparable to a file recorded as a 16-bit 44 kHz stereo file. If you are unsure as to the user's capabilities or bandwidth situation, use FM quality as your normal choice. This one is comparable to 16-bit 22 kHz stereo sound. In low bandwidth dial-up situations, use AM quality, which is comparable to 16-bit 22 kHz mono.

- Don't forget that you can control the sensitivity of a microphone by using the Voice Recording area of your computer's Sound and Audio Devices control panel. To do so, open the Control Panel, click the Voice tab, and click Volume in the Voice Recording section. When the Recording Control dialog box opens (**Figure 6.4**), adjust the volume slider for the microphone.

- If you make a mistake or the recording doesn't seem quite right, click the Remove Audio button (the button with the big red X) in the Record Audio dialog box. This deletes the sound from the slide.

To insert prerecorded audio into a slide:

1. Open a Captivate movie and either select the target slide in the Storyboard View panel or double-click a slide to open it in the Edit View panel.

2. Click the Audio button on the Main toolbar to open the Record Audio dialog box.

3. Click the Import button to open the Import Audio dialog box (**Figure 6.5**).

4. Navigate to the folder containing the WAV or MP3 audio file, and select the file.

   The filename appears in the "File name" area at the bottom of the dialog box.

5. Click Open. A progress bar appears, showing the progress of the conversion and import. When it finishes, the file's duration appears in the Record Audio dialog box.

✔ Tips

- Captivate ships with 29 MP3 files that you can use for a variety of situations. They are located in C:\Program Files\ Macromedia\Captivate\Gallery\Sound.

- Any slide with audio attached to it will have an audio icon. Click this Audio icon, and a context menu (**Figure 6.6**) with many of the choices from the Recording Options dialog box appear.

- You don't have to use the Audio button on the Main toolbar to add a sound. Select the slide in either the Slideshow View or Edit View panel, and select Audio > Import.

- How do you delete an audio file? Locate a slide that has an Audio icon, click the icon, and select Remove Audio from the pop-down menu.

Figure 6.5 Use the Import Audio dialog box to import sound into Captivate. Captivate can import only MP3 or WAV files.

Figure 6.6 You can access a number of audio properties by clicking a sound icon in the Thumbnail view of a slide.

A Quick Audio Primer

Some of the terminology used in this chapter may be new to you. Here's a brief overview of how sound is recorded and what some of the terms actually mean.

Sound travels in *waves* and is traditionally illustrated using a *sine waveform*. A single wave, measured from peak to peak, is called a *hertz* (**Figure 6.7**). Recorded audio usually has thousands of waves per second. A *kilohertz*, or kHz, is 1000 waves per second. Thus, the more waves per second, the more accurate the recording and the higher the resulting file size.

When a sound is digitized, each wave is broken into *samples* (**Figure 6.8**). The measurement for this is a *bit*. For example, an 8-bit sound will sample each wave 256 times. A 16-bit sound will have about 66,000 samples per wave. Again, the more samples there are, the more accurate the sound and the higher the resulting file size.

Bit rate has nothing to do with the actual sound but it is important. This number determines how fast the information is fed into the computer's processor. For example, a 16 kbps bit rate streams the audio into the computer at a rate of 16,000 bits of information (the 1s and 0s that are the sound data) per second.

All sound in Captivate is output in the MP3 format. The MP3 format is actually a *lossy* format, meaning information is lost upon conversion. In the case of MP3 files, sounds that are inaudible are discarded (**Figure 6.9**). The result is a lower file size. When you select a quality level in the "Audio quality" section of the Audio Options dialog box, essentially you are determining how much information will be tossed.

If you convert audio to the MP3 format before importing it or plan to use a WAV file in Captivate, be aware the application does not support the 5.5 kHz or 8.0 kHz frequencies for audio tracks. The Flash Player does not support these frequencies.

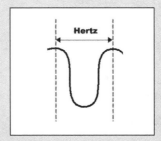

Figure 6.7 Traditionally, sound is illustrated as a sine wave.

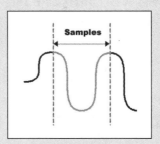

Figure 6.8 Each wave is sampled either 256 or 66,000 times. The more samples, the more accurate the sound.

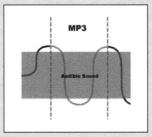

Figure 6.9 Generally, the inaudible high and low sounds are discarded in MP3 files.

Recording a Background Audio Track

You can add or record a background audio track—from a recorded narration or sound effect to a music track—that plays while the slides of the movie also play. You can also lower the volume of this track to avoid interference with other audio that may be playing. For example, you can import a music track from a CD or other source and have it loop—play continuously—for the entire movie. When slide-based sound starts to play—a voiceover explaining a technique, for example—the music track's volume will decrease.

To add background audio:

1. In either the Storyboard View or Edit View panel, select Audio > Movie Background.

   The Background Audio tab (**Figure 6.10**) of the Movie Preferences dialog box opens.

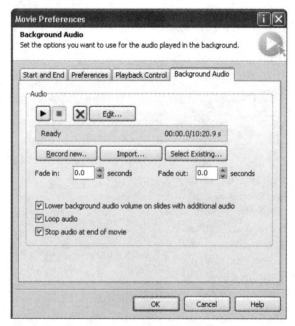

Figure 6.10 Add background audio in the Movie Preferences dialog box.

2. Add an MP3 or WAV audio track by clicking the Import button and navigating to the folder containing the audio track.

3. Select the track and click Open to return to the Background Audio tab.

4. To preview the track, click the Play button in the Audio controls.

5. If you want the audio to fade in or fade out, enter a value (in seconds) for the audio to fade in or fade out.

6. Select the "Lower background audio volume on slides with additional audio" option to lower the background sound's volume when a sound starts to play in a slide.

7. Select "Loop audio" to start playing the audio track from the beginning immediately after it ends.

8. Select "Stop audio at end of movie" to have the background audio stop playing, regardless of where the sound is currently playing when the movie stops playing.

9. Click OK.
   The audio is added to the movie.

✔ Tips

■ You can also access the Background Audio tab by selecting Movie > Preferences in either the Storyboard View or Edit View panel. When the preferences open, click the Background Audio tab.

■ You have no control over the background sound's properties such as stereo, frequency, sample rate, and so on. If this is a concern, make the changes in an audio application before adding the background sound track.

Editing Audio Tracks

Captivate contains a rather basic audio editor that enables you to perform the following tasks:

- Cut, copy, and paste sound selections elsewhere in the track or in another audio track.

- Delete sections of the audio track.

- Undo or redo your last action.

- Insert silence into an audio track.

- Adjust the volume of the audio.

- Zoom in or zoom out on the waveform.

Another interesting feature is the capability to import audio tracks directly into slides using the Audio Editor.

Keep in mind that the inclusion of an audio editor in Captivate does not replace the need for a regular audio editing application for more than the tasks outlined. In many respects, this feature is great for touching up sound more than anything else.

To open the Audio Editor:

1. In either the Storyboard View or Edit View panel, select a slide that has audio attached.

2. Single-click the Audio icon on the thumbnail to open the Audio pop-down menu.

3. Select "Edit audio" to open the Edit Audio dialog box (**Figure 6.11**).

✔ Tip

- If you prefer to use menus, select the slide and then select Audio > Edit Audio.

EDITING AUDIO TRACKS

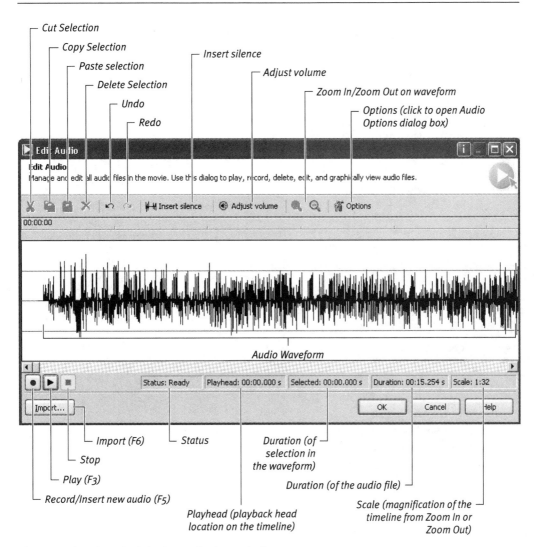

Cut Selection

Copy Selection

Paste selection

Delete Selection

Undo

Redo

Insert silence

Adjust volume

Zoom In/Zoom Out on waveform

Options (click to open Audio Options dialog box)

Audio Waveform

Import (F6)

Stop

Play (F3)

Record/Insert new audio (F5)

Status

Playhead (playback head location on the timeline)

Duration (of selection in the waveform)

Duration (of the audio file)

Scale (magnification of the timeline from Zoom In or Zoom Out)

Figure 6.11 The Edit Audio dialog box is a basic sound editor.

A Quick Tour of the Captivate Audio Editor

Here's a rundown of the buttons and other information presented in the Edit Audio dialog box, otherwise known as the Audio Editor:

- **Cut, Copy, Paste, and Delete** Click to add or remove selections of sound to the waveform.

- **Undo and Redo** Click if you make a mistake.

- **Insert silence** Click to add a predetermined length of silence to the waveform.

- **Adjust volume** Click to normalize or boost the volume of a selection.

- **Zoom In/Zoom Out** Click to change the visible detail in the waveform.

- **Options** Click to open the Audio Options dialog box.

- **Waveform** Displays the graphic representation of the sound.

- **Record/Insert new audio** Click (or just press F5) to automatically record and insert a new sound.

- **Play** Click (or press F3) to preview the sound file.

- **Stop** Click to stop playback.

- **Status** Indicates that the audio is ready to play.

- **Playhead** Displays the location of the playback head in the waveform.

- **Selected** Displays duration, in thousandths of seconds, of a section of the waveform, which you can select (see below).

- **Duration** Displays the duration of the entire clip, not just the selection.

- **Scale** Displays the view scale for the waveform. Clicking the Zoom In or Zoom Out icons changes this number.

- **Import** Click (or press F6) to import an audio file into the audio track at the location of the cursor.

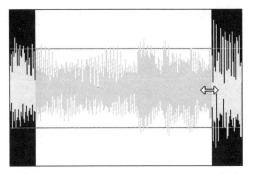

Figure 6.12 Change a selection by dragging the left or right edge of the selection inward or outward.

To select a section of the waveform:

1. Click in the waveform and drag the mouse across the selection (**Figure 6.12**).

2. To adjust the selection, roll your cursor to either side of the selection.

3. When the cursor changes to the double arrow shown in Figure 6.12, click and drag the edge to extend or reduce the selection.

To cut, copy, and paste a selection of the waveform:

1. Select the section of the waveform to be cut or copied.

2. Click the Cut button or the Copy button to place the selection on the clipboard.

3. Click once in the waveform where the selection on the clipboard is to be placed.

4. Click the Paste button or press Control-V to place the sound in the waveform.

✔ Tips

- You won't be able to use Edit > Cut or Edit > Copy for this operation. However, you can use the keyboard commands Control-X (Cut) or Control-C (Copy) after you make your selections.

- If you make a mistake, click the Undo or Redo button.

  You can't copy an audio selection in one Captivate movie or slide and paste it into the waveform of another Captivate movie or slide.

EDITING AUDIO TRACKS

Audio silence

In a waveform, silence is represented by a flat line. Use silence to start or end a sound file, or to break up sections of a sound file.

To insert silence into the waveform:

1. Click once in the waveform where the silence is to be added.

2. Click the Insert Silence button to open the Insert Silence dialog box (**Figure 6.13**).

3. Enter a silence amount or use the up and down arrows in the Insert area to set how much silence will be added.

4. Click the pop-down arrow and choose where the silence will be placed.

   Your options are "Playhead position," "Start of audio," and "End of audio."

5. Click OK.

   The dialog box closes and the silence appears on the waveform where you specified (**Figure 6.14**).

To adjust the volume of the waveform:

1. Click the Adjust volume button to open the Adjust Volume dialog box (**Figure 6.15**).

2. Make the necessary adjustments in the following three areas:

   ▲ **Volume** Use this slider to increase or decrease the sound level of the audio file. Drag the slider down to reduce the volume or up to increase the volume. (As you drag, the percentage increase or decrease in volume is displayed at the bottom, so you can adjust the sound precisely.)

   ▲ **Normalize (select best volume)** Select to have Captivate adjust the sound volume automatically. Normalizing audio helps keep the sound level consistent among slides. Think of

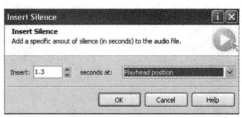

Figure 6.13 Use the Insert Silence dialog box to choose where silence will be inserted in the audio file.

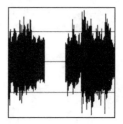

Figure 6.14 Silence, indicated by the flat line between the waveforms, has been inserted.

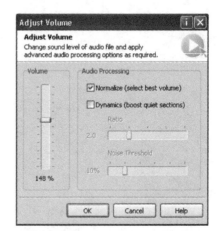

Figure 6.15 Use the Adjust Volume dialog box to adjust the volume level of the waveform.

Normalize as being a really smart volume knob that applies the volume shift of all of the sound to the level you set. This is a great way of adjusting volume without changing the dynamics of the sound.

▲ **Dynamics (boost quiet sections)**
Select to amplify quiet sections of the audio to help compensate for variations in audio volume. These areas are quite visible in the waveform. Loud sounds result in a large spike on the waveform, and quiet sounds have shorter spikes. In simple terms, the difference between these two levels is the dynamic range of the audio track. Changing the dynamics will alter the dynamic range. This is done through the use of two sliders:

Ratio Specifies the maximum amplification to be used. The default setting of 2.0 sets the quietest sections of the audio to be amplified by a factor of two. A higher setting can improve movies with large differences between quiet and loud sections, but can also amplify background noise.

Noise Threshold If you use audio editing software, this slider is comparable to a "noise gate," which is commonly used to get rid of background buzzes and noise that may have been recorded. This slider controls the amplification of background noise. Anything quieter than the noise threshold you set is not amplified. If background noise is amplified too much, setting a higher noise threshold may help solve the problem.

3. Click OK.

The dialog box closes, and the waveform changes to reflect your choices.

To insert a new recording into the audio track:

1. Click once in the waveform where the new audio recording is to be inserted.

2. Connect your microphone to the computer and click the "Record/Insert new audio" button.

   The microphone levels appear in the Edit Audio dialog box (**Figure 6.16**).

3. Record the sound.

4. When you're finished recording, click the Stop button.

   The new recording is added to the waveform.

✔ Tip

- If you make a mistake while recording, click the Stop button. When the recording appears in the waveform, click the Undo button.

To insert prerecorded audio into the waveform:

1. Click once in the waveform where the audio file is to be inserted.

2. Click the Import button to open the Import Audio dialog box.

3. Navigate to the folder containing the audio file, select it, and click Open.

   The dialog box closes, and the audio file is inserted into the waveform.

✔ Tip

- If the imported audio file is placed in the wrong position you can either click the Undo button and repeat the above steps, or select the audio in the waveform and cut and paste it into its new location in the waveform.

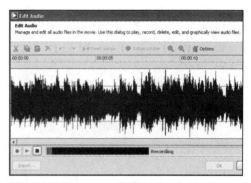

Figure 6.16 You can record audio directly into the audio file.

Audio timing

In the Audio dialog box is a menu item named Edit Timing. This really doesn't describe what this item does. The name implies that you can edit the timing of the audio track in the slide. Not quite.

There will be occasions where the sound file's length is either longer or shorter than the slide's duration. This dialog box lets you adjust the duration of each slide in the movie to match that of the audio track attached to the slide.

Audio Timing Tricks

After you understand how the Audio Timing dialog box works, you suddenly realize there are a bunch of other things you can do with the audio timing feature. Here are just a few:

◆ **Add individual audio tracks to all of the slides in one location** Your entire movie is laid out in front of you. Instead of importing audio to each slide in either the Storyboard View or the Edit View panel, click in the white area for each slide, and then click the Import button. This opens the Import Audio dialog box, and you can add an audio file to the slide.

◆ **Preview the audio track attached to your slides** Click once at the start of the audio attached to a slide and click the Play button.

◆ **Edit the audio** Zoom in on an audio track attached to a slide. You can insert silence or adjust the volume of the track.

◆ **Add narrations** Connect your microphone, click inside a slide, and click the "Record/Insert new audio file" button.

◆ **Add the same audio files to a number of slides** Select the entire waveform for the file to be used elsewhere. Copy the selection, click and drag across the white area of the target slide, and paste.

EDITING AUDIO TRACKS

To edit audio timing:

1. In either the Storyboard View or Edit View panel, select Audio > Edit Timing.

   The Edit Audio Timing dialog box opens (**Figure 6.17**). At first glance, this dialog box may appear to be a bit confusing. Essentially it's a graphical representation of each slide's duration and the waveform of any sound attached to the slide. A slide's duration is the distance between the red lines. Each red line represents the start of each slide in the movie.

2. Click and drag a slide marker to the edge of a sound to increase or decrease the duration of the slide.

3. Click OK to close the dialog box and accept the changes.

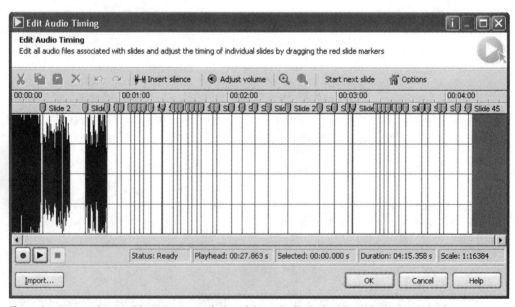

Figure 6.17 You can change slide timing to match that of the audio file in the Edit Audio Timing dialog box.

Using Advanced Audio Management

The Advanced Audio Management options are designed to give you a slide-by-slide overview of the audio attached to each slide and any audio that may be assigned as background audio. You can use this area to play or remove any audio files in the movie, as well as to export the files and manipulate them in audio editing software.

To open the Advanced Audio Management dialog box:

1. Open a Captivate movie.

2. In either the Storyboard View or Edit View panel, select Audio > Advanced Audio.

   The Advanced Audio Management dialog box opens (**Figure 6.18**, next page).

The Advanced Audio Management dialog box presents you with quite a bit of information:

- ▲ **Object** Lists each slide.
- ▲ **Sound** Indicates whether a sound file is attached to the slide.
- ▲ **Length** Displays the duration (in seconds) of each slide's audio track.
- ▲ **Fade In/Out** Displays the duration (in seconds) of any fades added to the sound.
- ▲ **Size** Displays the size of the file (in kilobytes).

- ▲ **Original Filename** Displays the name of the file, if any. Files you record in Captivate will be not be named.
- ▲ **Sample Rate** The frequency of the file, measured in kHz.
- ▲ **Bit Rate** Shows the number of samples per wave, measured in kilobits per second. The default in Captivate is 16-bit.
- ▲ **Preview** Select a sound and click the Play button to preview the audio file.
- ▲ **Show object level audio** Select to see any audio files that are attached to objects such as captions.

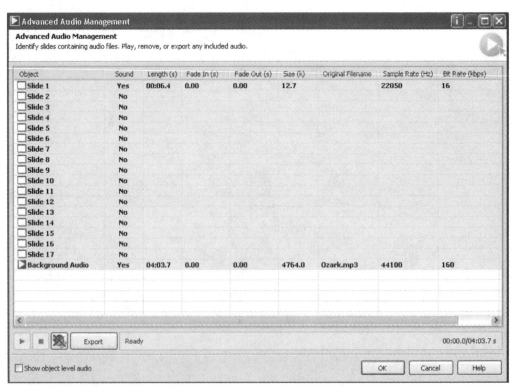

Object	Sound	Length (s)	Fade In (s)	Fade Out (s)	Size (k)	Original Filename	Sample Rate (Hz)	Bit Rate (kbps)
Slide 1	Yes	00:06.4	0.00	0.00	12.7		22050	16
Slide 2	No							
Slide 3	No							
Slide 4	No							
Slide 5	No							
Slide 6	No							
Slide 7	No							
Slide 8	No							
Slide 9	No							
Slide 10	No							
Slide 11	No							
Slide 12	No							
Slide 13	No							
Slide 14	No							
Slide 15	No							
Slide 16	No							
Slide 17	No							
Background Audio	Yes	04:03.7	0.00	0.00	4764.0	Ozark.mp3	44100	160

Export   Ready   00:00.0/04:03.7 s

☐ Show object level audio   OK   Cancel   Help

Figure 6.18 The Advanced Audio Management dialog box is an invaluable tool.

USING ADVANCED AUDIO MANAGEMENT

Figure 6.19 You will be asked if you really want to delete an audio file.

To delete a file in the Advanced Audio Management dialog box:

1. Open a Captivate movie.

2. In either the Storyboard View or Edit View panel, select Audio > Advanced Audio.

   The Advanced Audio Management dialog box opens.

3. Select the file to be deleted and press the Delete key, or click the Remove/Delete Audio button (the speaker with the red X through it at the bottom of the dialog box).

   An alert box (**Figure 6.19**) appears, asking you to confirm your decision.

4. Click Yes or No.

✔ Tip

■ Be very careful with deleting files in the Advanced Audio Management dialog box. The action cannot be undone. If you make this mistake, you will have to re-import the file into the slide.

Exporting an audio file

If you have an audio editing application, you can export any audio file out of Captivate and edit the file in the audio application.

To export an audio file:

1. In the Advanced Audio Management dialog box, select the slide containing the file to be exported.

2. Click the Export button or press the F10 key.

   The Browse For Folder dialog box opens (**Figure 6.20**).

3. Navigate to the folder where the exported sound will be placed and click OK.

   The dialog box closes, and you are returned to the Advanced Audio Management dialog box.

4. Finish what you are doing and close the dialog box.

5. Minimize Captivate by clicking the Window Minimize button and navigate to the folder where the sound was exported.

   There are two files in the folder: an MP3 version of the file and the WAV version (**Figure 6.21**).

6. Open your audio editor, import the WAV file into the editor, and make any changes.

7. Save the file as a WAV file and quit your audio editor.

   Now you can re-import the edited file back into Captivate.

✔ Tip

■ In your audio editor, use the WAV file, not the MP3 version (which is lossy). You should consider exporting the edited file out of the audio editor as a WAV file, as well.

Figure 6.20 Export audio to a separate folder and edit it in an audio editing application.

Figure 6.21 Exporting audio results in both an MP3 and a WAV version of the exported file.

USING ADVANCED AUDIO MANAGEMENT

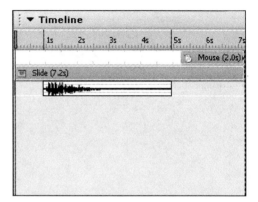

Figure 6.22 You can move audio files to different locations on the timeline.

Adjusting Audio on the Timeline

You can use the Captivate timeline for a couple of specific audio tasks, including:

◆ Have the audio file's duration match that of another object, such as a caption on the timeline.

◆ Adjust the slide's duration to match the audio.

◆ Remove audio from the slide.

To move audio to a new position on the timeline:

1. In the Edit View panel, open a slide containing audio.

2. Open the timeline.
   The audio file is on a separate layer.

3. Select the audio object and drag it to its new location on the timeline (**Figure 6.22**).

4. Release the mouse.

To remove audio from the timeline:

1. In the Edit View panel, open a slide containing audio.

2. Open the timeline.
   The audio file is on a separate layer.

3. Select the audio object and press the Delete key.
   An alert box opens, asking you to confirm your decision.

4. Click Yes.

Matching the duration of an object to a sound

You can't adjust the timing of an audio object on the timeline by selecting it and dragging an edge inwards or outwards. However, you can shorten the duration of an object to match that of a sound.

To match the duration of an object to a sound:

1. Open the timeline and place the cursor over the sound in the timeline.

   Note the duration and start time values in the resulting tool tip (**Figure 6.23**).

2. Double-click the caption to which the sound will be attached.

   The Caption Properties dialog box opens.

3. Click the Options tab and set the display time to match that of the sound's duration.

4. Set the caption's Appear After value to match that of the sound.

5. Click OK.

   The caption is placed precisely over the sound, and its duration matched the sound's duration precisely.

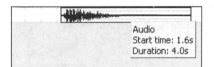

Figure 6.23 An audio tool tip.

ADDING
INTERACTIVITY

When it comes to the New Media field, the currency of "interactivity" has been cheapened. Just because you added navigation buttons to a presentation or found a clever way of adding a user's name to the presentation does not mean the presentation is interactive.

The best interactive process is a conversation you may have with a friend or colleague. If I speak to my friend Murray, he does three things: He first listens and deciphers what I am saying into a coherent whole. He then thinks about that "coherent whole" and formulates an equally coherent response. Finally, he responds verbally, which thrusts me into the three steps.

Obviously you can't replicate this human-to-human interaction process in a Captivate presentation, but you can simulate it. The speaking can be done through the use of a voiceover audio track (see Chapter 6, "Adding Audio") or through the use of words in the slide. The "thinking" is done by the user carefully considering the meaning of the aural or visual message presented. The response is the action that the user takes, either in the form of entering text or clicking a box.

continues on next page

This chapter focuses on the third step of the process: the response. In Captivate, a response is initiated using

- Highlight boxes
- Click boxes
- Text entry boxes
- Buttons used for the purpose of navigation.

Highlight boxes draw the user's attention to a specific area in a slide. These boxes, which function in a similar manner to highlighter pens, give the highlighted area more emphasis than the other objects in the slide. These objects are rather robust, and you can control their size, color, and transparency as well as how they appear in the slide.

You can use click boxes to test knowledge, navigate to other areas in the movie, navigate to Web sites, and even send an email message.

Text entry boxes require the user to formulate a response and then write the response into the slide. This feature is quite versatile and enables you to ask for responses ranging from the question answers to password entry into the movie.

Buttons require the user to make a navigation decision. For example, responses to a question may result in the user being asked to review a section before proceeding. In this case the button would be the element used for that purpose.

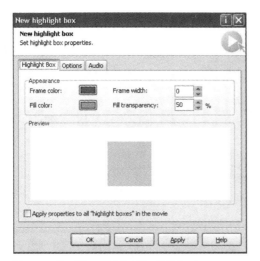

Figure 7.1 The "New highlight box" dialog box.

Adding and Using Highlight Boxes

As previously mentioned, think of highlight boxes as the digital equivalent of highlighter pens or underlining. The purpose of a highlight box is simply to add emphasis to an object or area in the slide. The user, seeing this emphasis, will instantly understand the item is more important than the rest and respond accordingly. Highlight boxes are also added during a recording to indicate mouse clicks.

To add a highlight box to a slide:

1. Open the target slide in the Edit View panel.

2. Select Insert > Highlight Box to open the "New highlight box" dialog box (**Figure 7.1**).

   Alternatively you can click the Highlight Box button on the Object toolbar or press Control-Shift-L to achieve the same result. Also, if you right-click a slide in the Storyboard View or Edit View panel, you can choose to add a highlight box from the Insert menu item of the resulting context menu.

3. Click the "Frame color" chip to open the color picker and select a color to be used as the box's border.

4. Click the "Fill color" chip and select a fill color from the color picker.

5. Use the "Frame width" arrows to set a width for the border.

   Your choices range from 0 to 20 pixels. Alternatively, you can simply enter the value into the "Frame width" area.

6. Select a fill transparency percentage using the arrows.

continues on next page

Your choices range from 0% (solid fill) to 100% (invisible fill). You can also enter a value into this area.

Note that using the arrows to increase or decrease the transparency value changes the current value by increments of 10 percent. If you need a transparency value of 55%, for example, enter **55** directly into the entry area.

7. Select "Apply properties to all 'highlight boxes' in the movie" to apply the settings that you choose to all highlight boxes that appear in the movie.

8. Select the Options tab of the "New high-light box" dialog box.

The highlight box's Options dialog box opens (**Figure 7.2**).

9. In the "Display time" box, use the arrows to select how long (in tenths of a second) the highlight box is visible on screen.

Alternatively, you can enter your own value. If you do enter your own value, keep in mind that the lowest value you can use is .1 second. For example, 1.5 seconds is legal, but 1.55 is not.

10. In the "Appear after" box, use the arrows or enter a value (in tenths of a second) indicating when the highlight box will appear on the screen.

This value is the amount of time that will elapse between the slide opening and the highlight box appearing on the screen. If the amount of time you need isn't one of the choices offered, enter the value in the input box.

11. Select a transition effect—"Fade in and out," "Fade in only," "Fade out only," or "No transition"—to determine how the highlight box appears and/or leaves the screen.

Figure 7.2 A highlight box's options.

Figure 7.3 You can add audio to all interactive elements, including highlight boxes, in your presentation.

Figure 7.4 A highlight box in a slide.

12. Select "Apply effect to all "highlight boxes" in the movie" to apply the transition effect to all highlight boxes in the movie.

13. Select the Audio tab (**Figure 7.3**) to add or record audio for the highlight box.

14. Click Apply to preview you choices or click OK to apply the changes and return the Edit View panel.

Your highlight box appears in the slide (**Figure 7.4**).

✔ Tip

■ If you want to change highlight box settings after they have been applied, double-click the highlight box in the Edit View panel. The Highlight Box dialog box opens. You can adjust the highlight box size and location in the slide by dragging the box within the slide. To adjust the size, select the highlight box; then click and drag a handle inward (to make the box smaller), or outward (to make it larger).

To delete a highlight box:

1. Select the highlight box to be removed.

2. When you see the handles, press the Delete key.

An alert dialog box opens, asking if you want to remove the highlight box.

3. Click Yes.

Adding and Using Click Boxes

Click boxes add an element of interactivity to your movie. They ask the user to click the item to make a decision, which could include navigating to another slide or the movie, sending an email, or opening a Web site. You can resize these boxes and place them anywhere in a slide.

Clicks boxes are not visible on the slide. If you are familiar with the button creation features of Fireworks MX 2004, Flash MX 2004, or Dreamweaver MX 2004, click boxes define both the "hit area" and the actions that occur when the object is clicked. You set these actions in the Click Box dialog box.

You can have multiple click boxes in a slide. If this is your intention, keep in mind these boxes must be attached to captions. If click boxes are not attached to any objects in the slide, all captions in the slide will display at the same time.

To add a click box to a slide:

1. Open the target slide in the Edit View panel.

2. Select Insert > Click Box. Alternatively, you can

   ▲ Click the Click Box button on the Object toolbar.

   ▲ Press Control-Shift-K.

   ▲ Right-click the slide in the Storyboard View or Edit View panel, then select Insert > Interactive Objects > Click Box (**Figure 7.5**).

   The "New click box" dialog box opens.

3. Select the Click Box tab (**Figure 7.6**).

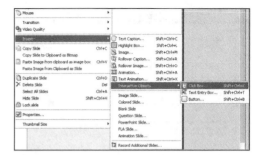

Figure 7.5 You can add click boxes using a slide's context menu.

Figure 7.6 Click boxes use events to determine what happens if a click is successful or if the click occurs elsewhere in the slide.

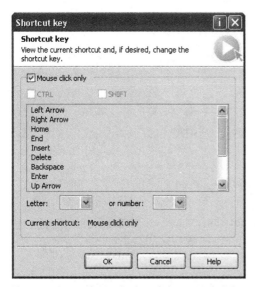

Figure 7.7 You can assign keyboard shortcuts to clicks.

✔ Tips

- To see the captions associated with a click box on the slide in the Edit View panel, click the object. Captions will appear.

- The Scoring tab on the "New click box" dialog box (Figure 7.6) is discussed in Chapter 12, "Creating eLearning Projects."

- Be very careful when assigning keyboard shortcuts to click boxes. You don't want to trigger a system shortcut. For example, theoretically you can use Control-C, but that is also the system shortcut for the Copy command. Also, always use a modifier key with shortcuts. Using just a letter or number, like C or 3, can be very confusing to the user. Function keys can't be used as shortcuts.

4. In the "On success" drop-down list, select what happens when the user clicks inside the click box.

   The options are Continue, "Go to next slide," "Go to previous slide," "Jump to slide," "Open URL of file," "Open other movie," "Send email to," and "Execute JavaScript."

   Depending upon your selection, the input box under the drop-down menu will change. How to work with each choice is presented later in this section.

5. If you want to add a key press instead of a mouse click to trigger the action, in the "Current shortcut" area, click the "Select keys" button.

   The "Shortcut key" dialog box (**Figure 7.7**) opens.

6. Deselect "Mouse click only."

7. Select a modifier key—Control, Shift, or both—and the key to be pressed.

   Alternatively, you can enter the key press manually.

8. Click OK.

   When you return to the "New click box" dialog box, the key combination appears in the "Current shortcut" area.

9. Back in the "New click box" dialog box, select what happens when the user clicks outside the click box.

   In the "Allow user" box, select how many clicks (1 to "Infinite attempts") are tracked before the action is triggered. In the "After last attempt" drop-down list, select what happens after the last attempt to click outside the box.

10. Select one or more options.

11. Click OK or Apply to see your changes.

Click Box Options

There is a lot of power "under the hood" when it comes to using click boxes. Essentially, the following options, on the Options tab of the of the "New click box" dialog box (**Figure 7.8**), determine what happens in a slide containing a click box:

◆ **Hint caption** Select to open a caption when the user rolls over the box.

◆ **Success caption** Select to add a success message caption.

◆ **Failure caption** Select to add a failure caption.

◆ **Show hand mouse cursor when over success "hit" area** Select to give the user a visual clue that the mouse is over a hot spot. This option should always be selected.

◆ **Stop audio when clicked** Select this if you want any audio to stop playing when the box is clicked. Selecting this option only stops the audio in the slide. It does not stop the background audio. As well, this option can only be initiated with a mouse click. You can't assign a Keyboard shortcut to stop the sound.

◆ **Pause movie until user clicks** Select to stop the movie until the user clicks the box.

◆ **Double mouse click** Select to assign a double-click action to a box.

If you choose to add one or all of the captions, they will appear in the slide (**Figure 7.9**). Double-click the caption to open the Caption dialog box and enter the appropriate text.

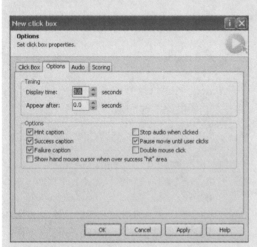

Figure 7.8 On the "New click box" dialog box's Options tab, you determine when the box appears on the slide, for how long, and what captions will appear when the box is clicked.

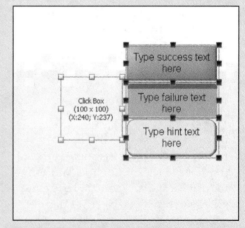

Figure 7.9 A click box with captions.

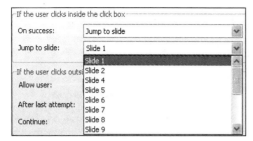

Figure 7.10 You can use click boxes to navigate to other slides in the movie.

To use click boxes to navigate throughout the movie:

1. Open the slide containing the click box in the Edit View panel.

2. Double-click the click box to open the "New click box" dialog box.

3. To assign a location if the user clicks inside the box, select "Jump to slide" in the "On success" area.

4. Select the slide from the pop-down list in the "Jump to slide" area (**Figure 7.10**).

5. To assign a location if the user doesn't click the box, set a number of attempts in the "Allow user" box, then select "Jump to slide" in the "After last attempt" area.

6. Select the slide from the pop-down list in the "Jump to slide" area.

7. Click OK.

✔ Tips

■ In many respects, movies are living documents. You can expand or contract them through the addition or deletion of slides. Navigating to a numbered slide is a dangerous practice, because the slide numbers change if slides are added or deleted. If you are using click boxes for navigation purposes, always navigate to a named slide. This way, if slides are added or deleted, the user doesn't run the risk of being taken to the wrong slide. To add slide names, select a slide's properties to open the Slide Properties box, and add the name in the Label area.

■ Selecting Infinite in the "Number of attempts" area results in the rest of the area being grayed out.

To use click boxes to open another Captivate movie:

1. Open the slide containing the click box in the Edit View panel.

2. Double-click the click box. The Click Box dialog box opens.

3. To open a new movie if the user clicks the box, in the "On success" area, select "Open other movie."

4. Select the movie to be opened from the "Open other movie" drop-down list (**Figure 7.11**).

5. Select a destination window by clicking the Destination button (the down arrow button to the right of the pop-down list).

   Your choices are Current (the default value), New, Parent, and Top.

6. If the movie is not listed, click the Browse button (it has three dots) and navigate to the movie.

7. To assign a location if the user doesn't click the box, set a number of attempts and, in the "After last attempt" area, select Movie.

8. Click OK.

To use click boxes to open a Web page:

1. Open the slide containing the click box in the Edit View panel.

2. Double-click the click box. The Click Box dialog box opens.

3. To assign a location if the user clicks the box, in the "On success" area, select "Open URL or file."

4. Enter the full URL address in the "Open URL or file" text entry box (**Figure 7.12**).

5. To assign a location if the user doesn't click the box, in the "After last attempt" area, select URL.

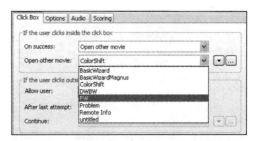

Figure 7.11 Click boxes can open Captivate movies.

Figure 7.12 Use a click box to open a browser.

Figure 7.13 You can send email when a click box is clicked.

6. Enter the full address in the "Open URL or file" text entry box and then click OK.

✔ Tips

■ When you enter a URL, always use the absolute address.

■ The down arrow in the URL input area enables you to choose, if the movie is playing through a browser, how the page selected appears in the browser. The choices are Current, New, Parent, and Top.

To use a click box to send email:

1. Open the slide containing the click box in the Edit View panel.

2. Double-click the click box.
The Click Box dialog box opens.

3. To assign a location if the user clicks the box, in the "On success" area, select "Send email to."

4. Enter the email address in the "Send e-mail to" text entry box (**Figure 7.13**).

5. To assign an email address if the user doesn't click the box, in the "After last attempt" area, select Email.

6. Enter the email address in the "Email address" text entry box.

7. Click OK.

✔ Tips

■ Be careful using click boxes to send email. If the movie is playing from a CD or even a kiosk, be sure that an email application is installed on the computer.

■ If you have a number of email applications on your computer, you can't choose which application opens. Captivate launches the computer's default mail application.

To execute a JavaScript:

1. Open the slide containing the click box in the Edit View panel.

2. Double-click the click box to open the Click Box dialog box.

3. To assign a JavaScript action if the user clicks the box, in the "On success" area, select Execute JavaScript.

4. Click the button with the three dots to open the JavaScript dialog box.

5. Enter the code and click OK (**Figure 7.14**).

Figure 7.14 You can use JavaScript to control the click box.

Adding and Using Buttons

Buttons are a more "visible" form of interactivity than click boxes. They are also a classic form of navigation. Users instinctively understand the purpose of a button. In Captivate, buttons are used for a number of activities ranging from navigation to opening URLs and sending email.

Captivate actually employs two types of buttons. The first type (discussed in Chapter 2, "Creating Captivate Movies") is used to create the elements of a movie playback controller. In this instance, there are only two possible states for the button: Up and Down. The second type of button, which is the subject of this section of this chapter, is the button as an object. In this case, the button has the traditional states of Up, Over, and Down to indicate it is live.

When creating a button as an object, you choose from among three button types:

◆ **Text button** With this type of button, the text you enter becomes live.

◆ **Transparent button** This button acts like a classic hot spot. Yet where it differs from a hot spot is that you can assign a fill color and transparency to the color. In this way, the viewer's attention is drawn to the area of the slide covered by the button.

◆ **Image button** This classic button type uses three separate images—Up, Over, and Down—for the button states.

To add a button:

1. Open the target slide in the Edit View panel.

2. Select Insert > Button, press Control-Shift-B, or click the Button button on the Object toolbar.

   The "New button" dialog box (**Figure 7.15**) opens.

3. Select the Button tab.

   This window functions in exactly the same manner as the "New click box" dialog box from the previous section.

4. Make your interactivity choices.

5. In the Type drop-down list (**Figure 7.16**), select one of the three button types—text, transparent, or image.

6. Click OK.

   The button appears in the slide (**Figure 7.17**).

✔ Tips

- The Scoring tab on the "New button" dialog box (Figure 7.15) is discussed in Chapter 12.

- If you need to change a button's properties or interactivity options, double-click the button in the slide to open the Button dialog box. This is simply the "New button" dialog box with its name changed.

- If the button text is a bit too long, click the button and drag a handle outward to resize the button.

Figure 7.15 The Button dialog box.

Figure 7.16 Three button types are available.

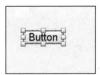

Figure 7.17 A button on the slide. Click the button in the Edit View panel to see any captions associated with it.

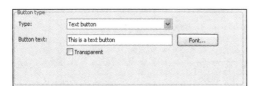

Figure 7.18 You can use text as a button. Selecting Transparent will make the text's background color invisible.

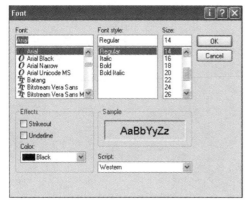

Figure 7.19 To format text, click the Font button.

To create a text button:

1. In the "New button" dialog box's Type drop-down list, select "Text button."

2. In the "Button text" text box, enter the text to be used on the button (**Figure 7.18**).

3. Click the Font button.
   The Font dialog box opens (**Figure 7.19**).

4. Select a font, style, and point size for the button text.

5. In the Effects area, select the text color from the Color drop-down list.
   Don't bother selecting Strikethrough or Underline. These are redundant.

6. If the style shown in the Sample box is acceptable, click OK.
   You are returned to the Button Type area of the dialog box.

7. If you simply want the text to function as a button, select Transparent.

8. Click OK to close the "New button" dialog box.

✔ Tip

■ You are limited to the choices available in the Color drop-down list. If you need to use a specific color, consider creating your own button. This is discussed in the sidebar "Rolling Your Own Buttons."

To create a transparent button:

1. In the "New button" dialog box's Type drop-down list, select "Transparent button" (**Figure 7.20**).

   The options for a transparent button appear in the "Button type" area.

2. Click the "Frame color" chip.

   The color picker opens.

3. Choose a color for the border and click OK.

4. Click the "Frame width" arrows to set the size of the border.

   Your choices range from 0 to 20 pixels. You can also enter your own value between 1 and 20.

5. Click the "Fill color" chip.

   The color picker opens.

6. Select a fill color and click OK.

7. Click the "Fill transparency" arrows to set the fill's transparency percentage.

   Your choices range from 0% (solid fill) to 100% (full transparency, or an invisible fill).

8. Click OK.

   The dialog box closes, and the button is placed in the slide.

✔ Tip

- Think of transparent buttons as being visible hot spots.

Figure 7.20 Think of a transparent button as being a hot spot. Add a color and a transparency value, and the hot spot becomes visible.

Figure 7.21 You can use graphic buttons from Captivate or that were created elsewhere.

✔ Tip

- Selecting "Transparent button" in the Image Button area of the Button dialog box does not make a button's fill color invisible. In this case, it treats the pixels outside of the button's border as being transparent. This is determined by the application sampling the color of the pixel in the upper left edge of the button's bitmap. The color value chosen from the "Transparency Pixel" will result in that color being made transparent throughout the entire image.

To create an image button:

1. In the "New button" dialog box's Type drop-down list, select "Image button."

   The options for an image button appear in the "Button type" area (**Figure 7.21**).

2. In the Up Image section, click the Browse button.

   The Open dialog box appears. A rather extensive button collection is available in C:\Program Files\Captivate\Gallery\Buttons.

3. Navigate to the folder containing the button's Up state.

4. Select the image and click OK.

   The image appears in the button preview.

5. In the Down Image section, click the Browse button.

   The Open dialog box appears

6. Navigate to the folder containing the button's Down state.

7. Select the image and click Open.

   The image appears in the button preview.

8. In the Over Image section, click the Browse button.

   The Open dialog box appears.

9. Navigate to the folder containing the button's Over state.

10. Select the image and click Open.

    The image appears in the button preview.

11. If you have chosen the wrong buttons, click "Use default buttons."

    The blank button replaces your choices.

12. Click OK.

    The dialog box closes, and the button's Up state appears in the slide.

Rolling Your Own Buttons

You aren't limited to using the button collection that ships with Captivate. You can create your own buttons using an imaging application such as Adobe Photoshop or Fireworks MX 2004. If you do create your own buttons, keep the following in mind:

- Create individual images for the Up, Over, and Down states of the button.

- Buttons can be saved in the .gif, .jpg, and .bmp formats.

- Build the buttons over a solid background color and select "Transparency color" in the Image Button area to remove that.

- Ensure the background color is unique to the image. For example, if you build a white button with beveled edges and black text over a black background, the text will disappear if you select the "Transparent buttons" check box for the button in Captivate.

- If you create the buttons in Fireworks MX 2004, create the button as a button symbol and then select Images Only in the Export Special dialog box. This will automatically create the three images for you.

- When naming the buttons, include the state in the button name. "Black_Marble_Up" is more intuitive than "Black_Marble_First."

- Buttons don't have to be massive. A button width of 100 pixels and a height of between 20 and 25 pixels is common.

- If you create the button in Fireworks MX 2004 and the button uses square corners, don't trim the canvas by clicking the Fit Canvas button in the Property Inspector. This will fit the canvas to the exact dimensions of the button, and the "Transparency Pixel" will be the one in the upper left corner of the button's border.

- Before saving your images in your imaging application, select the Crop tool and crop the image, being sure to leave an area of 10 to 15 pixels of the background or canvas color visible (**Figure 7.22**).

Figure 7.22 When creating a button in an imaging application, leave a 15-pixel canvas area visible around the button. Select Transparent in the Button Type area of the Button dialog box, and it will be removed in Captivate.

Figure 7.23 You can add text entry boxes as well as events based upon success or failure to a slide.

Adding and Using Text Entry Boxes

Another key interactivity feature is to give the user the opportunity to respond, in writing, to questions. This is the purpose of a text entry box. You can use text entry boxes to ask simple questions or to password-protect a presentation.

For example, you may have the image of an application's toolbar with the Text tool circled visible on the screen. On the screen is a question: "Enter the name of the circled tool." Beside the question is a blank text entry box. The user enters the words "Text tool" and presses the Enter key. A dialog box with the words "That is correct." appears, and the next question appears. If the student enters a wrong answer, such as "Grabber hand," a failure message appears, and the user is prompted to try again.

A password uses the same procedure. The user is presented with a screen and is prompted to enter the correct password to proceed. If the answer is wrong, the user can be given a few more attempts before being told to contact the system administrator. If the answer is correct, the user is taken to the correct screen immediately.

To add a text entry box:

1. Open the slide to contain the text entry box in the Edit View panel.

2. Select Insert > Text Entry Box, click the Text Entry Box button on the Object toolbar, or press Control-Shift-T.

   The "New text entry box" dialog box opens (**Figure 7.23**).

continues on next page

3. Select the Text Entry Box tab, where you'll decide how the movie will react to the user's input.

The Text Entry Box tab is not really that mysterious. It asks you to make only two decisions: "What do I do if the input text is correct?" and "What do I do if the text is incorrect?"

4. Click once in the "Correct entries" area.

5. Enter the correct response to your question in the text entry field (**Figure 7.24**).

When entering the text, place each possible text combination into a separate text box. Note that though the text entry box looks like it requires a rather short line of text, this is not the case.

6. Click the Add button to insert another text entry box, or click in the next text entry box area.

7. Click the Font button.

The Font dialog box opens.

8. Select the font, style, effect, and font color.

Note that these font settings apply to the text the user will enter into the text entry box. They do not apply to the text that you just entered into the Text Entry dialog box.

9. Click OK.

You are returned to the Text Entry dialog box.

10. In the "On success" drop-down list, select what happens when a correct answer is entered.

11. Select what happens when an incorrect answer is entered.

12. Select the Options tab.

The text entry box's options open.

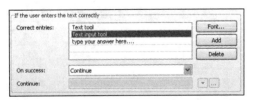

Figure 7.24 Enter the correct entries into the dialog box. You are not limited to the space given.

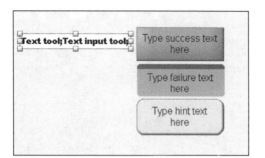

Figure 7.25 A text entry box with captions in a Captivate slide.

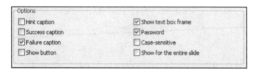

Figure 7.26 You can use text entry boxes to password-protect a movie.

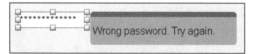

Figure 7.27 A password text entry box with failure caption on a Captivate slide.

13. Decide if the box should have a frame, if the box should be treated as a password, if the text input is case sensitive, what captions (if any) will appear, and the duration of the text entry box on screen.

14. Click OK.

The text entry box and any success or failure captions appear in the slide (**Figure 7.25**).

✔ Tips

■ Use a transparent caption for the actual questions requiring text entry.

■ Text entries that are too long are simply truncated to display in the correct entries list. When you double-click one of them to edit it again, the entire line of text is still editable and can be navigated using the arrow keys.

To create a user password:

1. Open the "New text entry box" dialog box.

2. Enter the password text into the "Correct entries" text entry box.

3. Choose the success and failure actions.

4. Select the Options tab.

5. Select Password and "Failure caption" (**Figure 7.26**). Also here, if a password contains upper and lowercase letters, select Case-sensitive.

6. Click OK.

The Password text entry box with the password visible as a series of asterisks and the failure caption appear in the slide (**Figure 7.27**).

✔ Tip

■ Always include a failure caption. This lets the user know, unequivocally, that the text just entered is incorrect.

ADDING AND USING TEXT ENTRY BOXES

Adding JavaScript to Extend Functionality

JavaScript is a common coding language for interactivity on the Web and elsewhere. For example, ActionScript, Flash's coding language, is an implementation of JavaScript. As well, Macromedia Director MX 2004, has added JavaScript as a coding alternative to its native object-oriented language, Lingo. It should not come as any great surprise, then, to discover you can write your own JavaScript code to drive many of the interactive objects and features of this application, providing the movie is destined for playback through a browser.

To add JavaScript to a box or a button:

1. Open a movie and double-click the slide to which a button or box will be added.
   The Edit View panel opens.

2. Add a click box, button, or text entry box.

3. Click the properties tab for your object and select the JavaScript option to determine what happens if the user clicks inside or outside of the box.

4. Click the Change button (it has three dots). The JavaScript dialog box opens.

5. Enter the JavaScript into the text box.

6. Click OK.
   The JavaScript dialog box closes.

7. Determine what happens, including using JavaScript, if the user clicks outside of the object.

8. Click OK.

✔ Tips

■ The example shown earlier in Figure 7.14 is very basic. You can copy and paste complex code into the JavaScript input box from other sources, such as word processing applications.

■ You can add JavaScript to objects that have already been added to a slide. Simply double-click the object and, when the object's dialog box opens, select JavaScript from the Success or Failure areas. Then enter or copy and paste the JavaScript into the JavaScript dialog box.

ADDING RICH MEDIA

New Media developers can't avoid encountering the term *Rich Media*. Unfortunately, the term is very difficult to define. It seems to adopt whatever definition is tagged onto it at the time.

Macromedia has embraced the term and, for the past couple of years, has seemingly added it to every document and presentation put in front of its clients and the public at large. Thus it makes sense, for the purposes of this book, to use their version of the term.

Macromedia does not have a "corporate" definition of *Rich Media*. They have neither "codified" it nor defined it consistently. Actually, this is a rather wise approach, because the term is rather chameleon-like.

Listen to Macromedia use the term in a variety of situations, and you will come to understand that their interpretation of the term is "any media added to any other media that engages the user and enhances the user experience."

continues on next page

For example, adding an interactive Flash presentation to a Web page falls into this interpretation. A Web page, by nature, is a fairly static piece of media composed of text and images. Adding a Flash animation and allowing the user to interact with that animation adds a new dimension to, or "richens," the experience of the static page. Toss sound into the Flash animation and you make the experience even "richer." This brings us to Captivate.

At first glance you could rightfully claim the movies are Rich Media. They start out fairly static but, through the addition of sound, interactivity, and so on, they develop to the point where they meet Macromedia's interpretation. But not quite. To meet Macromedia's interpretation, media from other sources—including video, GIF animations, Flash animations, and animated screen captures—will have to be added.

Figure 8.1 Select the file to be imported into Flash's Library.

Preparing Video for Captivate

Video in Captivate is a classic Good News/ Bad News story.

The bad news? Captivate doesn't do video. The good news? Says who?

You *can* add video to your Captivate presentation. It just requires you not to think of it as video. Instead, think of it as a Flash presentation. Flash MX and Flash MX 2004 both have the ability to convert a video file into a format—FLV—that is able to read by Flash. This means the video can actually be played in Captivate, because you can place a Flash file— both the SWF (the final compiled file) and the FLA (the working file)—into Captivate.

There are two methods of adding video to Flash:

◆ Let Flash do the conversion to FLV.

◆ Create the FLV file in Sorenson Squeeze before adding it to Flash.

✔ Tip

■ Providing you have QuickTime 4.0 or later installed on your PC, you can import MOV, MPG, DV, and AVI files into Flash. You can also use DirectX 7 or later to import ASF, MPEG, and AVI files into Flash.

To create an FLV file in Flash MX 2004:

1. Open Flash MX 2004 and select File > Import > Import to Library to open the Import to Library dialog box (**Figure 8.1**).

2. Navigate to the folder containing the video, select the folder, and click Open. The Video Import dialog box opens.

continues on next page

3. Select "Embed video in Macromedia Flash document."

Note that selecting "Link to external video file" here defeats the purpose of this exercise. The resulting Flash movie will have to be output as a QuickTime file.

4. Click Next.

The Editing section of the dialog box opens.

5. Select "Import the entire video" and click Next.

The Import Encoding options window opens.

6. In the "Compression profile" pop-down list, select the optimization setting that is best suited to the final use of the video (**Figure 8.2**).

7. Click the Finish button.

The Import dialog box opens, showing the progress of the conversion process from QuickTime to FLV. When the conversion process is finished, the Import dialog box closes.

8. Open the Flash Library by selecting Window > Library or pressing the Control-L (PC) or Command-L (Mac) keys.

The file, containing a little video camera icon, is the FLV file in the Library (**Figure 8.3**).

✔ Tip

■ You can import the video to the stage rather than the Flash Library. Yet the advantage of importing the video to the Library is that you can add the video to the Flash timeline when you need it.

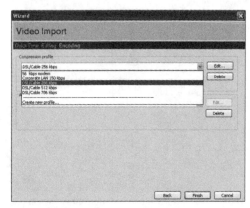

Figure 8.2 The video encoding options in Flash enable you to target the file to the user's modem speed.

Figure 8.3 An FLV file in Flash has a small video recorder icon.

Figure 8.4 The Sorenson Squeeze (Version 4) interface is relatively simple to learn.

The Video Compression Options

When you compress video, you will have to determine a target bandwidth for playback. The choices are as follows:

◆ **56 kbps modem** Select if your Captivate movie is destined for Web playback. This is the reference standard for a dial-up connection.

◆ **Corporate LAN 150 kpbs** Select if the Captivate movie will be played back through a corporate network.

◆ **DSL/Cable *XXX* kbps** Select one of these values if the Captivate movie will be played back through a DSL connection or cable modem. If you are unsure of which speed to choose, pick the slowest. If the Captivate movie is destined for CD or hard drive playback, choose the fastest speed.

To create an FLV file using Sorenson Squeeze:

1. Open Sorenson Squeeze.

   This exercise uses the latest version of Sorenson Squeeze, version 4.0. If you are at all serious about using Flash video in your Captivate products, then upgrading to this version is a must. The FLV format now requires a metadata header that contains a bit of information—file length and so on—if a video is to be streamed from your server. Further, Macromedia's Flash Video Kit for Dreamweaver requires that the FLV files used contain this metadata.

2. Click the Import File button.

   The Open dialog box appears.

3. Navigate to the folder containing the video file to be used.

4. Double-click the file to be imported.

   It is added to the Settings area of the Squeeze interface.

5. Double click Macromedia Flash Video in the Format and Compression Settings.

   The streaming options open.

6. Select 56K_Dial_Up_Stream from the pop-down list and click the Apply button.

   The selection appears in the settings under the imported video file (**Figure 8.4**).

   continues on next page

7. Double-click either the Audio compression or Spark Pro compression setting.

The Audio/Video Compression Settings dialog box opens (**Figure 8.5**).

8. Select the Video checkbox, and set the frame rate to 12 frames per second (fps).

9. Set the method to Sorenson 2-Pass VBR.

10. Set the frame size to match that of the original video.

11. Select the Audio check box.

12. In the Audio section's Codec field, select Fraunhofer MP3.

Don't change any of the resulting settings. (The reason is explained in "Squeezing Out Quality Video.")

13. If your compression settings resemble those shown in **Figure 8.6**, click OK.

14. Click the Squeeze It button.

A video is "squeezed," and progress bars in the Settings area of the Squeeze interface indicate the progress of the operation (**Figure 8.7**).

15. When the compression finishes, quit Squeeze.

The new FLV file appears in the same location as the original video (**Figure 8.8**).

To import an FLV file into Flash:

1. Open a new document in Flash.

2. Select File > Import > Import to Library.

The Import to Library dialog box opens.

3. Navigate to the FLV file location and click Open.

4. When the Working dialog box closes, open the Flash Library.

The imported file appears.

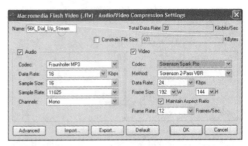

Figure 8.5 Double-clicking the settings in Squeeze opens the Audio/Video Compression Settings dialog box, which you can use to change the settings and the filename, or even to remove the settings.

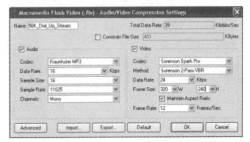

Figure 8.6 The Squeeze compression settings enable you to make a number of changes. If the file is destined for Flash, select Sorenson 2-Pass VBR in the Video area.

Figure 8.7 The progress of the conversion appears right in the Sorenson Squeeze interface.

Figure 8.8 There is a serious file size difference, thanks to the compressed audio and video, between the original and the resulting FLV files.

Squeezing Out Quality Video

Sorenson Media, the makers of Squeeze and the Spark Video codec that comes packaged with Flash, have developed a rather solid reputation among developers as a company that produces amazing video tools. Squeeze 4.0 is the latest version and, if you are a Flash or Captivate developer looking to add video to your projects, it will become an indispensable tool.

Your first clue that it is vital is obvious in Figure 8.8. The original QuickTime video weigh in at 16.8 Mb, and the FLV file and FLA files are only 900 K. The SWF file, though, is only 823 Kb.

The reason the file size dropped so dramatically is due to not compressing the audio in Squeeze and, instead, letting Flash do the audio compression work. Here are a few other pointers to keep in mind if you do use Squeeze:

- Match the FLV frame rate to that of the Flash movie.

  Flash movies traditionally play back at a rate of 12 fps. If the video frame rate is faster or slower than that in Flash, you will lose the synchronization of the sound in the video to the images in the video.

- Use the Sorenson 2-Pass VBR option.

  Sorenson compression uses Variable Bit Rate (VBR) compression. VBR encoding adjusts the data rate according to the amount of movement between the frames and the number of scene changes. 2-Pass means it repeats the process twice, resulting in an even smaller file.

- If you are producing a .SWF file, feel free to apply audio compression.

- Don't play with the aspect ratio.

  If you need a physically smaller file than the original, maintain the 4:3 aspect ratio of the original to avoid potential distortions in the final product.

- Use mono, not stereo, audio output.

  Stereo sound only adds "weight," especially when the Captivate movie is being played through a browser.

- You can download a trial version of the application at www.sorenson.com.

- If you simply want to add the metadata to an FLV file without the expense of Squeeze, Mac and PC versions of a "donationware" application designed for this purpose are available at www.swfx.org/flv-duration. A freeware PC-only application, named "FLVMetaData Injector," is available at http://buraks.com/flvmdi/.

Working with AVI Video

AVI is short for Audio-Video Interleave, the file format for Microsoft's Video for Windows standard. It is an audio-video standard designed by Microsoft and is as close to being a video standard on the PC as you can get because it has been around since the introduction of Windows 3.1. It is a format developed for storing video and audio information, and files in this format have an .avi extension. These files are limited to a play-back rate of 30 fps, which is adequate for full screen, full motion video. However, Video for Windows does not require any special play-back hardware, making it the lowest common denominator for multimedia applications. AVI is the only video format that you can add to your movie with no extra effort or helper applications on your part.

Captivate imports an AVI file as an animation and converts the video into a Flash SWF file during the import process.

To import an AVI file:

1. Open the Storyboard or Edit view, and select or open the slide to contain the AVI file.

2. Select Insert > Animation.

    The Open dialog box appears.

3. Navigate to the folder containing the AVI file, select the file, and click the Open button.

    A progress bar appears, showing the progress of the conversion process from AVI to SWF (**Figure 8.9**). When the conversion process is completed, the "New animation" dialog box opens (**Figure 8.10**).

4. Add any transitions or audio effects, and click OK.

    The "New animation" dialog box closes, the new movie appears in the slide.

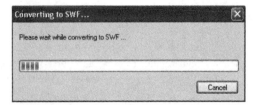

Figure 8.9 AVI movies imported into Captivate are converted to SWF files.

Figure 8.10 AVI videos open in the "New animation" dialog box.

Importing Movies from Other Screen Recording Software

Captivate is an amazing product, though it is not the only screen recording software on the market. There are a number of very good ones out there, such as Camtasia Studio 2 from TechSmith and Snapz Pro X (Macintosh) from Ambrosia Software.

If you have projects created in either of these applications, or if you need a Macintosh capture, your work is not lost. You may also have been given these files with instructions to include them in your project. Here is how to add files created in these applications to your movie.

To import a Camtasia Studio 2 movie:

1. In the Storyboard View panel's Task Launch areaselect either Insert > Animation to add the video to the slide or Insert > Animation Slide to create a slide used solely to play the video. The Open dialog box opens.

2. Click the Browse button and navigate to the folder containing the Camtasia Studio AVI file to convert it to an SWF on import.

✔ Tips

- Camtasia Studio works with a number of formats ranging from FLV and QuickTime to AVI and SWF.

- You can no longer import AVI files in this way. Instead you must import it as an animation as described previously in the AVI section.

Importing a SnapzPro X movie

Though Captivate is a PC-only product, you can show Macintosh demos that are captured using SnapzPro X on the Macintosh. SnapzPro captures are output only to the QuickTime format, which uses the .mov extension. The great thing about the MOV format, though it is the QuickTime native format, is that it works equally well on both platforms.

Before importing a MOV file into Captivate, you should decide which format you need: FLV or AVI. If the file is to be converted to an AVI format, you will need to do this either using QuickTime Pro or a video editing software.

The file can then be imported into a Captivate Animation slide by selecting Insert > Animation slide or adding it directly to a Captivate slide by selecting Insert > Animation. In both cases the AVI movie will be converted to a Flash .SWF before placement into Captivate.

Figure 8.11 An animated GIF is previewed in the Open dialog box.

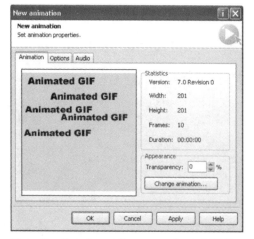

Figure 8.12 If you import the wrong animated GIF file, click the "Change animation" button to open the Open dialog box.

Importing Animations into Your Movie

The addition of video to your movies enhances the Rich Media experience. You can also make the slides more engaging by including GIF and Flash animations in your movies.

The advantage of a GIF animation is size. Traditionally, GIF animations were designed not to take up a great deal of space in the browser. This makes them ideal for use in slides. Further, their relatively small file size is due to the use of no more than 256 colors.

Flash animations are also very small and use a larger color palette. What makes them so appealing is the fact that Captivate imports the SWF directly into an Animation slide.

To insert a GIF animation:

1. Open a movie in the Storyboard View or Edit View panel, and select the slide to contain the animation.

2. Select Insert > Animation.
   The Open dialog box opens.

3. Navigate to the folder containing the GIF animation and select it.
   The animation is previewed on the right side of the dialog box (**Figure 8.11**).

4. Click Open.
   A progress bar appears, showing the conversion of the GIF to a Flash SWF file. When it finishes, the dialog box closes, and the GIF appears in the "New animation" dialog box (**Figure 8.12**).

5. If you have converted the wrong animation, click the "Change animation" button.
   This returns you to the Open dialog box, where you can select another GIF animation.

continues on next page

6. In the "New animation" dialog box, click the Options and Audio tabs to change how the animation appears on the slide and to add any audio to the animation.

7. Click OK.

   The animation appears on the selected slide (**Figure 8.13**).

✔ Tip

■ When an animated .GIF is converted to a Flash .SWF file, the original file is not lost. The new .SWF file will appear in the same folder as the original file. This new .SWF file can then be used in web pages and even other Flash movies.

To insert a Flash SWF file:

1. Open a slide in the Storyboard View or Edit View panel, and select the target slide for the Flash animation.

2. Select Insert > Animation or press Control-Shift-A.

   The Open dialog box displays.

3. Navigate to the folder containing the Flash SWF file, and either double-click the file or select it and click the Open button.

   The "New animation" dialog box opens, and the SWF starts to play in the preview area.

4. If the SWF is the wrong file, click the "Change animation" button.

   This returns you to Open dialog box opens, where you can select another file. The Statistics section provides valuable information regarding the file, including the movie's width and height as well as how many slides it contains. It also displays the movie's duration, which is invaluable when making decisions in the Play Options.

Figure 8.13 An animated GIF placed in a Captivate slide.

Figure 8.14 You can set what happens when a Flash SWF animation starts in the Options area of the "New animation" dialog box.

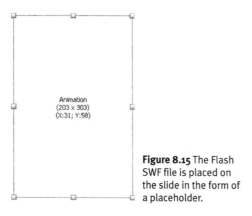

Figure 8.15 The Flash SWF file is placed on the slide in the form of a placeholder.

✔ Tips

- You can use this technique to place a GIF animation in a slide as well. Keep in mind that the file will be converted to a SWF file before the "New animation" dialog box opens.

- Like their GIF animation counterparts, Flash movies can also be placed into animation slides.

5. Select the Options tab and choose the desired settings for the animation (**Figure 8.14**):

   ▲ **Display for specific time** Select this option and enter how long (in seconds) the Flash animation should remain onscreen.

   ▲ **Display for rest of slide** Select this option from the drop-down menu to show the animation for the remainder of the slide's duration.

   ▲ **Display for rest of movie** Select to have the animation remain onscreen until the end of the movie.

   ▲ **Display for duration of animation** Select to have the animation appear only for the original length of the Flash movie.

   ▲ **Appear after** Enter the number of seconds that should pass before the animation appears on the slide.

   ▲ **Synchronize with movie** Select to force the imported animation's frame rate to match that of the Captivate movie. Be careful, as this may produce rough/choppy animations in some cases.

   ▲ **Loop** Select to have the animation file play repeatedly until the "Show for" time has elapsed. Otherwise, the animation will play once and simply stop on the last frame.

6. Optionally, set the transition effect options.

7. In the Appearance area of the Animation tab, set the transparency.

8. Click OK.

   The animation appears in the slide as a bounding box (**Figure 8.15**).

Captivate and the Macromedia Studio MX 2004

The Macromedia Studio MX 2004 is composed of Freehand MX, Flash MX 2004, Fireworks MX 2004, and Dreamweaver MX 2004. These content creation tools are an absolute development powerhouse when used together. Unfortunately, most developers tend to align themselves with one tool and tend to ignore the others. This is a huge mistake.

Each tool supports the other. For example, a vector drawing such as a company logo can be created in Freehand, imported into Flash, subsequently animated, output as a Flash SWF file, and placed in a Captivate movie. If you need fine typography, create the text in Freehand, save the file as a JPG, and import it into Captivate. In the previous chapter, you learned how to work with buttons. These, too, can be greatly improved by creating the button in Fireworks, placing the button in Flash, adding a link to a Web page in Flash, and then adding the SWF file to your Captivate movie. As long as the file can either be "fed" into Flash or saved in a format used by Captivate, the power of the Studio is available to you.

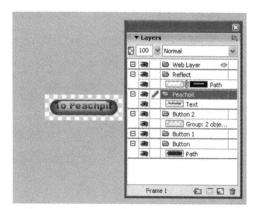

Figure 8.16 The button artwork is constructed in Fireworks MX 2004.

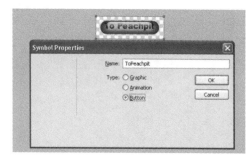

Figure 8.17 The artwork is converted to a Fireworks button symbol and given a name.

From Fireworks to Flash to Captivate: The Studio workflow

This example demonstrates how to create a simple three-state (Up, Over, and Down) button in Fireworks MX 2004. The button will then be placed in Flash MX 2004, where a link to the Peachpit site will be added to the button. The file will then be compiled into an SWF file and added to a Captivate movie.

The button used will be an Aqua type button (**Figure 18.16**) that is used in the Mac OSX interface. Creating the button would be out of the scope of this book, but there are a number of tutorials out there that show you how to do this.

For this exercise, I created the button and saved the master as a PNG file. I then flattened the layers in the Layer panel and saved that image as PeachpitUp.png. I created the other two states—Over and Down—using a LiveEffect to change the color of the glow in the image. From here I was ready to build the button.

To create a button symbol in Fireworks MX 2004:

1. Open the Up, Over, and Down button images in Fireworks MX 2004.

   The button names appear in tabs at the top of the document window.

2. Click the Up button's tab and right-click the image to open the context menu.

3. Select Convert To Symbol.

   The Symbol Properties dialog box opens (**Figure 18.17**).

4. Name the button and select Button as the symbol type.

continues on next page

5. Click OK.

The green overlay indicates the object under it is interactive or is a slice. The small arrow in the bottom left corner indicates the object is a symbol.

6. Right-click the object and select Symbol > Edit Symbol from the pop-down menu.

The Button Editor opens. Note the X and Y positions of the button in the Fireworks Property Inspector.

7. Click the Over tab in the Button Editor.

8. Click the tab for your Over button image (mine was named *PeachPitOver*) to open it.

9. Select the button on the Canvas and copy the button to the clipboard.

10. Click the image's tab at the top of the document window containing the name of the symbol (my symbol is named *ToPeachpit*).

You are returned to the Button Editor.

11. Paste the button into the Over area (**Figure 8.18**).

12. When the button appears, enter the X and Y coordinates of the Up button into the Property Inspector.

13. Repeat step 10 for the Down button, and click Done to close the Button Editor.

The button is created. Do not close the image or quit Fireworks.

Figure 8.18 Use the Fireworks Button Editor to add the button symbol's Up, Over, and Down states quickly.

Figure 8.19 Dragging and dropping the button symbol from Fireworks into Flash results in the creation of a Flash button symbol.

To add a Fireworks button symbol to Flash MX 2004:

1. Launch Flash and open a new Flash document.

You should have both the button open in Fireworks and a blank stage open in Flash.

2. Noting the canvas size for the Fireworks button in the Fireworks Property Inspector, click the Fireworks button, and drag and drop the button symbol slice (the green overlay) onto the Flash stage.

A progress bar appears.

3. Save the button and quit Fireworks.

4. Click the Flash stage and select Window > Library.

The Library opens. Notice that there are three bitmaps and a folder named "Fireworks objects."

5. Double-click the folder in the Library to open it.

In the folder are a movie clip and a button symbol (**Figure 8.19**).

6. Single-click the button symbol.

In the preview, you will see that the button symbol from Fireworks has been converted to a Flash button.

7. Click the Size button on the Flash Property Inspector.

The Document Properties dialog box opens.

8. Change the stage's width and height to match that of the button, and click OK.

9. Single-click the button on the stage and press the F9 key to open the ActionScript editor.

continues on next page

CAPTIVATE AND THE MACROMEDIA STUDIO MX 2004

10. Enter the following code into the ActionScript editor:

```
on (release){
   →getURL("http://www.peachpit.com",
   "_blank");
}
```

11. Close the ActionScript editor and save the file.

To create a Flash SWF file for Captivate playback:

1. Select File > Publish settings or press Control-Shift-F12.

The Publish Settings dialog box opens.

2. Select the Formats tab and deselect HTML (**Figure 8.20**).

The SWF uses the name set for the Flash file. You can change the name by selecting the SWF in the File text box and entering a new name.

3. Select the Flash tab.

Here, you can choose Player settings and other actions to be performed when the SWF file is created.

4. Select Flash Player 6 in the Version drop-down list (**Figure 8.21**).

5. Click Publish.

A progress bar appears, showing the progress of the compilation process.

6. When the process finishes, click OK to close the Publish Settings dialog box.

7. Save the movie and quit Flash.

8. Select Insert > Animation.

9. Navigate to the folder containing the Flash button you have just created and either double-click it or select it and click Open in the Open dialog box.

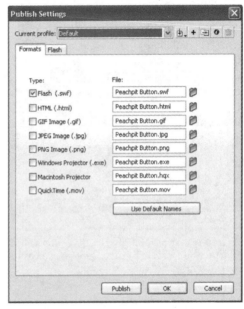

Figure 8.20 You need only the SWF file in the Formats area of the Flash Publish Settings dialog box.

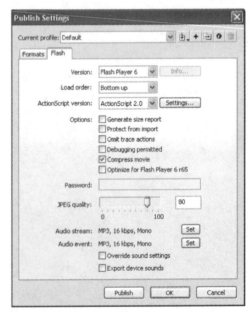

Figure 8.21 Captivate uses only Flash Player 6 for SWF playback. You choose this on the Flash tab of the Publish Settings dialog box.

Figure 8.22 Test a Captivate slide by selecting "From this slide" from the Preview pop-down list in the Main toolbar.

Figure 8.23 Click the Flash button to open the Web page.

10. Drag the button to its final location in the slide.

11. Click the arrow beside the Preview button on the Main toolbar and select "From this slide." (**Figure 8.22**) Alternatively you can press the F8 key.

The Generating progress bar appears. When the movie has been generated, the slide containing the button appears.

12. Click the button.

The browser opens and goes to the Web address entered in the Flash movie (**Figure 8.23**).

13. Click the Close button in the window to return to the slide.

✔ Tip

■ At the time of this writing, Captivate can play only SWF movies that use Flash Player version 6 or earlier.

The Power of the Studio

This exercise, showing the creation of a simple button using Fireworks MX 2004, Flash MX 2004, and Captivate, just scratches the surface of the possibilities open to you. For example, you could design the button in Fireworks as an element in a navigation menu. Instead of the capsule shape, you could make it a square and use it as a part of a navigation menu that is assembled in Flash. You could add a click sound to the button in Flash as well as the jump to a Web page or even have the button trigger an MP₃ sound when it is pressed.

This exercise also addresses a Fireworks/Captivate issue. The JavaScript generated by a button symbol in Fireworks can't be used in Captivate. This exercise is a back-door solution to this constraint.

You can add an entirely new dimension to the use of corporate logos. For example, you can draw a logo in Freehand and then place it in Flash. From there, you can add sound and animation to it. Suddenly the static logo becomes more engaging and offers a richer user experience.

If you draw objects and shapes in Freehand, when you place them in Fireworks MX 2004, you can apply a range of effects—from drop shadows to color changes—using the LiveEffects. You can then be save those images as JPG images. You can even animate objects in Freehand and output the SWF files from Freehand.

Finally, you can create GIF animations using the Frames feature of Fireworks MX 2004.

PREPARING CONTENT FOR CAPTIVATE

Though Captivate does quite a job of preparing content for playback using a wide assortment of buttons and controllers, there will be occasions where you will have to prepare your own content for the presentation. This could involve creating a custom controller or button using Macromedia Fireworks MX 2004, or adding a Captivate demonstration to a PowerPoint presentation rather than adding a PowerPoint slide to Captivate. You may have been handed an EPS version of a corporate logo and been asked to add it to all of the slides in the movie. It is at this point that the value of the other tools in the Macromedia MX Studio really becomes apparent.

This chapter covers how to:

◆ Create a custom playback controller in Fireworks.

◆ Create a three-state button in Fireworks for use in Captivate.

◆ Use Macromedia Freehand MX and Fireworks MX 2004 to prepare a logo for a Captivate movie.

◆ Use Adobe Illustrator CS and Freehand MX to create Flash animations without knowing Flash MX Professional 2004.

◆ Make your Captivate movie accessible to those with disabilities.

✔ **Tip**

■ Many of the techniques demonstrated in this chapter can be reproduced easily in other imaging or drawing applications. The key is the ability to output the work in a format that Captivate recognizes.

Creating a Custom Controller in Fireworks MX 2004

If you are a New Media designer, you are quite used to creating custom controls and adding the code that makes them function. Captivate makes your life easier because it writes the code for you. The major difference between your normal approach to building buttons and Captivate's approach is: Buttons in Captivate have only Up and Down states. There is no Over state.

If you create your own controllers, follow these guidelines:

◆ All buttons must have the same width and height.

◆ Playback controls can have only the following buttons:
  ▲ Play
  ▲ Back
  ▲ Forward
  ▲ Pause
  ▲ Exit
  ▲ Rewind
  ▲ Info

◆ All buttons must use the following naming convention: *controlstylename-buttonamebuttonstate.fileextension*. For example, assume you create a style named VQSGray. A rewind button for this style would have two files associated with it: VQSGray-backbuttonup.bmp and VQSGray-backbuttondown.bmp. The composite image for this controller that would appear in the Preview area of the Playback Control dialog box would be named VQSGray-preview.bmp.

This example assumes the controller to be constructed contains a Play button, a Rewind button, and an Info button. The plan is to have the buttons be a dark gray color and to name the controller VQSGray.

✔ Tips

- You can make areas of your control transparent by changing the name from *style*-playbuttonup.bmp to *style*-playtransbuttonup.bmp (add *trans* before the word *button*). The transparent color will be obtained from the top left pixel; any other pixels of the same color will appear transparent.

- Controls you create don't always have to use a horizontal orientation. You can make your controls appear vertically by using the word *vertical* in the name of your playback control (for example, *style*vertical-playbuttonup.bmp).

Building a custom controller in Fireworks

Fireworks is a great New Media imaging application. At its heart it is a paint program; in other words, it essentially works with pixels. The roots of this application stretch right back to the introduction of the personal computer, and MacPaint on the Macintosh was one of the first commercially available paint applications. Though a number of paint applications have evolved over the past 20 years, two have established themselves as de facto standards: Adobe Photoshop and Fireworks. If you are looking for advanced image manipulation and imaging for print, Photoshop is your tool. If you are displaying images on a Web page or other digital media, use Fireworks.

Knowing that controllers require a composite image in Fireworks—all of the elements must appear on a single flattened bitmap—it makes sense to construct the bar and then create the bitmaps used for the buttons from that composite image.

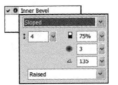

Figure 9.1 The first step in the process of creating custom Playback Controller is to build the background for the buttons.

✔ Tip

■ Though Captivate is a PC-only application, Fireworks MX 2004 is available in both Macintosh and PC versions. This means you can construct controllers on either platform.

To build a custom controller in Fireworks MX 2004:

1. Launch Fireworks MX 2004 and, in the Create New area of the start page, select Fireworks File.

2. Select the Rectangle tool from the toolbar and draw a rectangle on the stage.

3. Select the rectangle and enter these values in the Property Inspector:
   ▲ Width: 130
   ▲ Height: 30
   ▲ Fill color: #666666
   ▲ Fill type: Solid
   ▲ Grain: 21%

4. With the rectangle still selected, in the Property Inspector, select Effects > Bevel & Emboss > Inner Bevel.

5. When the Inner Bevel dialog box opens (**Figure 9.1**), select the following values:
   ▲ Bevel edge shape: Sloped
   ▲ Bevel width: 4 pixels
   ▲ Contrast: 75
   ▲ Softness: 3
   ▲ Angle: 135
   ▲ Button preset: Raised

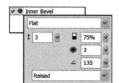

Figure 9.2 The button is given a 3D look using these settings.

6. Select the Ellipse tool and draw a circle on the bar.

7. If the Property Inspector isn't open, select Window > Properties to open the Fireworks Property Inspector. Select the circle and enter these values in the Property Inspector:
   ▲ Width: 20
   ▲ Height: 20
   ▲ Fill color: #666666
   ▲ Fill type: Solid
   ▲ Grain: 21%

8. With the circle still selected, in the Property Inspector, select Effects > Bevel & Emboss > Inner Bevel.

9. When the dialog box opens (**Figure 9.2**), enter these values:
   ▲ Bevel edge shape: Sloped
   ▲ Bevel width: 3 pixels
   ▲ Contrast: 75
   ▲ Softness: 3
   ▲ Angle: 135
   ▲ Button preset: Raised

10. Press the Alt key (PC) or the Option-Shift keys (Mac); then click and drag a copy of the circle to the left side of the bar. Drag another copy to the left.

11. To create the Info button for the controller, select the Text tool and single-click in the circle on the right.

12. Enter the letter *I*.

13. Enter these settings for the letter in the Property Inspector:
   ▲ Font: Arial Black
   ▲ Size: 16 points
   ▲ Color: #FFFFFF

continues on next page

CREATING A CUSTOM CONTROLLER

14. Select the Zoom tool (the magnifying glass) and marquee the interface to zoom in on it.

15. Select the Pen tool and, on the middle circle, draw an arrow pointing to the Info button.

16. Fill the arrow in the Property Inspector's Fill area with #FFFFFF.(White) by clicking the fill color chip to open the Fill Colors and clicking in the white chip.

    This will be the Play button.

17. Press the Alt key (PC) or the Option-Shift keys (Mac), and click and drag a copy of the arrow to the circle on the far left.

18. Select the copied arrow and select Modify > Transform > Flip Horizontal.

19. Move the arrow into place.

    This will be the Rewind button.

20. Your image should resemble **Figure 9.3**; Save it.

Figure 9.3 The completed controller uses an Info button as well as buttons for Play and Rewind.

Preparing the controller for use in Captivate

With the controller constructed, you must break it apart into the required images for use in Captivate. This means you will have to create six buttons plus the flattened composite image Captivate needs to construct the controller. This may seem like a lot of extra work, but it isn't if you follow that old adage, "Let the software do the work."

To construct the controller:

1. Press the Shift key and then select the *I* and the button graphic that make up the Info button.

2. Select Modify > Group to combine the letter and the graphic into one object.

CREATING A CUSTOM CONTROLLER

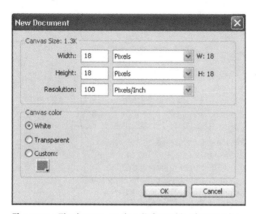

Figure 9.4 The button on the clipboard is about to be placed into a new Fireworks document.

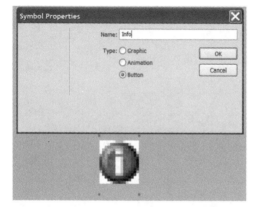

Figure 9.5 Converting an object to a button symbol enables you to quickly create the various bitmaps that Captivate needs.

3. Select the grouped object, and select Edit > Copy and then File > New.

   A new Fireworks document opens. The first thing you will notice is the dimensions of the new document match those of the object on the clipboard. This is a great way of sizing documents to the precise size of an object on the clipboard.

4. When the New Document dialog box opens (**Figure 9.4**), change the resolution, if necessary, to 100 pixels/inch and set the background color to white (#FFFFFF). Click OK.

   A blank document opens.

5. Select Edit > Paste to paste the button on the clipboard into your new document.

   Note that if you changed the resolution in the New Document dialog box, pasting will result in a dialog box informing you that the resolution of the object on the clipboard doesn't match that of the document. Simply click the Resample button to have the clipboard object's resolution match that of the document. Though this process is generally frowned upon, both the change in values and the object itself are so small that no one will notice the image has been "down sampled."

6. Select the button and, in the Property Inspector, click the Fit Canvas button.

   This shrinks the canvas to the exact dimensions of the button and centers it in the canvas.

7. Right-click (PC) or Control-click (Mac) the button.

   The context menu opens. Select Convert to Symbol.

   The Symbol Properties dialog box opens (**Figure 9.5**).

continues on next page

8. Name the symbol *Info*, select Button as the type, and click OK.

The green overlay that appears over the button is a nonvisible Web layer.

9. Double-click the target in the Web layer.

The Button Editor dialog box opens. As mentioned earlier, note that Captivate buttons can have only Up and Down states. This means you need only two bitmaps of the button: one showing the Up state and the other showing the Down state. In this procedure, you will use the Over tab in the Button Editor to create the Down button for the controller.

10. Select the Over tab and click the Copy Up Graphic button.

The button appears in the window.

11. Select the Subselect tool—the hollow pointer—and single-click the button shape.

12. Select the Inner Bevel effect by clicking the I button beside the effect's name in Property Inspector.

The Bevel dialog box (**Figure 9.6**) opens.

13. Select Inverted from the Button preset pop-down.

This reverses the coloring of the button and gives it the appearance of being pressed.

Click Done. You are returned to the canvas.

14. Select File > Export Preview.

The Export Preview dialog box opens.

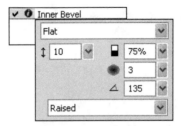

Figure 9.6 Fireworks button states are regarded as offspring of the original image, meaning that they can be changed without affecting the original image. This occurs in the Button Editor.

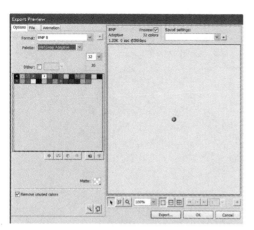

Figure 9.7 Set the output format and color depth of the image in the Export Preview dialog box.

Figure 9.8 Use the Export dialog box to name the file and create individual bitmaps for the buttons when the slices are exported.

15. Choose the following settings:
    - ▲ Format: BMP 8. This is an 8-bit (256) color space.
    - ▲ Palette: Web Snap Adaptive. This moves the colors in the image to their nearest Web-safe equivalents.
    - ▲ Minimum Number of Colors: 32. The number under this pop-down shows the actual number of colors in the image.

16. If your screen resembles that shown in **Figure 9.7**, click the Export button.

    The Export dialog box opens. Note that Fireworks saves images a little differently than many imaging and drawing applications. Selecting File > Save or File > Save As saves the image only in one format: PNG. The Export Preview dialog box is where images are saved in the JPG, GIF, and BMP formats.

17. Navigate to the folder in which the button pieces will be saved, and choose the following settings:
    - ▲ File name: VQSGray-infotransbuttonup.bmp
    - ▲ Save as type: Images only
    - ▲ Slices: Export slices
    - ▲ Include areas without slices: Deselect

18. If your settings resemble those shown in **Figure 9.8**, click Save. Saving a JPG, GIF, or BMP image in Fireworks is a two-step process. The step shown in Figure 9.7 optimizes the image. The step shown in Figure 9.8 is where the file is named and saved.

    When the image is saved, the button appears, sitting on a white background. To remove it, in Captivate, you add *trans* to the filename.

continues on next page

CREATING A CUSTOM CONTROLLER

19. Select File > Save As and save the button as a PNG image.

This way, if changes are needed, you have the original artwork available.

20. Repeat these steps for the Play and Forward buttons.

The play button will be named VQSGray-playtransbuttonup.bmp, and the Rewind button will be named VQSGray-backtransbuttonup.bmp

21. Return to the composite image containing the bar and the buttons. Select File > Export Preview. Set the format to bmp8, change the color depth, and click the Next button.

22. Save the file as VQSGray-preview to the same folder as the three buttons.

You must use this naming convention.

23. Save the file and quit Fireworks MX 2004.

24. Open the folder in which you saved the images.

The Down button names all end with _F2. Replace the _F2 with the word *down* (**Figure 9.9**).

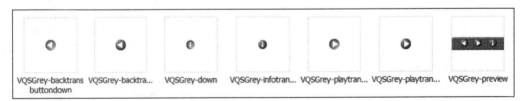

VQSGrey-backtrans buttondown VQSGrey-backtra... VQSGrey-down VQSGrey-infotran... VQSGrey-playtran... VQSGrey-playtran... VQSGrey-preview

Figure 9.9 The Playback Controller elements have been constructed and are ready for use in Captivate.

CREATING A CUSTOM CONTROLLER

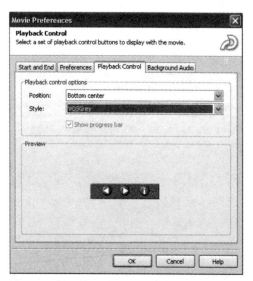

Figure 9.10 The playback controller created in Fireworks is available for use in Captivate through the Movie Preferences dialog box.

To use the custom controller in Captivate:

1. Navigate to the folder in which you saved the controller pieces.

2. Select and copy all of the BMP files.

3. Navigate to C:\Program Files\ Macromedia\Captivate\Gallery\ Playback Controls.

4. Paste the BMP files to add them to the folder.

5. Open a Captivate movie and select Movie > Preferences.

    The Movie Preferences dialog box opens.

6. Select the Playback Controls tab and select the controller from the Styles pop-down menu.

    The preview appears in the Playback Control dialog box (**Figure 9.10**).

7. Click OK.

    The new controller appears in the preview window.

Building a Fireworks Button for Captivate

As you saw in the previous exercise, it is possible to create a playback controller that can be used in Captivate. You can also create buttons used to navigate to various slides, sections, and even Web sites in Captivate.

Where Captivate buttons differ from those used on Playback Controllers is the addition of a third button state (**Figure 9.11**). In Captivate, buttons can have Up, Over, and Down states, whereas playback controllers can have only Up and Down states.

Though buttons can be any size, it is best to keep them small. The width can range from 60 to 100 pixels, and the height can range from 20 pixels to the width of the button (if it is to be square). Buttons also must be saved as BMP images and should fill the entire canvas in Fireworks.

This exercise won't give you the step-by-step instructions for creating the artwork used in the button. Those instructions were presented in the previous section.

To create a Fireworks button:

1. Open a new Fireworks document with a canvas size of 150 pixels wide and 150 pixels high. Set the canvas color to white. Draw a rectangle that is 70 pixels wide by 20 pixels high, fill it with a color or pattern, apply a small bevel to the image, and add the word *Next* to the image (**Figure 9.12**).

2. Single-click the canvas and, in the Property Inspector, click the Fit Canvas button.

   The canvas shrinks to the exact dimensions of the button.

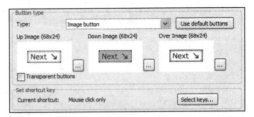

Figure 9.11 Add buttons to Captivate slides using the Button dialog box. Note the three button states.

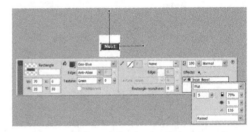

Figure 9.12 The artwork for the Captivate button has been created in Fireworks MX 2004.

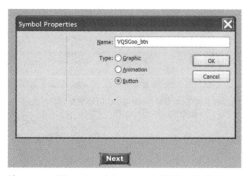

Figure 9.13 The artwork is converted into a button symbol in Fireworks.

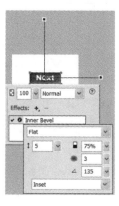

Figure 9.14 Changing the preset to Inset causes the button to darken when the user rolls the mouse over it in Captivate.

3. Press Control-A (PC) or Command-A (Mac) to select all of the objects on the canvas. Press Control-G (PC) or Command-G (Mac) to group the selected objects.

4. With the objects still selected, press the F8 key (Mac and PC) or select Modify > Symbol > Convert To Symbol.

The Symbol Properties dialog box opens. Name the symbol and select Button as the symbol type (**Figure 9.13**).

5. Double-click the green overlay on the button.

The Button Symbol Editor opens.

6. Select the Over tab and click the Copy Up Graphic button.

7. In the Property Inspector, open the Bevel effect and select Inset from the Preset Values pop-down menu (**Figure 9.14**).

8. Select the Down tab, click the "Copy Over Graphic" button and change the preset to Inverted. Click Done.

You are returned to the Fireworks canvas.

9. Select File > Export Preview and select BMP 24 as the format. Click the Export button.

The "Export options" dialog box opens.

10. Navigate to the C:\Program Files\ Macromedia\Captivate\Gallery\ Buttons folder.

11. Name the image.

In this example, I used VQSGoo_up.

12. From the "Save as type" pop-down, select Images Only.

13. From the "Export slices" pop-down, select "Export slices." Click Save.

continues on next page

BUILDING A FIREWORKS BUTTON FOR CAPTIVATE

14. Select File > Save As to save the button as PNG image, and save it to another folder on your computer. This will be the back up copy containing the all of the button states should you have to revisit the button. Quit Fireworks.

15. Open the Buttons folder in which you saved the images, and rename the Over and Down buttons.

16. Open the Captivate movie in which the button will be used.

17. Select Insert > Button (which opens the New Button dialog box) or, if a button already exists, double-click the button in the Edit View panel (opens the Button dialog box).

18. In the Type pop-down, select "Image button."

19. Click the Navigate button (it has three dots) under the Up image preview. Navigate to the Buttons folder and select the Up button (VQSG00_up).

Do this for the other two buttons (VQSG00_over and VQSG00_down). Click OK.

The button appears in the slide (**Figure 9.15**).

Figure 9.15 Add the Fireworks button to Captivate using the Button dialog box.

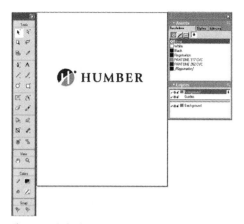

Figure 9.16 The logo is created in Freehand MX and ready for placement in Captivate.

Figure 9.17 You can usually export EPS documents out of a drawing application as bitmaps.

Using Freehand MX to Prepare a Logo for Captivate

When you work, as I do, for a post-secondary educational institution, much of what you do requires the addition of the college or university's logo to your Captivate slides. Inevitably these logos will come from the marketing or graphics department and be in the EPS (Encapsulated PostScript) format. Or you may be required to place clip art into your Captivate presentation. Depending on the clip art vendor, the odds are good that it, too, will be in the EPS format.

The problem: Captivate can't use EPS graphics. They must be bitmaps. The solution: Follow these steps.

✔ Tip

- This exercise uses Freehand MX to create the Captivate image. You can also use another drawing program such as Adobe Illustrator CS.

To use Freehand MX to prepare a logo:

1. Open the logo file in Freehand MX (**Figure 9.16**).

2. Select File > Export.
   The Export Document dialog box opens.

3. Navigate to the folder in which the file is to be saved, name the document, and select "JPEG (*.jpg)" from the "Save as type" pop-down menu (**Figure 9.17**).

4. Quit Freehand MX and open the Captivate movie in which the graphic will be placed.

5. Open the slide that will receive the image in the Edit View panel, and select Insert > Image.

continues on next page

6. Navigate to the folder containing the graphic, select it. and click Open.

   The New Image dialog box opens.

7. Click OK.

   The image is placed in the slide (**Figure 9.18**).

✔ Tips

■ If you are an Illustrator CS user, you can create the JPG file by selecting File > Export and selecting "JPEG (*.jpg)" in the Format pop-down menu. You can also place the logo in Fireworks MX 2004 or Photoshop CS and export it as a JPG image.

■ Don't feel like using the Insert menu to place graphics in your Captivate slides? Open the folder in which the graphic is located, and drag and drop the graphic file into the slide.

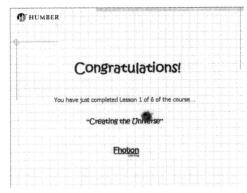

Figure 9.18 A file created in Freehand MX is placed into a Captivate slide.

Figure 9.19 The text is formatted in Illustrator CS. Keep in mind you do not have to use text; you can also animate logos and other artwork.

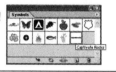

Figure 9.20 The text is converted to a symbol in Illustrator CS.

Creating Flash Animations for Captivate Without Using Flash

Though they are two of the more important Web applications on the market, Flash MX 2004 and Flash MX Professional 2004 are not exactly the easiest programs to master. The learning curve is quite steep, and it takes time to become proficient in Flash. Still, you don't have to know a thing about Flash to create Flash animations for your Captivate projects.

The advantages to using the SWF format over the animated GIF format are file size and smoothness of playback. This section discusses how to create SWF animations in Illustrator CS, Freehand MX, and Fireworks MX.

To create an SWF file in Illustrator CS:

1. Open a new Illustrator document.

2. Open the Layers palette and click the Create New Layer button 11 times.
   You now have 12 layers.

3. Single-click in Layer 1, select the Text tool, and single-click the page.

4. Enter the words "Captivate Rocks!," set the point size to 24 points, choose Verdana as your font, and set the weight to bold (**Figure 9.19**).

5. Select Window > Symbols.
   The Symbols Palette opens.

6. Hold down the Shift key, and click and drag the words from the page into the Symbols palette.
   When you release the mouse, the words appear in the Symbols palette, and the words on the page will be an instance of the symbol (**Figure 9.20**).

continues on next page

CREATING FLASH ANIMATIONS FOR CAPTIVATE

7. Select Layer 2 and drag an instance of the symbol from the Symbol palette onto the page.

8. Repeat this for the remaining layers (**Figure 9.21**).

9. Select File > Export.

The Export dialog box opens.

10. Select "Macromedia Flash (*.SWF)" from the "Save as type" pop-down list, name the file, and click Save.

The Macromedia Flash (SWF) Format Options dialog box opens.

11. In the Export As pop down menu, select AI Layers to SWF Frames.

12. Click OK.

13. Save the file and quit Illustrator.

14. Open the Captivate movie in which the animation will appear and either add the SWF to an animation slide or import the file into an existing slide as an animation (**Figure 9.22**).

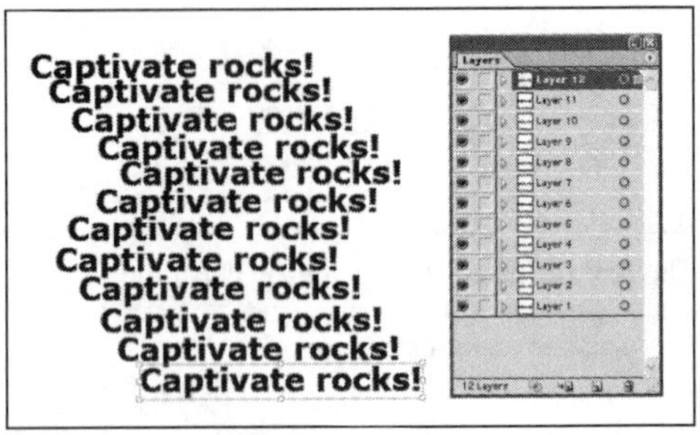

✔ Tip

■ Be careful with the Illustrator SWF Format Options dialog box. If you select AI File to SWF, you are simply converting the page—including layers—into a flat SWF file. If you select AI Layers to SWF Files, each layer becomes a separate SWF file.

Figure 9.21 The animation is created by changing each instance's position in the layer.

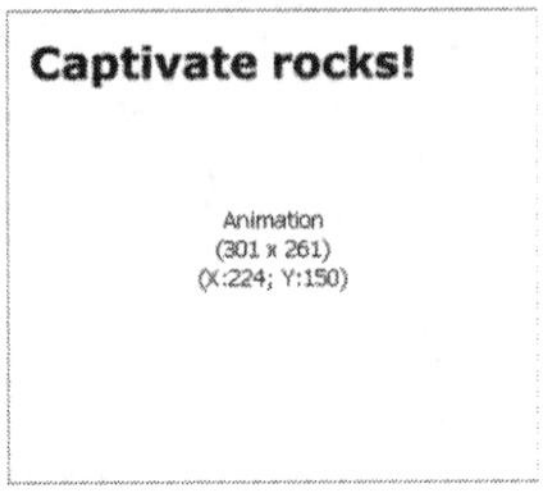

Figure 9.22 The Illustrator CS file is converted to a Flash SWF file and placed in a Captivate slide.

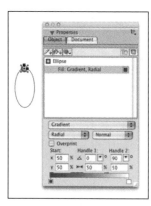

Figure 9.23 The first electron is created, filled with a radial gradient, and placed into its start position.

Symbols and Instances

Symbols and instances are quite common in today's Web-based production environment. Think of a symbol as being the original artwork, and the copy of it on the page is called an *instance*. In many respects, an instance is like a pointer or shortcut to the original artwork. The really great thing about symbols and instances is they can have a huge impact on final file size.

Let's assume the artwork is 25K in size. If you create 12 copies of that artwork in 12 layers, it is reasonable to assume the file size will increase to 300K. An instance is significantly smaller—in this case, let's assume 3K. Suddenly the file size drops to 61K ((12*3) + 25).

Further, you can manipulate—resize, distort, add new colors—instances without affecting the original symbol.

If your drawing, paint, or animation program enables you to work with symbols and instances, use them. It is a great work habit to develop.

Creating an SWF animation in Macromedia Freehand MX

Macromedia Freehand and Flash have a symbiotic relationship. As a vector drawing application, Freehand creates content for use in Flash, which is a vector-based animation application. It isn't surprising, therefore, to discover that Freehand MX has some rather powerful animation tools that can create an SWF file. In this exercise, rather than animate the words "Captivate rocks!," you are going to have electrons revolve around the phrase.

Keeping in mind that Freehand comes in Macintosh and PC versions, this example uses the Mac version of Freehand MX, and the SWF is imported into the Captivate movie. The steps work on both Macintosh and PC versions of the application.

To create an SWF animation in Freehand MX:

1. Launch Freehand MX. Select the Ellipse tool and draw an oval shape that is 60 pixels wide and 120 pixels high.
   Don't fill the oval.

2. Draw a circle that is 20 pixels wide by 20 pixels high. Fill the circle with a Radial gradient by selecting Gradient from the pop-down list in the Fill panel and then selecting Radial Gradient from the list. Drag the small circle to the top of the large circle (**Figure 9.23**).

3. Select View > Keyline to turn off the fills.

4. Zoom in on the circle and drag the small circle so that its center point, the X in the middle, is sitting on the large circle.

continues on next page

5. Press the Option (Mac) or Alt (PC) key and drag copies of the circle to the three, six, and nine o'clock positions on the circle.

6. Create four more copies of the small circle placed between the copies just created (**Figure 9.24**). Delete the large circle.

7. Select Edit > Select > All and select Modify > Group to group the electrons a into one object.

8. Select Xtras > Animate > Release to Layers.

   The Release to Layers dialog box opens (**Figure 9.25**).

9. Select Sequence from the Animate pop-down and click OK.

   The dialog box closes.

10. Select Windows > Layers.

    The Layers panel opens, and eight new layers are created in your Freehand document. The electrons will not be in the order you would expect. They will follow the order in which they were created.

To reorder the electrons

1. If it is closed, open the Layer panel and deselect the check marks (which indicate layer visibility) beside all of the layers except for the Foreground layer.

2. Double-click the Foreground layer name and rename it One.

3. Moving up the layers, click the check marks until the next electron in the sequence becomes visible.

4. Drag that layer above the layer named One and name it Two (**Figure 9.26**).

5. Repeat steps 3 and 4 for the remaining layers.

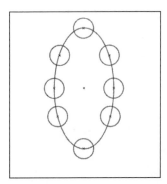

Figure 9.24 The electrons are placed on the path they will follow in the final animation.

Figure 9.25 Releasing grouped object to layers using Freehand's Animate Xtra places each object in its own layer.

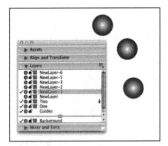

Figure 9.26 Reorder and rename the layers to have the animation move the electrons in the proper direction.

Figure 9.27 By placing electrons in front of and behind the lettering, you give the illusion of depth.

To set text and visibility:

1. Click the Lock icon in Layers 8 to 2. This locks the layers and prevents changes.

2. Select Frame One and select the Text tool.

3. Enter the phrase "Captivate rocks!" Set the point size to 48 points, the font to Verdana, and the weight to Bold.

4. Drag the phrase over the circles.

5. Select the text and click the Object tab. The Object panel opens. Note the Left and Top values in the Dimensions area. They are the object's X and Y coordinates on the page.

6. Copy and paste the selection and enter the L and T values in the new object to those noted in the previous step. The words will move into the same position as the original.

7. With word "Captivate" selected, turn on the visibility in Layer 2.

8. Click the Layer name and, when you see the pen icon in the layer name, lock the layer.
   The selection moves to that layer.

9. Lock Layer 2 and turn off the visibility of Layer 2.

10. Select Layer 1 and repeat steps 6 to 9 for the remaining layers.
    The electrons are in front of the words in Layers 3 and 4.

11. To give the illusion of the electrons moving around the words, select the text in each of the two frames and select Modify > Arrange > "Send to back."
    Your artwork should resemble **Figure 9.27**.

continues on next page

CREATING FLASH ANIMATIONS FOR CAPTIVATE

12. Select File > Export and select Macromedia Flash (SWF) from the Format pop-down menu.

13. Click the Setup button.

The Movie Settings dialog box opens. Choose the settings shown in **Figure 9.28**. Note that in the Movie Settings dialog box, you always want to select Autoplay. This allows the animation to loop. The animation occurs using the frames, thus it is also important that you select Animate in the Layers area.

14. Click OK.

The Movie Settings dialog box closes.

15. Name the file and click Export. Save the file and quit Freehand MX.

16. Open the Captivate movie and place the SWF in an animation slide or into an existing slide as an animation (**Figure 9.29**).

✔ Tip

■ When using Illustrator CS or Freehand MX to create SWF files, try to create the files using a document that is the same size as the area used for the SWF file in the Captivate slide. If you create the Freehand SWF using a letter-size page, that will be the size of the SWF file. If it uses only 10 to 15 percent of the page, all you are doing is adding to the bandwidth required to play the movie.

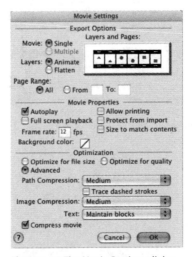

Figure 9.28 The Movie Settings dialog box determines how the Flash SWF will be created and how it will play.

Captivate rocks!

Figure 9.29 Even SWF files created using a Macintosh version of Freehand MX can be placed into Captivate movies.

Creating an SWF animation in Fireworks MX 2004

Though Captivate can use an animated GIF file created in Fireworks MX 2004, don't overlook creating an SWF instead. I created an animated GIF in Fireworks that had the words "Captivate rocks!" reduce in opacity from 100 percent to 35 percent over 12 frames. The animated GIF file was 24K in size; the resulting Flash SWF file was 4K. Though that may not seem like much, if your Captivate movies are being prepared for Web delivery, every extra "K" of file size adds to the bandwidth requirement.

To create an SWF file in Fireworks MX 2004:

1. Create the GIF file in Fireworks MX 2004.

2. Select File > Export Preview.
   The Export Preview dialog box opens.

3. Select Animated GIF from the Format pop-down menu.

4. Click the Export button.
   The Export dialog box opens.

5. Navigate to the folder in which the file will be saved and name the file.

6. Select Macromedia Flash SWF from the "Save as type" pop-down menu.

7. Click OK and save the file as a PNG file by selecting File > Save As.

✔ Tip

■ Get into the habit of saving all Fireworks MX 2004 images and animations as PNG files. This format preserves all effects, including frames used in animations. It will pay for itself the first time a client requests a change to an animation.

CREATING FLASH ANIMATIONS FOR CAPTIVATE

Accessibility and Captivate

Accessibility is not creating a Captivate movie that is easy to navigate or find. Accessibility is publishing a Captivate SWF that meets the compliance requirements in Section 508 of the United States Rehabilitation Act. This act essentially mandates that any work done for any form of government must meet accessibility standards. Captivate falls into that category.

To those of you who claim, "I am not doing any government work in the U.S.," my response is, "You don't have a choice." The bottom line is that accessibility is now entrenched in legislation, and you are going to have to make your work accessible to those with disabilities whether you choose to or not. The European Union is requiring that all sites be accessible, too. Educational institutions have the same requirement, and it is only a matter of time before business adopts accessibility standards as well.

Consider this rather interesting fact: Over 70 percent of the U.S. population who are legally blind are either unemployed or underemployed. Of that group, only 1 percent has access to the Web content that could potentially change their situation. This means that, in effect, 99 percent of the blind population is locked out of the Web.

One of the companies leading the accessibility movement is Macromedia. They not only see accessibility in business terms, but they see it as a societal issue and have a number of accessibility experts on staff charged with helping Macromedia's clients prepare accessible content for their clients.

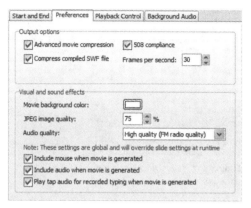

Figure 9.30 Selecting 508 compliance in the Movie Preferences dialog box makes the navigation accessible.

Figure 9.31 Screen readers will read concise descriptions in the Movie Properties dialog box.

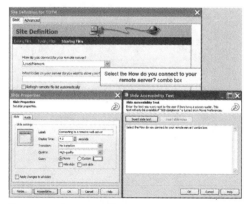

Figure 9.32 Screen readers can read captions by clicking the Accessibility button in the Slide Properties dialog box.

To create a Section 508–compliant movie:

1. Select Movie > Preferences.

   The Movie Options dialog box opens.

2. Select the Preferences tab.

3. In the Output Options area, select "508 compliance" (**Figure 9.30**).

4. Click OK.

Hints for using 508 compliance

In Captivate, selecting "508 compliance" makes the SWF's navigation accessible, but you can go further than that with the various objects in your movies.

Start with a name that means something and a concise description of the project in the Movie Properties dialog box (**Figure 9.31**).

For those with hearing impairments, if you are narrating a slide, consider placing the narration in a caption on the slide. Conversely, for those with visual impairments, consider narrating the contents of captions.

To make captions accessible to screen readers, select the slide where the captions appear and click the Slide Properties button. When the Slide Properties dialog box opens, enter a concise label and click the Accessibility button to open the Slide Accessibility Text dialog box (**Figure 9.32**). Click the Insert Slide Text button, and the caption text appears in the input area.

You don't have to use the captions in the Insert Slide Text dialog box. You can use the text input area to enter text that describes the slide. This text will be read only by screen readers.

continues on next page

ACCESSIBILITY AND CAPTIVATE

All navigation dialog boxes contain keyboard equivalents. Use them for those who are visually or mobility impaired (**Figure 9.33**).

Finally, use the Captivate Help Files to learn more about making your Captivate movies accessible. Select Help > Captive Help or press F1. When the Help screen opens, click the Index tab. Accessibility is the first entry in the Captivate Help list.

Figure 9.33 A keystroke instead of a mouse click is added to a click box.

CAPTIVATE & MACROMEDIA FLASH MX 2004

10

If ever there were two Macromedia applications just made for each other, it would have to be Captivate and Flash MX 2004. Both output to the SWF format, both are interactive, and both are used in eLearning. As well, Captivate's EXE format is a Flash EXE and, like Flash, a Captivate SWF can be used easily in Breeze. On the other side of the relationship, Flash SWF files that are compatible with Flash Player 6 can be placed into Captivate movies as animations or as animation slides.

An obvious question: "Why should I export a Captivate movie to Flash?" The answer lies in Captivate's enabling technology: Flash Player 6. The latest version of the Flash Player—version 7.0—allows, for example, streaming rich media such as video. In Captivate, video can't be added efficiently to your Captivate movie. If the movie is exported to Flash MX 2004, suddenly video is doable because the movie can be published using the Flash Player 7.

Also, through the use of ActionScript 2.0, Flash's scripting language, you can extend the functionality of your Captivate movie to include, for example, dynamic delivery of content into a Captivate movie published in Flash.

continues on next page

Captivate will export only to either Flash MX 2004 or Flash MX Professional 2004. If you own a copy of Flash MX or versions of Flash prior to Flash MX, you will not be able to import Captivate files into Flash. Also, if your Captivate movie contains Question slides, these slides will not import into Flash.

Obviously, fully exploring the potential relationship between Flash and Captivate is well beyond the scope of this book. Instead, this chapter sticks to the basics and shows you how to:

◆ Export a Captivate movie to Flash.

◆ Import a Captivate movie into Flash.

◆ Navigate through a Captivate movie placed in Flash.

◆ Optimize a Captivate movie for Flash.

◆ Use the Flash MX 2004 frame effects to add some zip to a Captivate movie.

◆ Add Flash video to a Captivate movie.

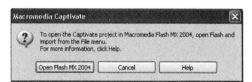

Figure 10.1 Exporting your Captivate movie to Flash starts with clicking the Open Flash MX 2004 button.

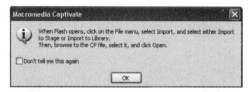

Figure 10.2 The CPT file gets imported into either the Flash Library or to the Flash timeline.

Figure 10.3 The Captivate Options dialog box is where you can prevent elements of the Captivate movie from being imported into Flash.

Exporting a Captivate Movie to Flash MX 2004

As mentioned earlier in this chapter, exporting a Captivate movie to Flash enables the user to view your movie with Flash Player. The power of streaming video can be yours!

To export a Captivate movie to Flash MX 2004:

1. Open a Captivate movie.

2. Select File > Import/Export > "Export the movie to Flash MX 2004."

   The Macromedia Captivate dialog box opens (**Figure 10.1**).

3. Click the Open Flash MX 2004 button.

   You are prompted to save the Captivate movie as a Flash Project file. The Saves As dialog box opens.

4. Navigate to the folder in which the file will be saved, name the file, and click the Save button.

   A message box opens, giving you instructions for importing the file into Flash (**Figure 10.2**).

5. Click the OK button.

   Flash opens.

6. Select File > Import > Import to Stage.

7. Navigate to the folder containing the Captivate movie (the CPT file), select it, and click Open. If you have some experience with Flash, you also import the CPT file directly into the Library.

   The Captivate Options dialog box (**Figure 10.3**) opens.

continues on next page

8. Select the features to be imported into Flash and click Import.

A progress bar appears, showing you the import process. When the file has been completely imported, the progress bar closes and you are informed of any elements that couldn't be imported (loading screens, Question slides, and any Section 508 compliance features built into the Captivate movie will be likely candidates).

9. Click OK.

If you have slides containing full motion captures, these captures are compiled as separate SWF files. A slide containing a Full Motion capture causes the Captivate Importer dialog box (**Figure 10.4**) to open. Carefully note the location of these files; if they are not in the same directory as the Flash movie, the movie will not play correctly.

10. Click OK.

A progress bar appears in the Working dialog box. Once the files are imported into Flash, the dialog box closes, and the project appears on the Flash stage (**Figure 10.5**).

✔ Tip

■ If you create Captivate movies for export to Flash, consider saving them to a folder on your hard drive separate from the My Captivate Projects folder where Captivate movies are saved by default. This way, any extra files—such as full motion SWF files—will always be in the same location as the parent movie.

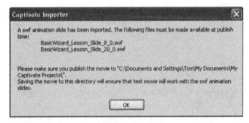

Figure 10.4 Slides containing full motion recording elements will import the slide elements into Flash and include a link to the SWF containing the full motion recording.

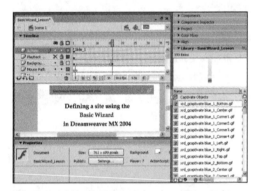

Figure 10.5 A Captivate movie has been imported to the Flash timeline, and the files created during the Import process are moved into the Flash Library.

Importing a Captivate Movie to Flash MX 2004

When performing the import, you may be wondering why you were asked to create the FLA file and then import the Captivate file into Flash. It would seem to make sense to simply open the FLA file. The reason is the inclusion of full motion captures. When the FLA is created, full motion captures are converted to external SWF files, and the links to those files are embedded into the FLA created by Captivate. These links are relative links because files get moved around. If the links were absolute, they would break. Relative links actually make the file portable.

To import a Captivate movie into Flash MX 2004:

1. Save the Captivate movie and quit Captivate.

2. Launch Flash MX 2004 or Flash MX Professional 2004.

3. On the Flash start page, select Create New > Flash Document.

4. When the new document opens, select File > Import > "Import to stage."
   The Import dialog box opens.

5. Navigate to the folder containing the Captivate CP file, select the file, and click Open.
   Flash starts to import the file.

Navigating Through a Captivate Movie Placed in Flash MX 2004

When you place a Captivate into Flash MX 2004, everything in the movie is converted to bitmaps. This includes background images, mouse pointers, captions, and so on. These bitmaps are then converted to Flash Graphic symbols and imported into folders in the Captivate Objects folder, which is created in the Flash Library. The original bitmaps will sit loose in the Flash Library along with any sounds used in the Captivate movie (**Figure 10.6**).

✔ Tip

■ To avoid a cluttered Flash Library, create a folder in the Library named Bitmaps and another named Sounds. Drag the bitmaps and sounds into their respective Library folders. Do not delete any of the bitmaps—they have tree icons—because they are referenced by the symbols in the Captivate Objects folder.

Inside the Captivate Objects folder are a number of subfolders (**Figure 10.7**) containing the Graphic symbols used in the Flash movie created from your Captivate movie:

◆ **Backgrounds (Captivate)** Any backgrounds, including the slide background color, are converted to bitmaps, broken apart in Flash, grouped, and then saved as a Graphic symbol. This is a rather clunky approach; if you are familiar with Flash, feel free to replace the object in the symbol with a vector object drawn with the Rectangle tool in the Flash toolbar.

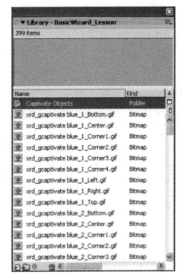

Figure 10.6 All objects in the Captivate movie are converted to bitmaps and placed in the Flash Library.

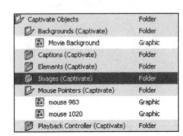

Figure 10.7 The subfolders found in the Flash Library's Captivate Objects folder.

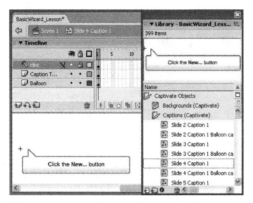

Figure 10.8 You can change, reformat, or edit caption text in Flash.

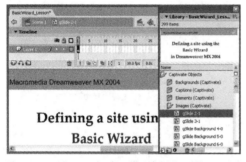

Figure 10.9 The Images (Captivate) folder will contain the screen shots of the interfaces captured along with any images used in the Captivate movie.

◆ **Captions (Captivate)** All of the captions used in the movie, including the balloons, are placed in this folder. If you double-click a caption in this folder, the symbol opens, and you can change the text (**Figure 10.8**).

◆ **Elements (Captivate)** The contents of this folder comprise all of the bits and pieces used to construct the interface elements, such as the balloons used in captions. Don't change a thing in this folder.

◆ **Images (Captivate)** All of the interfaces and other images used in the Captivate movie are moved to this folder (**Figure 10.9**).

continues on next page

◆ **Mouse Pointers (Captivate)** Any mouse pointers captured during the recording are converted to bitmaps and placed in this folder.

◆ **Playback Controller (Captivate)** If you chose to import the controller, the controller movie clip, buttons, and sliders that are in the controller, and the Captivate Info box, are placed in this folder (**Figure 10.10**).

Navigating through the Flash timeline

When you create your Captivate movie, it is designed to playback through the Flash Player 6 at 30 frames per second (fps). Assuming you have a Captivate movie that is 30 slides long and each slide takes up 15 seconds on the Captivate timeline, you can reasonably assume you are going to need well over 13,000 frames in a Flash movie. This explains why the timeline in a Flash movie is so long. In the case of the movie shown in **Figure 10.11**, 1,149 frames are used.

How this occurs is a result of how the Captivate movie is reconstructed in Flash. Each slide of the Captivate movie is brought onto the timeline. The duration of the slide is calculated, and the appropriate number of Flash frames is added. Any transitions, such as fade in and fade out, are created using a Flash Tween and, if there are any full motion SWF files attached to the slide, Flash writes the appropriate ActionScript to load the SWF into the movie when it is needed.

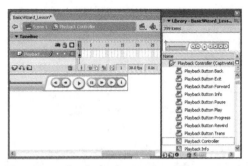

Figure 10.10 The playback controller will be converted to a series or Flash buttons and movie clips if it is imported into your Flash movie.

Figure 10.11 Each Captivate slide is reconstructed in Flash. Captions and highlight boxes are placed on separate layers in the Flash timeline, and any actions or labels are added also.

```
7  nAttempts = undefined;
8  // Add any actions to be taken on success here
9  _parent.gotoAndPlay("Slide_13");
10
```

Figure 10.12 If you change a frame label, be sure to change the name in the ActionScript attached to any navigation elements in the slide.

Layers are created for objects such as captions, highlight boxes, sounds, mouse movement, and the playback controller. The start point of each slide is indicated by the use of a label (a little flag). As well, any actions that control the playback head are added.

If you find the label names or layer names to be confusing, you can change them.

To change a label name:

1. Click the frame containing the frame label.

2. In the Property Inspector, select the name in the Frame area and enter the new name.

✔ Tip

■ Be careful with this step. If there are any buttons in the movie that navigate to different areas of the Flash timeline, they will be included in a folder named Interactive (Captivate). It isn't the button that will cause a problem—it is the movie clip that will be the issue. When the Captivate movie is imported into Flash, navigation will use the frame labels. If you change the label, be sure to locate the script containing the navigation and change the name of the label in that script (**Figure 10.12**).

To change a layer name:

1. Double-click the layer name on the Flash timeline to select it.

2. Enter the new name.

3. Press the Enter key.

It is standard Flash practice to have frame labels appear on a separate Flash layer named Labels. As you can see, Captivate doesn't exactly mirror this "best practice."

To create a separate Labels layer:

1. Click the "New layer" button.
   The new layer appears in the timeline.

2. Drag the new layer to the top of the timeline and name it Labels.

3. Click the hollow dot in Frame 1 of the new layer, and in the Frame area of the Property Inspector, select <Frame Label> and enter the name of the current frame label.
   A red flag with the name entered appears in the layer.

4. Single-click on the frame containing the "old" label name.

5. Select the name in the Property Inspector, press the Delete key, and press the Enter key.
   The flag and frame name disappear.

6. Right-click (PC) or Control-click (Mac) on the frame in the Labels layer that is directly above the next frame label.
   The context menu opens.

7. Select Insert Keyframe.
   A hollow dot appears in the frame.

8. Create the new frame label and delete the old one (**Figure 10.13**).

9. Repeat steps 6 and 7 for the rest of the frames that require labels.

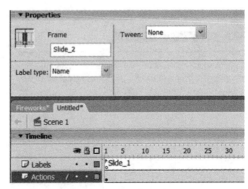

Figure 10.13 It is common practice to have a separate Labels layer in Flash. The Slide_2 label created during the import of the Captivate movie into Flash is about to be deleted.

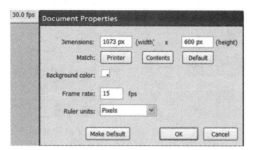

Figure 10.14 You can change the frame rate of the Flash movie by double-clicking the Frame Rate area of the timeline and changing the rate in the Document Properties dialog box.

Figure 10.15 If the playback rate needs to be changed, make the change in Captivate.

Changing the frame rate

To the average Flash developer, 30 fps (Captivate's default rate) is quite fast. Again, it is best practice among Flash developers to produce Flash movies with frame rates between 12 and 15 fps. You can change the frame rate of the Flash movie from 30 fps to 12 or 15 fps by double-clicking the frame rate on the timeline to open the Document Properties dialog box (**Figure 10.14**) and changing the frame rate.

You should approach changing the frame rate with a high degree of caution. Keep in mind that full motion video being "called" into the Flash movie will be affected because these SWF files will adopt the frame rate of the Flash SWF calling them.

If a movie is destined for Flash, it might be a better idea to change the frame rate in Captivate. There could be a lot of extra work that could be done more easily in Captivate.

To change the frame rate:

1. Open a Captivate movie in Captivate and select Movie > Preferences.

   The Movie Preferences dialog box opens.

2. Select the Preferences tab and change the "Frames per second" from the default value of 30 to the new rate (**Figure 10.15**).

3. Click OK.

   Most likely, you will see an alert box notifying you that changing the frame rate may affect the playback of any animation objects in the movie.

4. Click Yes to accept the change.

5. Locate the frames containing animation objects, if any, and adjust their timing on the timeline.

6. Save the movie and export the movie to Flash.

NAVIGATING THROUGH A CAPTIVATE MOVIE

Optimizing a Captivate Movie for Flash MX 2004

Being able to utilize the best of Captivate with the power of Flash MX 2004 is a very strong incentive to look for ways to make Captivate "play nice" with Flash. Here are some ideas:

◆ Keep the Captivate movie small. The fewer Captivate slides, the better. The end result is a shorter Flash timeline.

◆ Keep the Captivate slide duration to a minimum. Shorten the duration of mouse movements or other timeline objects. Remember, each extra second on the Captivate timeline adds 30 frames to the Flash movie.

◆ Consider adding buttons or other navigation elements in Flash rather than inserting them into the Captivate slide. These items are converted to movie clips, buttons, and bitmaps in Flash and add only to the "weight" of the final Flash movie.

◆ If the plan is to add an AVI video animation to the Captivate movie, consider using a more efficient FLV file in Flash. AVI movies are imported into Captivate as a series of slides.

◆ If you are using a background sound track to the Captivate movie, consider adding it to the Flash movie using the more efficient Flash Sound Object. This way the sounds are not embedded in the Flash timeline.

◆ If a Captivate movie is a self-running demonstration, don't add a controller to it.

◆ If Question slides are necessary, consider using the Quiz templates that are installed with Flash MX 2004 (**Figure 10.16**).

Figure 10.16 Knowing Quiz slides can't be imported into Flash, consider using one of the Quiz templates that are installed with Flash.

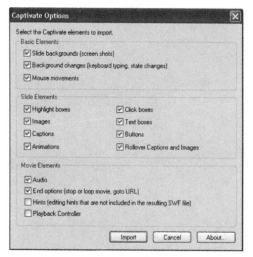

Figure 10.17 Judicious deselection of various Captivate features during import will slim down the Captivate movie. You can always replace deselected items—more efficiently—in Flash.

♦ Change the frame rate of the Captivate movie to match that of the Flash movie before inserting sound into Captivate slides. This will ensure that the timing of the slide and the sound match.

♦ If a Captivate movie is to be included in a Flash movie, consider using the ActionScript LoadMovie function in Flash to load the Captivate SWF file rather than importing the Captivate movie into Flash.

These are just a few suggestions. You can also pare down the weight of your Captivate movie during the Import process. When the Captivate Options dialog box (**Figure 10.17**) opens during import, deselect the elements that aren't important to the movie.

For example, if the movie is a self-running demonstration, you won't need the playback controller. Highlight boxes that result from mouse clicks are also good candidates to be jettisoned if they do nothing more than add "eye candy" to the movie. Deselect the End Options if you are comfortable writing your own ActionScript code and if you are familiar with either creating and coding your own buttons in Flash or using the combination of buttons in the Flash Library—Window > Other Panels > Common Libraries > Buttons—and Flash's behaviors to control them, then deselect Buttons in the Slide Elements area of the Captivate Options dialog box.

The Flash MX 2004 to Captivate Connection

If you are an experienced Flash developer, you know there is a lot that you can do to add to the Captivate experience. As long as you stay within the parameters of the Flash Player 6—no ActionScript 2.0 and no streaming video, for example—moving Captivate movies to another level of interactivity through the addition of Flash animations to your Captivate movies is now an option.

If you are a RoboDemo or Captivate developer with little or no experience with Flash you can still use Flash to add a little zip to your Captivate movies. The easiest way of getting going with Flash, without having to really know Flash, is through the use of a feature new to Flash MX 2004—Timeline Effects. Though Flash developers tend to regard this feature with more than a little disdain, it wasn't added to the application to please them. Timeline Effects were designed to give the new Flash user an opportunity to add special effects to his or her movie without having to know how to code using ActionScript.

There are four Timeline Effects:

- **Explode** You control how an object explodes on the screen.

- **Expand** Give objects the effect of growing and shrinking over time.

- **Blur** Make objects simultaneously fade in and out, and grow larger or smaller.

- **Drop Shadow** As the name says...

If used sparingly, you can use these small animations in your Captivate movies as a bridge between subject changes, new captures, and even mode changes.

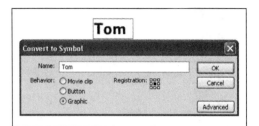

Figure 10.18 Get into the habit of converting everything you create in Flash into a symbol.

Figure 10.19 The Explode Timeline Effect enables you to control how many aspects of the object will shatter.

Figure 10.20 The effect is added to the main timeline, and the frame rate is changed to 30 fps.

To use the Explode Timeline Effect:

1. Open Flash MX 2004 and from the start page, select Create New > Flash Document.

2. Select the Text tool, single-click the stage, and enter your name.

3. Select your name on the stage and press the F8 key.

   The Convert to Symbol dialog box opens.

4. Name the symbol, select Graphic as the behavior (**Figure 10.18**), and click OK.

   The dialog box closes.

5. Right-click (PC) or Control-click (Mac) the symbol.

   The context menu opens.

6. Select Timeline Effects > Effects > Explode.

   The Explode dialog box opens (**Figure 10.19**).

7. Enter the following settings:
   ▲ Effect Duration: 30 frames. This will result in a one-second animation in Captivate.
   ▲ Rotate Fragments by: 45 degrees
   ▲ Change Fragments Size by: X = 20 pixels

8. Click the Update Preview button to review the effect.

9. Click OK.

   This accepts the changes, closes the dialog box, and adds the effect to the main timeline.

10. Change the frame rate of the Flash movie to 30 fps to match that in Captivate (**Figure 10.20**).

continues on next page

THE FLASH MX 2004 TO CAPTIVATE CONNECTION

11. If you want to preview the effect, press Control-Enter (PC) or Command-Return (Mac), or select Control > Test Movie. Click the Close button when you're finished.

12. Save the movie and select File > Publish Settings.

The Flash Publish Settings dialog box opens.

13. Select the Formats tab and deselect the HTML option.

There is no need for the document because the SWF is going to be placed in a Captivate movie.

14. Click the Browse folder beside the name of the Flash (SWF) file, navigate to the folder where the SWF will be saved (**Figure 10.21**), and click Save.

15. Select the Flash tab.

The Flash Player settings open.

16. Enter the following values:

▲ Version: Flash Player 6

▲ ActionScript version: ActionScript 1.0

17. Your settings should resemble **Figure 10.22**; click Publish.

A progress bar appears.

18. When the progress bar disappears, click OK.

The dialog box closes.

19. Save the file and quit Flash.

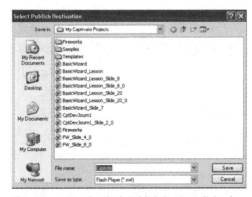

Figure 10.21 Use the Flash Publish Settings dialog box to indicate the folder in which the Flash SWF file is to be saved.

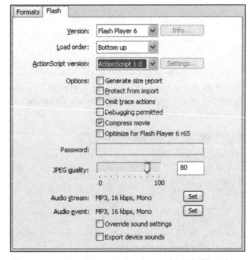

Figure 10.22 Captivate can accept only SWF files that are compatible with the Flash 6 Player and that use ActionScript 1.0.

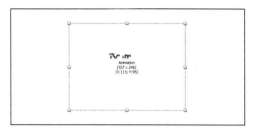

Figure 10.23 A Timeline Effect created in Flash MX 2004 is placed in a Captivate slide.

20. Open the Captivate movie in which the animation will be placed.

21. In the Storyboard view, double-click the slide where the effect will be placed.

The slide opens in the Edit View panel.

22. Select Insert > Animation.

The Open dialog box opens.

23. Navigate to the folder containing the SWF you just created and double-click the file.

The New Animation dialog box opens.

24. Set the properties and options, and add any necessary audio.

25. Click OK.

The animation appears in the Captivate slide (**Figure 10.23**).

Adding Flash Video to Captivate

Video is becoming a major aspect of many demonstrations and simulations. Captivate uses a rather klunky frame-by-frame method of AVI import into the movie, which makes one wonder if there isn't a better way. There is.

If you are creating a Captivate movie for playback through an EXE or Web delivery, you can include Flash video in the project as long as you are aware of the following:

◆ You must use an FLV (Flash Video) file.

◆ The video has to be embedded into the Flash SWF file. Flash Player 6 does not allow Progressive Downloading of the Flash Video file (FLV) from a web server into the SWF file.

◆ The frame rate of the FLV and the Flash file containing it should match that of the Captivate movie.

◆ Try and keep the video as short as possible. Embedded video must be read into memory before it plays. This isn't an issue with an EXE, but it is a reason for preloaders on the Web.

To add a Flash video to your Captivate movie:

1. Open Flash and on the start page, select Create New > Flash Page.

2. When the blank Flash page opens, select File > Import > Import to Library.
   The Import to Library dialog box opens.

3. Navigate to the folder containing the FLV file, select the file, and click Open.
   A progress bar appears, showing the progress of the import. When it finishes, the file appears in the Library (**Figure 10.24**).

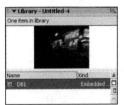

Figure 10.24 An embedded video is contained in the Flash Library and can be dragged to the Flash stage.

4. Drag the embedded video file from the Library to the stage.

   When the video is placed on the stage, an alert box appears, informing you that the frame will have to be added to the timeline to accommodate the video.

5. Click OK.

6. Select Modify > Document.

   The Document Properties dialog box opens.

7. Click the Contents button and click OK.

   This shrinks the Flash stage to the size of the video on the stage. If you don't do this, you will create a movie that sits on a stage that is seriously larger than the content. It is a waste of space and potential bandwidth.

8. You could publish the movie at this point, but it will loop continuously. To fix this, add a new layer named Actions to the Flash timeline.

9. In the Actions layer, select the last frame of the video, and right-click (PC) or Control-click (Mac) the frame.

   The context menu opens.

10. Select Insert Keyframe.

11. Select the new keyframe and press the F9 key or select Window > Development Panels > Actions.

    The ActionScript editor opens.

12. Enter the following code into the editor:
    ```
    stop();
    ```
    This line stops the playback head on the last frame of the movie, preventing the video from looping.

13. Close the ActionScript editor and save the file.

continues on next page

ADDING FLASH VIDEO TO CAPTIVATE

14. If you want to preview the video at this point, press Control-Enter (PC) or Command-Return (Mac).

The Preview window opens.

15. Select File > Publish Setting.

The Publish Settings dialog box opens.

16. Deselect the HTML option and click the Browse button beside the Flash (.swf) input box.

17. Navigate to where the SWF will be saved and click the Save button.

18. Select the Flash tab, set the version to Flash Player 6, and set the ActionScript version to ActionScript 1.0 (**Figure 10.25**).

19. Click the Publish button to create the SWF.

A progress window appears.

20. When the progress alert disappears, click OK to close the window, save the file, and quit Flash.

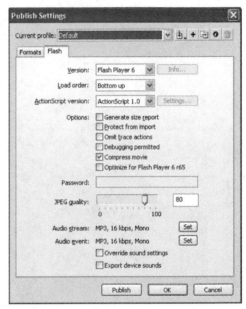

Figure 10.25 The video is ready to be published to a Flash Player 6 using ActionScript 1.0.

ADDING FLASH VIDEO TO CAPTIVATE

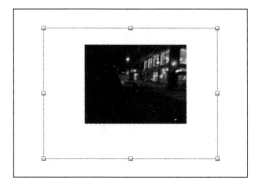

Figure 10.26 The Flash video is placed in a Captivate slide.

21. Launch Captivate and open the Captivate movie in which the video will be placed.

22. Open the slide to contain the video in the Edit View panel.

23. Select Insert > Animation, navigate to the folder containing the SWF you just created, and double click the file.

The New Animation dialog box opens.

24. Set the properties and options, and add any necessary audio.

25. Click OK.

The animation appears in the Captivate slide (**Figure 10.26**).

CREATING eLEARNING APPLICATIONS

To consider Captivate as being nothing more than an "industrial strength" screen capture utility or application would be a huge mistake. The simple fact that you can add interactivity through the use of click boxes and so on means you can also create extremely effective eLearning presentations.

For example, instead of showing the viewer which button on the interface to click, why not ask the user to click the appropriate button? A caption could then appear explaining if the choice was the correct one. Alternatively, rather than ask a question, ask the viewer to enter the answer into a text box and, again, provide the appropriate feedback.

You can even provide the viewer with feedback captions. *Hint captions* suggest a correct answer, while *Success* and *Failure captions* appear in response to a specific action. Text boxes also give the viewer the opportunity to enter the answers to questions, and Captivate lets you define multiple correct answers to a question. For example, a question might be: "Captivate is an example of _____." The correct answer could be either "program," "application," or "software." In this case, the answer typed into the text box will be checked against the three possible answers, and the appropriate feedback to the answer will be presented.

continues on next page

You can also add an extra dimension to your movies by adding true/false or multiple-choice quizzes to your movies. Quizzes are useful for providing the viewer with feedback regarding how well he or she comprehended the content. For multiple-choice quizzes, you have quite a degree of flexibility. You can include a single correct answer or multiple correct answers. You can even *branch* to other Captivate movies based upon the viewer's responses.

Branching permits you to create what Captivate calls *Learning Objects (LOs),* which are individual Captivate movies focusing on a single aspect of the overall learning objectives. These objects use buttons, click boxes, text boxes, and quizzes to jump to different slides in the movie or to even different movies. In this manner, the content is tailored to the viewer's learning style. For example, if a viewer is having problems understanding a particular concept or operation, you automatically redirect the presentation to another presentation that offers a bit more practice or a slightly less complex version of the subject matter.

Captivate provides three types of movies than you can use for eLearning purposes:

◆ **Demonstration** This is a straight screen capture of a software procedure or technique. It employs the use of captions and highlight boxes to demonstrate the lesson. This is a linear presentation format, which is, essentially, self-running (requiring no interactivity).

◆ **Simulation** The student proceeds through the movie performing the tasks—clicking boxes, entering information, etc.—that one would perform normally when using the technique.

◆ **Training** This mode adds the all-important element of eLearning—the quiz. In Captivate, answers can be graded and sent to your Learning Management System (LMS). Also, the use of branching and feedback enable you to mold the movie to the student's knowledge.

Finally, all of the interactivity in your movie can be tracked and scored because Captivate content is both SCORM (Sharable Content Object Reference Model) 1.2 certified and AICC compliant. This makes your movies able to integrate fully with any LMS by automatically generating the XML manifest that the LMS requires.

An LMS is, essentially, a database that uses LOs as the presentation to the student. The LMS then brings the "results" of the LO into the LMS database for storage. Typically an LMS contains information such as when, where, and how often has this student taken this test; the student's name and position; and passing and failing grades or efforts.

Standards and Learning Management Systems

There are several LMSs that range from off-the-shelf software to custom applications. The key to any system is how the scoring data moves from Captivate, for example, into the LMS. How that happens is the role of standards. If standards weren't in place, organizations switching from one LMS to another would also have to change all of their courseware.

LMS standards, therefore, describe the metadata involved in the course definition. This data—containing, for example, the author, objectives, and course structure—is usually contained in an XML document referred to as a *manifest*.

These standards are not independent of each other. In fact, they are interrelated because the members of standards organizations are usually members of the other standards organizations. There are four major LMS standards:

- **Advanced Distributed Learning (ADL or ADL SCORM)** This is a U.S. government–sponsored initiative to facilitate instructional content development and delivery using current and emerging technologies. SCORM focuses on the next generation of open architectures for eLearning applications.

- **Aviation Industry Computer-Based Training Committee (AICC)** The AICC has developed the most widely accepted interoperability standards for computer-based training (CBT) or eLearning applications. AICC-compliant applications meet the guidelines for deployment, delivery, and evaluations of digital training materials.

- **IMS Global Consortium (IMS)** This organization sets the standards for K-11 and post-secondary education. Its focus is maintaining an open standard for locating and using educational content, student progress, and tracking, and enabling the exchange of student records between various administrative systems.

- **Institute of Electrical and Electronics Engineers (IEEE) Learning Technology Standards Committee** This group focuses on software components, tools, and technologies used for digital learning.

Storyboarding the eLearning Project

When it comes to eLearning, the worst thing you can do is make it up as you go along. A lot of planning should go into the project, and the most important and time-consuming step in the process is the creation of the storyboard.

The *storyboard* includes the text, media (sound, images, and video), and interactive elements that support the project's learning outcomes and objectives. As well, the storyboard serves to keep you focused on both the audience and design consistency.

There are as many approaches to storyboard creation as there are developers. The approaches range from a pencil and a sheet of paper to, in the case of extremely complex or technical projects, commercial software designed for this purpose.

If you are like most developers, the odds are you already have software that can be used for building a storyboard on your computer. For example, Macromedia Freehand MX and Fireworks MX 2004, which are bundled with the MX 2004 Studio, are great tools. Storyboards created in these applications can be printed as well as output in a Web format and posted to a staging site for client review. Page-layout applications such as Adobe InDesign CS, Illustrator CS, and Photoshop CS can also be used, as can the common applications Microsoft PowerPoint and even Microsoft Word.

At this stage of the process, you don't need a Fine Arts degree. What you are developing is a plan that communicates what happens on the screen and where it happens on the screen. You should also create a content inventory that lists all of the media elements. This will give you a good overview of what you need to acquire and/or create.

What you need at this stage is consistency of design by repeating what interactions are required and the page types used. The key to learning is consistency and predictability. If you use a particular caption style to indicate a question, then that style is to be rigorously used throughout the entire movie. After the student becomes familiar with the style, consistency and predictability become intuitive as the learner recognizes the functions of the various onscreen elements in the movie.

Use the storyboard to identify logical groupings of the content. For example, there may be a blank slide used to separate the sections of the movie, a series of captions that present the information during the movie's playback, a series of slides that engage the learner through rollovers, and so on; and, at the end of each section, there is a multiple-choice quiz. Each of these "sections" should be presented to the learner in a similar manner. For example, the blank slide used to introduce each section uses the same design throughout the movie. The best way of doing this is to use a template for the content. Not only does a template inject consistency into the look and feel of the groupings, but it can also contain the style guide you develop (see the following Tip) and speed up the process.

Finally, test the design. This is simply showing the storyboard to people and asking them to use it. Listen carefully to their feedback; they can help isolate design flaws, which are best (and easily) addressed at this stage of the process. Discovering and addressing these flaws in the midst of the development process is, at the very least, an expensive proposition.

✔ Tips

■ Here's an interesting approach to storyboarding from Captivate Product Manager Silke Fleisher: Use Captivate to create the storyboard by doing an initial capture of the procedure or movie, and then output the capture as a Word document. From there, you can add notes to the storyboard and make subsequent changes. "It is an extremely rapid and effective approach."

■ It isn't difficult to apply a style guide to your movie. One way to do this is by inserting a couple of blank slides into the movie. You can then add a series of captions and error/success messages with specific fonts, color, and sizes to those slides, which are then applied to the entire movie. Simply copy and paste them into the slides where they are needed. When you are ready to export the movie, simply delete the blank slides with the caption styles.

Preparing a Movie for eLearning

Creating a full-bore eLearning presentation is out of the scope of this book. Instead, the bulk of this chapter is devoted to the features of Captivate that you will use in the creation of eLearning tutorials. These features include:

◆ Assigning captions to buttons and boxes

◆ Text entry boxes

◆ Hints

◆ Quiz slides

◆ Answer prompting

As mentioned earlier, depending on the complexity of the learning objectives and the presentation, you can use these elements to branch to other areas of the presentation. Branching (the official eLearning term is *contingency branching*), in the context of New Media, should be regarded as nonlinear navigation.

A Captivate movie is a linear production, moving in a straight line from the start to the end of the movie. Branching is the exact opposite. For example, a learner answers a question in a slide. Depending upon the response, the playback head could move to a slide later on in the movie or to a completely different movie.

The whole process starts with setting the eLearning output options, setting the pass rate, and indicating whether the scoring will be presented to the student.

To set the eLearning output options:

1. Open a Captivate movie and select Movie > Quiz Manager (**Figure 11.1**). The Quiz Manager dialog box opens.

2. Select the Reporting tab and select "Enable output options."

   Your choice in this area determines which type of output is required (**Figure 11.2**):

   ▲ **AICC** Select if your LMS uses this standard. Be aware that because AICC output uses slide sets, selecting this option will not allow you to use a full screen display during export.

   ▲ **SCORM** Select if your LMS uses this standard.

   ▲ **Questionmark Perception** Select if you use this system.

   ▲ **Authorware** Select if the file is destined for inclusion in an Authorware project. If you do use Authorware, be sure to identify the separator. The default is a comma. Change this if you use a semicolon or other character as your separator.

   ▲ **E-mail** Select if the results are to be sent via email and enter the email address into the adjacent text input box.

3. In the "Reporting level" drop-down list, select a reporting level from the two options.

4. Select how a pass or fail is reported.

   The choices are Report (this is traditionally used where no formalized grading structure is in place) or Report Pass/Fail.

5. Choose whether the score should be reported as a percentage or fixed number.

Figure 11.1 Select the Captivate eLearning options from the Quiz Manager.

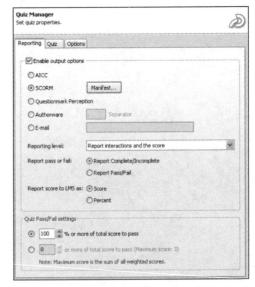

Figure 11.2 The first step is to determine which type of output is required.

✔ Tip

■ Two of the choices—Questionmark Perception and Authorware—are stand-alone products. Questionmark Perception is eLearning software available from the UK-based Question Mark Computing Limited. Selecting this option will output the results as a QML file, which Perception can then use. More details on this product can be found at www.questionmark.com/uk/home.htm. Authorware is a Macromedia product that has evolved from a New Media application into a robust eLearning and presentation software application. Details can be found at www.macromedia.com.

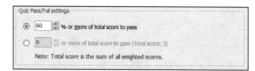

Figure 11.3 Set the passing or failing grade in this area.

Setting the quiz Pass/Fail level

In the "Quiz Pass/Fail settings" area of the Quiz Manager dialog box, you set the value for a passing grade. This number is usually determined by institutional grading standards (at some colleges, for example, a passing grade is 60% or higher) or other corporate/institutional standards.

To set the quiz pass/fail level:

1. Open a Captivate movie and select Movie > Quiz Manager. The Quiz Manager dialog box opens.

2. Select the Reporting tab.

3. In the "Quiz Pass/Fail settings" area, select the first item and (**Figure 11.3**) enter the passing percentage or use the arrows to change the value. Alternatively, select the second item and enter the minimum number of correct questions that will result in a passing grade.

4. Enter the maximum number of incorrect questions that will result in a passing grade.

To set the eLearning scoring display:

1. Open a Captivate movie and select Movie > Quiz Manager.
   The Quiz Manager dialog box opens.

2. Select the Quiz tab.

3. Select "Show score at end of quiz."
   When the student finishes answering the questions during movie playback, he or she is presented with the results.

✔ Tip

■ Click the Settings button to open the Results dialog box. You can enter the text of a pass or fail message, which score to display, and the background color of the caption used for the score display.

PREPARING A MOVIE FOR ELEARNING

To set the SCORM course manifest options:

1. Open a Captivate movie and select Movie > Quiz Manager.

   The Quiz Manager dialog box opens.

2. Click the Reporting tab.

3. Select "Enable output options," select SCORM, and click the Manifest button.

   The Manifest dialog box opens (**Figure 11.4**).

4. Enter a course identifier (**Figure 11.5**).

   The course identifier is the keyword used to identify various manifests. The default value, which you can change, is the name of the movie that is currently open. This is a required field.

5. Enter a title.

   Students using the LMS will see the title. The default value, which you can change, is the name of the movie that is currently open. This is a required field.

6. Enter a description.

   This is a required field.

7. Enter a version number.

   This number will be used to differentiate manifests that have the same course identifier. This is a required field.

8. Enter a duration value.

   This is the amount of time the student will be given to work with the movie. This value must use the *hh:mm:ss* format. This is an optional field.

9. Enter a subject—a short description of the movie using key words or phrases. This is an optional field.

Figure 11.4 In the Manifest dialog box, determine how the score is moved from Captivate to your LMS.

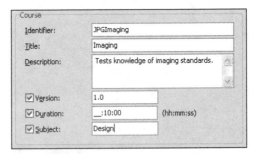

Figure 11.5 Enter a course identifier and other information used by the manifest document.

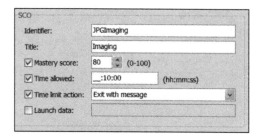

Figure 11.6 Shareable Content Objects (SCOs), if any, are identified.

✔ Tip

■ If you have selected SCORM as your output option, you must set how the manifest file is created. If you selected another output option, you can skip this section.

If your LMS uses Shareable Content Objects (SCOs), you can also set their properties and options. These objects are a key part of SCORM's XML-based framework used for learning objects so they can be shared easily among different LMSs. SCOs are reusable self-contained learning units that can be combined and assembled into a package for the LMS to use.

To set SCO options:

1. In the Manifest dialog box, if required by the LMS, enter an SCO identifier (**Figure 11.6**).

   The default value is the name of the movie being used. Identifier is a required field.

2. Enter a title for the SCO.

   This is a required field.

3. Enter a mastery score.

   The value should be between 0 and 110. Only movies containing score reporting objects such as quiz slides and text entry boxes need to include this option. This is an optional field.

4. Set the time allowed for the test.

   This value must use the *hh:mm:ss* format. This is an optional field.

5. If you set a time limit for movie completion, select the action to be taken from the "Time limit action" drop-down menu.

6. Select "Launch data" to specify initialization data expected by the SCO.

   The adjacent text entry field is optional.

Providing Student Feedback

Feedback is an important eLearning element. The student should be able to respond to questions and then receive an immediate response that either reinforces the decision or suggests alternatives. In Captivate, feedback can be provided via click boxes, buttons, and text entry boxes. This feedback takes the form of three types of captions—Success, Failure, and Hint—that you can add to these interactive elements. The Hint caption traditionally appears on a rollover. As well, the results of the decision can be used for scoring purposes.

To use a click box to provide feedback:

1. Select the slide to which the click box will be added.

2. Insert a click box by either clicking the Click Box icon on the Object toolbar, selecting Insert > Click Box, or pressing the Control-Shift-K keys.

   The "New click box" dialog box opens.

3. Select the Click Box tab and indicate the event that occurs upon success. (Full details regarding these choices are found in Chapter 7, "Adding Interactivity.")

4. Select the Options tab and, in the Options area (**Figure 11.7**), indicate how long the box is visible on the screen, when it appears, and whether the caption will indicate success (a correct choice) or failure (an incorrect choice).

5. Also here, select "Hint caption" to have a Hint caption appear when the mouse rolls over the click box.

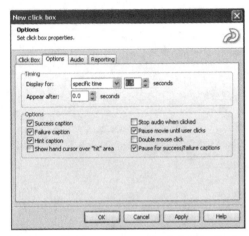

Figure 11.7 Click boxes can provide student feedback.

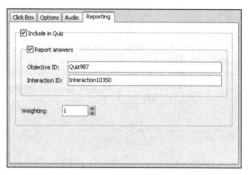

Figure 11.8 The score can be tied to the LMS.

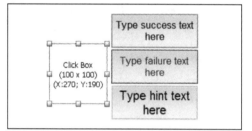

Figure 11.9 A click box with feedback on a slide.

6. If the results of the click box are to be graded or scored, click the Scoring tab to and select "Keep score" (**Figure 11.8**).

7. In the Weighting text entry box, enter a nondecimal value for the answer.

   For example, if the question is worth one mark or point, enter 1 here.

8. If necessary, enter an objective ID.

   This parameter refers to the objective for the action, which could be related to one set in your LMS. This is an optional field.

9. If necessary, enter an interaction ID.

   This parameter refers to the interaction name of the action. Enter this information if you want the final SWF file to send tracking information to your LMS. This ID must match that specified by your LMS.

10. Click OK.

    The "New click box" dialog box closes. The click box and the captions appear in the slide, and you can edit and reposition them on the screen (**Figure 11.9**).

✔ Tip

■ You can change the timing options of a click box on the timeline as well.

To use a button to provide feedback:

1. Select the slide to which the button will be added.

2. Insert a button by either clicking the Button icon on the Object toolbar, selecting Insert > Button, or pressing the Control-Shift-B keys.

   The "New button" dialog box opens.

3. Select the Button tab and indicate the event that occurs upon success. (Full details regarding these choices are found in Chapter 7.)

4. In the Options area of the dialog box, indicate whether the caption will indicate success (a correct choice) or failure (an incorrect choice) (**Figure 11.10**).

5. Also here, select "Hint caption" to have the button contain a Hint caption that appears when the mouse rolls over the button.

6. If the results of the button are to be graded or scored, click the Reporting tab and select "Report answers" (**Figure 11.11**).

7. In the Weighting text entry box, enter a nondecimal value for the answer.

   For example, if the question is worth one mark or point, enter 1 here.

8. If necessary, enter an objective ID.

   This parameter refers to the objective for the action, which could be related to one set in your LMS. This is an optional field.

9. If necessary, enter an interaction ID.

   This parameter refers to the interaction name of the action. Enter this information if you want the final SWF file to send tracking information to your LMS. This ID must match that specified by your LMS.

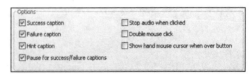

Figure 11.10 You can use the Option area of the dialog box to provide student feedback.

Figure 11.11 You can use button clicks to keep score.

PROVIDING STUDENT FEEDBACK

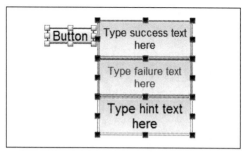

Figure 11.12 A button and its associated captions are added to the slide.

Figure 11.13 The Text Entry Options dialog box.

10. Click OK.

The "New button" dialog box closes. The button and the captions appear in the slide (**Figure 11.12**), and you can edit and reposition them on the screen.

To use a text entry box to provide feedback:

1. Select the slide to which the text entry box will be added.

2. Insert a box by either clicking the Text Entry Box icon on the Object toolbar, selecting Insert > Text Entry Box, or pressing the Control-Shift-T keys.

The Text Entry Box dialog box opens (**Figure 11.13**).

3. Select the Text Entry Box tab, enter the correct answer or answers, and choose the event that occurs upon success.

continues on next page

PROVIDING STUDENT FEEDBACK

4. Select the Options tab and choose which options in the list will be applied to the text entry box (**Figure 11.14**).

   One of your options is to include a button with the text entry box. This is a rather handy way of including a Submit button rather than using a keystroke to submit the answer. If you do include a button, it will appear as a text button in the slide beside the text entry box. Double-click the button to open the Button Options dialog box and change the text in the button from "..." to "Submit."

   Select "Case-sensitive" if the phrase entered must be exact. For example, if the correct answer is "Captivate," entering "captivate" will result in a wrong answer.

5. Choose whether the caption will indicate success (a correct choice) or failure (an incorrect choice).

6. Also here, select "Hint caption" to have the text entry box contain a Hint caption that appears when the mouse rolls over the box.

7. If the results of the text entry box are to be graded or scored, click the Scoring tab and select "Keep score."

8. In the Weighting text entry box, enter a nondecimal value for the answer.

   For example, if the question is worth one mark or point, enter 1 here.

9. If necessary, enter an objective ID.

   This parameter refers to the objective for the action, which could be related to one set in your LMS. This is an optional field.

Figure 11.14 A text entry box and its associated captions are added to the slide.

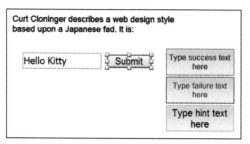

Figure 11.15 A text entry box and its captions on a slide.

10. If necessary, enter an interaction ID.

This parameter refers to the interaction name of the action. Enter this information if you want the final SWF file to send tracking information to your LMS. This ID must match that specified by your LMS.

11. Click OK.

The "New text entry box" dialog box closes. The text entry box, Submit button, and captions appear in the slide (**Figure 11.15**), and you can edit and reposition them on the screen.

✔ Tips

- The text in a Submit button will default to an ellipsis (…). Double-click the button to open the Button dialog box, in which you can change the text.

- You can't use a text entry box to provide the question. Use a transparent caption instead.

Creating Question Slides

In many respects a Question slide can be regarded as a test embedded into the Captivate movie. The addition of Question slides provides you with:

◆ The ability to quickly add single-choice, multiple-choice, matching, and true/false quizzes to your movie. You can even have a variety of these quiz types throughout the movie.

◆ The use of radio button responses for single responses or check box responses for multiple correct answers.

◆ The flexibility to determine the actions that occur based upon the user's decisions. This could include going to a slide if the answer is correct and going to a completely different slide if the answer is incorrect.

◆ A student feedback mechanism.

◆ Integration of the scoring features of Question slides with your LMS. This includes the number of attempts, the number of correct and incorrect answers, and the ability to send the pass/fail data to the LMS.

Keep in mind, though, that the inclusion of Question slides in the movie means the student must complete the entire movie if the scoring is going to be sent to your LMS. You might want to include a message such as, "This movie includes a number of questions that will have to be answered. You must complete the entire movie." A great location for this would be the first slide of the movie or a blank slide at the start of the movie.

Figure 11.16 You can add Question slides using the Insert menu.

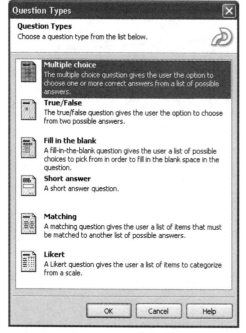

Figure 11.17 There are six types of Question slides that you can create.

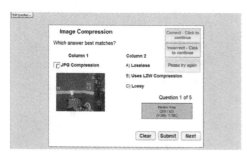

Figure 11.18 A typical Question slide.

To add a Question slide:

1. Open a Captivate movie in either the Slide View or Edit View panel, and select Insert > Question Slide (**Figure 11.16**). The Question Types dialog box opens (**Figure 11.17**).

2. Choose the question type:
   - ▲ Fill in the blank
   - ▲ Likert
   - ▲ Matching
   - ▲ Multiple choice
   - ▲ Short answer
   - ▲ True/false

3. Click OK.
   Depending upon your choice, the appropriate dialog box opens.

4. Create the questions and answers based upon the requirements of the dialog box.

5. Click OK to accept your choices.
   The dialog box closes, and the data that you entered appears on the slide (**Figure 11.18**).

6. To edit the questions and answers, click the Edit button in the upper left corner of the Question slide.
   The relevant dialog box opens.

7. Make your changes and click OK.

✔ Tip

- A Question slide is no different from any other slide in the movie. If you have a slide selected, the Question slide will be added after the selected slide.

To "link" the Question slide answers to your LMS:

1. Click the Reporting tab of the Question options panel (**Figure 11.19**).

2. Enter an objective ID and interaction ID (if needed).

3. In the Weighting text entry box, enter the mark assigned to the question.

   For example, if the question is worth five marks or points, enter 5 here.

4. Click OK.

✔ Tips

■ The objective ID is used with an LMS and is a fairly advanced feature. There is a concept in many LMSs called an *objective set*. If you create a quiz question in Captivate that is part of a defined objective set in the LMS, then enter a unique objective ID for the quiz question. This associates the quiz question with the appropriate objective in the LMS. The objective ID is an optional parameter and does not *have* to be set for the quiz question to work properly in Captivate.

■ The interaction ID is another piece of communication between Captivate and an LMS. If you want a quiz question to send tracking information to a server-side LMS, then each quiz question needs an interaction ID. This ID will be used in the LMS reporting. The interaction ID should be unique and should correspond to the correct interaction ID in the LMS.

Figure 11.19 You can link the responses in Question slides to your LMS.

Figure 11.20 The "New fill-in-the-blank question" dialog box.

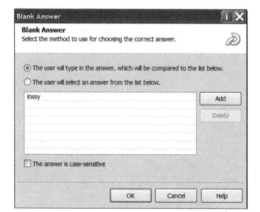

Figure 11.21 The fill-in-the-blank answer is determined. You can have multiple answers.

Creating a fill-in-the-blank question slide

A great way to test knowledge is to actually have the student enter missing words or phrases, or select from a list of words the missing word in a statement. This is the purpose of a fill-in-the-blank slide.

To create a fill-in-the-blank question slide:

1. Select Insert > Question Slide.
   The Question Types dialog box opens.

2. Select "Fill in the blank."
   The "New fill-in-the blank question" dialog box opens (**Figure 11.20**).

3. Enter a slide title and a description of what needs to be done.

4. In the Phrase text entry box, enter the phrase, including the word to be entered by the student.

5. Highlight the word that the student must enter, and click the Add Blank button.
   The Blank Answer dialog box opens (**Figure 11.21**). There are a couple of choices to be made here. You can enter a series of words or phrases that the student must match, or you can provide the words or phrases from which the student can then choose. You can add these by clicking the Add button or remove them by selecting the word or phrase and clicking the Delete button. You can also decide whether or not the word to be entered is case-sensitive.

6. When you have finished adding the words or phrases, click OK.
   You are returned to the "New fill-in-the-blank question" dialog box.

continues on next page

CREATING QUESTION SLIDES

7. Select the Options tab to open the fill-in-the-blank options.

8. Indicate whether the questions are to be graded by making a selection in the Type pop-down menu, and enter the text and select the event for success and failure.

9. Indicate which buttons, if any, will appear.

10. Select the Reporting tab to enter the appropriate eLearning data.

11. Click OK.

    The "New fill-in-the-blank question" dialog box closes, and you can view the slide in the Edit View panel (**Figure 11.22**).

✔ **Tip**

■ You can change the wording of the captions by double-clicking a caption to open the Caption dialog box, or by clicking the Quiz button in the "New fill-in-the-blank question" dialog box to open the Quiz Manager. Select the Quiz Manager's Quiz tab and change the text. You can also change the size of the buttons to a uniform size by right-clicking a button and selecting Size from the context menu to open the Size menu. Select Custom Width and Custom Height, and enter the width and height (in pixels) of the button.

Creating a Likert questionnaire

If you have ever been approached by a polling organization doing any sort of consumer or other research, the odds are you have completed a Likert questionnaire. These questions don't look for precision; rather, they ask you to rate your response using, in most cases, a five-point scale. A typical Likert question would be:

Captivate is one seriously cool tool.

Strongly agree___ Agree___ Neutral___
Disagree ___ Strongly disagree___

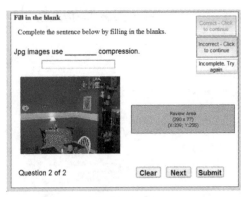

Figure 11.22 A fill-in-the-blank slide.

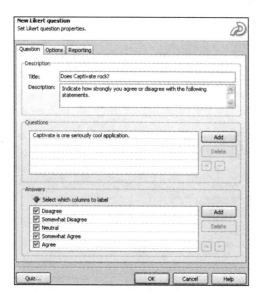

Figure 11.23 Likert questions use a scale of responses.

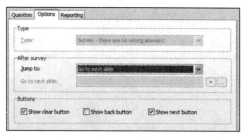

Figure 11.24 Likert questions don't have Success, Failure, or Hint captions.

To create a Likert Question slide:

1. Select Insert > Question Slide.
   The Question Types dialog box opens.

2. Select Likert and click OK.
   The "New Likert question" dialog box opens (**Figure 11.23**).

3. In the Title text input box, enter a title for the slide, and enter the instructions to the user in the Description text input box.

4. In the Questions text input box, enter the statement.

5. Click the Add button to add more statements, or select a statement and click the Delete button to remove it.

6. In the Answers area, select the columns to be labeled.

7. Select the Options tab to open the Likert question options, and indicate what occurs after the survey is completed and what buttons, if any, will appear on the slide (**Figure 11.24**).

8. Select the Reporting tab to open the Likert question reporting options, and enter the eLearning information.

continues on next page

CREATING QUESTION SLIDES

9. Click OK.

The "New Likert question" dialog box closes, and you can view the slide in the Edit View panel (**Figure 11.25**).

✔ Tip

■ If the categories seem to be somewhat "squashed," remember they are objects. You can select them and drag the handles to spread out the categories. The radio buttons attached to them move also.

Creating a Matching Question slide

When using a Matching Question slide, the viewer is presented with a question and is asked to match the best possible answer from a list to the item being questioned. When the user is viewing the slide, he or she can either enter the answer into the text input box or drag the choice into the input box. Depending upon the choice, the appropriate message appears. As well, you can use the responses to these slides in your eLearning application.

To create a Matching Question slide:

1. Select Matching Questions.

The Matching Question dialog box opens (**Figure 11.26**).

2. Select the Question tab.

3. Enter a name for the question.

This name will not appear on the slide.

4. Enter the question into the Question text input box.

5. Click in the text input box in Column 1 and enter the answer.

6. Click in the text input box in Column 2 and enter the first matching item.

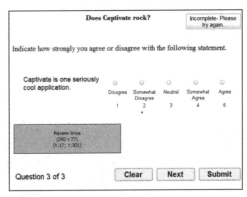

Figure 11.25 A Likert Question slide.

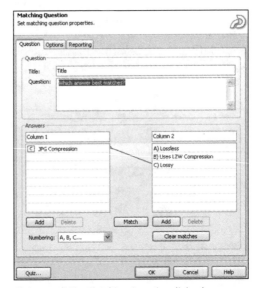

Figure 11.26 The Matching Question dialog box.

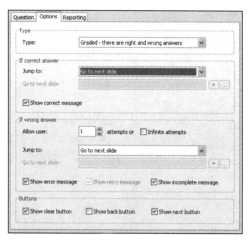

Figure 11.27 Use the Matching Question dialog box's Options tab to indicate the event and the matching caption.

Figure 11.28 You can have the question responses sent to an LMS.

7. Press the down arrow, click the Add button at the bottom of the column, or click once in the second line of Column 2, and enter the second matching item.

8. Repeat step 7 until you have entered all of the items in the list of potential matches.

9. Select the answer in Column 1 (the "item" column) and the correct match in Column 2 (the "answer" column), and click the Match button.

   A line appears that links the item to the correct answer.

10. If you have made a mistake with the match, click the "Clear matches" button to remove the link.

11. Select the Options tab (**Figure 11.27**) and indicate the type of test you are administering. If there are right and wrong answers, select Graded from the pop-down. If you are just surveying knowledge, select Survey.

12. Select the events for the correct and the wrong answers.

13. Select the button type to be used for the slide's buttons.

14. Select the Reporting tab (**Figure 11.28**) and, if the answers are to be part of a report, assign objective and interaction IDs.

15. In the Weighting text entry box, enter the mark assigned to the question.

    For example, if the question is worth five marks or points, enter 5 here.

16. Assign a time limit, if any, to the slide.

17. Click OK.

    The Matching Question dialog box closes, and you are returned to the Edit View panel.

To link the Matching Question slide to your LMS:

1. Open a Matching Question slide in the Edit View panel and click the Edit button in the upper left corner of the slide. The Matching Question dialog box opens.

2. Click the Quiz button.

   The Quiz Manager dialog box opens (**Figure 11.29**).

3. Select the Reporting tab and set the reporting options.

4. Select the Quiz tab to open the quiz settings (**Figure 11.30**).

5. Assign a name to the quiz.

6. If there are user requirements, choose them from the Required pop-down list.

   There are four options (you can choose only one):

   ▲ **Optional** Allows the student to skip the quiz.

   ▲ **Required** Does not allow the student to move forward in the movie without completing the quiz.

   ▲ **Pass required** Does not allow the student to move forward without passing the quiz.

   ▲ **Answer all** Does not allow the student to move forward without answering all of the quiz questions.

7. Select "Allow backward movement" if the student can move backward in the quiz.

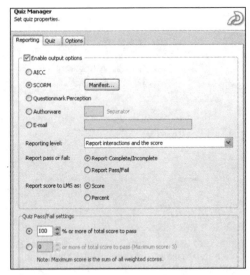

Figure 11.29 The Quiz Manager can be accessed directly from the Matching Question dialog box.

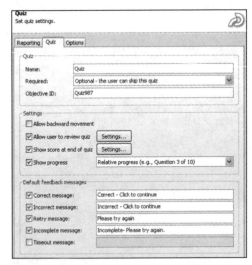

Figure 11.30 A number of the actions based on response are set in the Quiz area of the Quiz Manager.

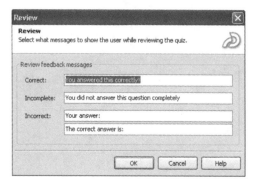

Figure 11.31 The student can review the answers submitted.

Figure 11.32 The student can be shown the score results at the end of the test.

8. If the student will be able to review the answers, select "Allow user to review quiz" and click the Settings button.

    The Review dialog box opens (**Figure 11.31**).

9. Enter the appropriate messages and click OK.

    The Review dialog box closes, and the messages you added to it appear in the gray review area on the slide when the movie is playing. Double-clicking this gray box opens the Review dialog box. (The gray color is strictly to let you know where the review will appear on the slide; it will not appear when the movie plays.)

10. Back on the Quiz tab, if the student will be able to see his or her score, select "Show score at end of quiz" and click the Settings button.

    The Results dialog box opens (**Figure 11.32**).

11. In the Messages area, enter the pass and fail messages.

12. If the results are to be emailed, enter the text for the button used to send the email.

13. In the Score area, indicate how the score will be displayed.

    Keep in mind that although you can select each of the three choices, you might consider using only one. Having three scoring responses could be confusing to the user.

14. In the Background area, indicate the background color of the caption used to display the results, or assign a background image to the caption.

15. Click OK.

    You are returned to the Quiz Manager dialog box.

continues on next page

16. Select the Options tab to open the Quiz Manager options (**Figure 11.33**).

17. Select the pass or fail events from the appropriate pop-down lists.

18. In the Buttons area, enter the buttons' text and the event associated with the buttons.

19. Click OK.

You are returned to the Matching Question dialog box.

Editing objects on a Matching Question slide

When the Matching Question slide appears in the Edit View panel, you can select and edit everything in that slide (**Figure 11.34**). This means you can change the layout, fonts, words, colors, and any other property of the objects in the slide. You can even, as shown in Figure 11.34 add an image to the slide.

Figure 11.33 You can determine the events, button text, and Hint captions in the Options area of the Quiz Manager.

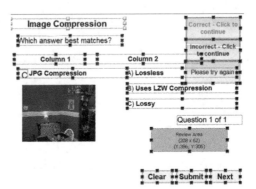

Figure 11.34 You can select and edit everything in a Question slide.

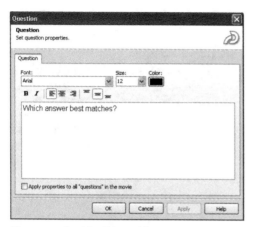

Figure 11.35 Double-click an object on a Question slide to change its properties.

Figure 11.36 The Multiple Choice Question dialog box.

To edit the objects on a Matching Question slide:

1. Double-click any object on the slide to open the relevant properties dialog box (**Figure 11.35**).

2. Make any necessary changes and click OK.

   If you have a number of Matching Question slides, select the "Apply properties to all 'questions' in the movie" check box to apply the change to all objects to which the change applies. This makes life easier for you, because you have to make the change only once to have it applied globally to the movie.

3. Double-click the grey Review Area box that appears on the slide as shown in Figure 11.34.

   The Review dialog box opens.

Creating Multiple-Choice Question slides

Multiple-Choice Question slides are quite robust. In fact, they are used for more than multiple-choice questionnaires. They can be used for single-choice questions, true/false questionnaires, and yes/no questions. This section focuses solely on the use and application of Multiple-Choice Question slides. All of the other options and so on used by these slides match those of the section on Matching Question slides, above.

To create a Multiple-Choice Question slide:

1. Select Insert > Question Slide and, in the Question Types dialog box, select Multiple Choice.

   The Multiple Choice Question dialog box opens (**Figure 11.36**).

continues on next page

CREATING QUESTION SLIDES

2. Enter the answers to the quiz in the order in which they will appear.

3. Select the check box or boxes beside the correct answer or answers of the answers you entered.

4. From the Style pop-down menu, select Multiple Answers.

5. From the Numbering pop-down menu, choose a numbering scheme.

6. Click OK.

   The dialog box closes, the questionnaire appears on the slide, and the correct answers are checked (**Figure 11.37**).

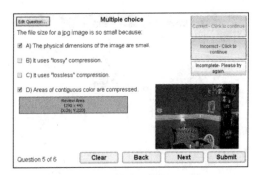

Figure 11.37 A Multiple Choice slide.

✔ Tip

■ You can change the order of the answers by dragging them to different locations on the slide. This will not affect the ordering of the answers in the dialog box. In this way, you can put the correct answer in the same position for each slide in the dialog box but have it appear in a different location in each slide.

To create a single-choice slide:

1. Select Insert > Question Slide and, in the Question Types dialog box, select Multiple Choice.

2. Enter the answers to the quiz in the order in which they will appear.

3. Select the check box beside the correct answer.

4. From the Style pop-down menu, select Single Answer.

5. From the Numbering pop-down menu, choose a numbering scheme.

6. Click OK.

   The dialog box closes, the questionnaire appears on the slide, and the correct answer is checked.

Figure 11.38 The "New short answer question" dialog box.

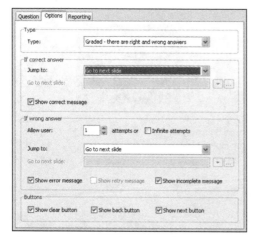

Figure 11.39 The "New short answer question" dialog box's Options tab.

Creating a Short-Answer slide

A Short-Answer slide requires the student to enter a short phrase into a text box as the answer to the question. That answer is then compared to a list of possible answers, and the appropriate Success, Failure, or Hint captions are displayed.

To create a Short-Answer slide:

1. Select Insert > Question Slide and, in the Question Types dialog box, select Short Answer.

   The "New short answer question" dialog box opens (**Figure 11.38**).

2. Enter a slide title and the question.

3. Select "Compare answer with the list below" if the answer is to contain a specific phrase.

4. Enter the correct response in the text input area beneath the "Compare answer with the list below" check box. If there is more than one correct response, click the Add button and enter the next response. If you make a mistake or want to remove a response, select the answer and click the Delete button.

5. If the spelling or phrase must be exact, click "The answer is case-sensitive."

6. Select the Options tab (**Figure 11.39**).

7. From the Type pop-down menu, select Graded or Survey.

8. Indicate the events that occur if the answer is correct or incorrect.

9. Select which buttons will appear on the slide.

10. Select the Reporting tab and enter the eLearning information.

11. Click OK.

    The slide appears in the Edit View panel.

To create a True/False slide:

1. Select Insert > Question Slide and, in the Question Types dialog box, select True/False.

   The New Multiple Choice dialog box opens (**Figure 11.40**).

2. In the Question text input box, enter the statement.

3. From the Style pop-down list, select "True or false."

4. In the Answers area, select whether the statement is true or false.

5. In the Numbering pop-down list, choose a numbering scheme.

6. Click OK.

   The dialog box closes, the question appears on the slide, and the correct answer is checked (**Figure 11.41**).

Figure 11.40 The True/False Question dialog box.

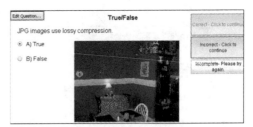

Figure 11.41 A True/False question shows you the correct answer on the slide. It won't be visible when the movie plays.

Figure 11.42 True/False questions can be yes or no questions.

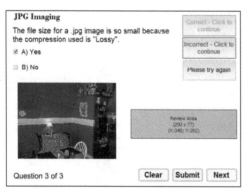

Figure 11.43 A Yes/No Question slide.

To create a Yes/No Question slide:

1. Select Insert > Question Slide and, in the Question Types dialog box, select True/False.

   The True/False Question dialog box opens (**Figure 11.42**).

2. In the Question text input box, enter the statement.

3. From the Style pop-down list, select "Yes or no."

   You will be asked if you want to change the style to "Yes/No."

4. Click OK.

5. In the Answers area, select whether the answer is Yes or No.

6. In the Numbering pop-down list, choose a numbering scheme.

7. Click OK.

   The dialog box closes, the question appears on the slide, and the correct answer is checked (**Figure 11.43**).

Creating Branching in Captivate

Branching is a critical element of any eLearning application. Branching—sometimes referred to as contingency branching—leads the learner through the application based upon his or her responses to questions. In this way, the eLearning application is molded to the individual's learning style. Branching can be added based on correct answers, wrong answers, a choice made by the student, or the student's current knowledge base.

Here are just a few ways in which you can incorporate this critical feature into your movies. Each one includes the ability to include the scoring results, so they can be used individually or cumulatively:

◆ Create a series of question slides and specify paths based upon correct and incorrect answers. This is the obvious method, because the Question slide options make provisions for navigation based on correct and incorrect answers.

◆ Add a path to the click box and have the learner move to other sections of the movie based on clicking inside or outside of the click box. The advantage to using click boxes over Quiz slides is they can be added to existing slides.

◆ Use the Text Entry Box dialog box to set the path based upon a correct or incorrect answer. You can also password-protect them and make them case-sensitive.

◆ Buttons are another method of branching. Buttons are a common navigation technique, and many users will intuitively understand a button's purpose.

◆ Use a variety of techniques in one slide. You could use a series of buttons as a toolbar for a slide and still have click boxes and text entry boxes in the slide as well.

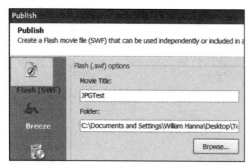

Figure 11.44 Select Flash (SWF) as the publish option for eLearning applications.

Creating PIF Files

Captivate enables you to create a Package Interchange File (PIF), which the SCORM guidelines recommend but do not require.

A PIF file allows for smooth movement of files between systems. This means that to avoid a Tower of Babel scenario of conflicting languages and standards, the contents of the file must be packaged in a similar manner. The standard used is PIF. At the root of the package, there must be an XML file called imsmanifest.xml, which is the manifest file created when you set the manifest options earlier in this chapter. This file, the manifest, describes the learning materials that make up the eLearning application.

To create a PIF file:

1. Open a Captivate movie and select File > Publish.

2. Select the Flash SWF file (**Figure 11.44**).

3. In the Movie Title text entry box, enter a name for the file, but don't add a three-letter extension.

4. In the Folder area, click the Browse button and navigate to the directory to which the ZIP file will be sent.

5. Select the "Zip file" and Export HTML check boxes.

6. Click Publish.

If you open the directory, you will see the ZIP file and a folder named SCORM_support. Inside the ZIP file (**Figure 11.45**) are the SWF file, the HTML file, and the SCORM manifest file, imsmanifest.xml.

Overall, the SCORM_support files/folder are required to facilitate two-way SCORM communication. These files (the ones under the line in Figure 11.45), must be available when playing back a file after publishing to the SCORM standard. The files prefaced by SCORM_support should be placed in the SCORM_support folder. You should be able to open the SCORM_support.js file in Notepad or another text editor unless there is some corruption in the publish process.

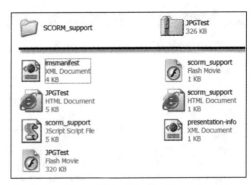

Figure 11.45 The published file. The files in the ZIP file, shown below the line, should all be placed in the SCORM_support folder.

USING MENUBUILDER TO LINK MOVIES

12

MenuBuilder enables you to break complex demonstrations into user-friendly, stand-alone movies that are linked to each other. One of the best ways of dealing with complexity is from a position of simplicity. New Media developers, for example, can break complex projects into manageable chunks that, when combined, form the final project. It is no different in Captivate and MenuBuilder.

Imagine you have to demonstrate how to create a new site in Dreamweaver MX 2004. This requires you to capture a movie that:

◆ Captures the variety of screens, text input, and mouse clicks required to define a new site using Dreamweaver's New Site Wizard.

◆ Demonstrates how to use the Advanced Site Definition feature of Dreamweaver.

The result, due to the linear nature of a Captivate movie, will be a rather long movie that walks the user through the process of defining a new Dreamweaver site. However, it does not enable the user to access precise areas of the movie. To learn how to enter the login information in the Advanced Site Definitions, the user must either click the through the movie using the playback controller or simply sit there and wait for the playback to arrive at the point in the movie they are looking for.

MenuBuilder Overview

MenuBuilder is a rather interesting component that enables you to link a number of movies to each other. In this way, even the most complex demonstrations can be reduced to a series of manageable linked movies that all contribute to the overall goal of the project.

You can use this tool to link movies to other files. For example, use it to create a menu page and link to the movies that demonstrate the individual steps, to URLs, and to other files. What makes MenuBuilder so appealing is you don't have to know Action-Script or other programming languages. And you can export MenuBuilder projects in the following formats:

◆ HTML

◆ Flash SWF

◆ PC EXE

◆ Macintosh projector

◆ Word DOC

Another interesting aspect of MenuBuilder is the fact the menu page does not necessarily have to be constructed in MenuBuilder. If you know how to build a PowerPoint template page, you know how to construct a MenuBuilder menu page.

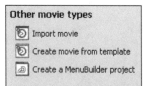

Figure 12.1 The MenuBuilder application is accessed through the Captivate Start page.

Figure 12.2 The MenuBuilder project dialog box lets you choose between using a wizard or a blank project to build the application as well as letting you choose to open an existing project if the project needs to be edited.

To open the MenuBuilder application:

1. Open Captivate and, on the start page's Other movie types area, double-click the MenuBuilder icon (**Figure 12.1**).

   The MenuBuilder Project dialog box opens (**Figure 12.2**).

2. Select Project Wizard if you would like some help in constructing a MenuBuilder project. Blank project if you intend to start with a blank screen and construct the project using elements such as graphics and buttons you have created elsewhere.

3. In the "Open an existing project" area, select the project on which you are currently working or a previously constructed project.

4. Click OK.

✔ Tips

- Don't bother clicking the "Don't show this dialog box again" check box in the MenuBuilder Project dialog box. It is quite useful and provides handy one-click access to your MenuBuilder projects.

- MenuBuilder projects are saved to C:\Program Files\Captivate\ MenuBuilder\Projects.

MENUBUILDER OVERVIEW

Creating a MenuBuilder Project

MenuBuilder approaches the development process from a slightly different angle than Captivate. In fact, MenuBuilder files are called "projects," not "movies."

You can construct projects using templates that come prepackaged with Captivate, using a blank page and constructing the project in MenuBuilder, or through the use of a template you construct.

There are also two methods to constructing a project. MenuBuilder contains a wizard that walks you through the process. If you choose not to use the wizard, you can simply start with a blank page and proceed with constructing the project using files from a variety of sources.

MenuBuilder Template Basics

There are a few things you should be aware of regarding the template wizard used in MenuBuilder:

◆ Templates are stored in a couple of locations. The first is C:\Program Files\ Macromedia\Captivate\MenuBuilder\ Templates, the default storage location for Captivate templates. If you have PowerPoint installed on your computer, the two other locations are C:\Program Files\Microsoft Office\Templates\1033 and C:\Program Files\Microsoft Office\ Templates\Presentation Designs.

◆ PowerPoint templates used in Menu- Builder must be saved, in PowerPoint, as a template and contain the .pot extension.

◆ Templates can be stored anywhere on your computer. Use the template wizard's Browse button to navigate to their location.

◆ The three view buttons beside the Browse button enable you to change the view of the template list to Large Icons, List, or Details views.

◆ When you select a template, a low- resolution preview of the template's design appears in the Preview area of the dialog box.

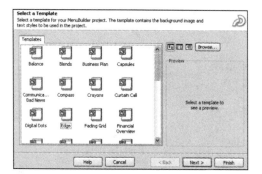

Figure 12.3 PowerPoint templates can be used to create a MenuBuilder project.

Figure 12.4 The text entered will be added to the PowerPoint template.

Figure 12.5 Subitems in a template can be linked to other Captivate movies, web pages, sent to recipients via email, or uploaded to an FTP server.

To use the MenuBuilder Wizard:

1. Launch MenuBuilder and select Project Wizard in the MenuBuilder project dialog box. Click OK.

   The MenuBuilder Wizard launches, and the Select Template window opens (**Figure 12.3**).

2. Select the PowerPoint template to be used for the project.

3. Click Next to open the Add Text Items dialog box (**Figure 12.4**).

4. Enter the text that will appear on the screen. This text is what will be entered into the text area of the template and will follow the style set for the PowerPoint template. Click the New Item button to add a new Level 1 heading, the New Sub Item button to add a Level 2 heading, and the New Sub Item button again to add a Level 3 heading.

5. If the item is to be linked to another file, make a selection in the "Link area" pop-down list (**Figure 12.5**):

   ▲ **Macromedia SWF file** Select to links only to the SWF file.

   ▲ **Web address** Enter the entire address (for example, http://www.macromedia. com).

   ▲ **Email address** Select to add the HTML mailto: function to the file. Enter the recipient's full email address.

   ▲ **FTP address** Enter the entire address (for example, ftp://www.mysite.com).

   ▲ **Newsgroup address** Enter the entire newsgroup address (for example, news://servername.ca).

   ▲ **Browse** Click to link to files other than the ones shown, and navigate to them.

   continues on next page

CREATING A MENUBUILDER PROJECT

6. In the Tooltip field, enter the text that will appear when the mouse rolls over the link.

Note that you don't have to use a tool tip for its obvious purpose. It can also be used as an Alt tag.

7. Click the Next button.

The Project Options dialog box opens (**Figure 12.7**).

8. Enter a name for the project.

This name will appear in the top of the Project dialog box and in the resulting HTML file.

9. If the file is destined for an EXE file on a PC, select the ICO file that will be used for the project's icon.

10. In the Background pop-down list, select a border style.

11. In the transparency pop-down list, select the amount of transparency to be applied to the background of the template file.

12. Set the screen size to either "Full screen" or Custom.

13. Click Finish.

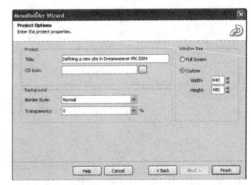

Figure 12.7 The MenuBuilder Project Options allow you to name the project and even add a custom icon to the MenuBuilder output.

Mac users, note that in step 9, you don't really need to create an ICO file.

To add an icon to your Macintosh projector:

1. On a Mac, create the graphic to be used for the icon and copy the bitmap to the clipboard.

2. Select the projector on the Macintosh desktop and select File > Get Info.
   The Info dialog box opens.

3. Single-click the file's icon to select it.

4. Select File > Paste.
   The icon on the clipboard replaces the one shown in the Info dialog box.

5. Close the dialog box.
   The file has the new icon.

To open an existing project:

1. Open MenuBuilder.
   The MenuBuilder wizard opens.

2. Click Cancel.

3. Click the Open button on the Main toolbar or select File > Open.

4. Double-click the file you want to open.

A Few Words About Linking

When you link to a Captivate movie, MenuBuilder links to the movie's HTML file, not the actual SWF. Keep this in mind when you are publishing Captivate movies. The HTML file, published with the movie's SWF file, contains the information necessary to play the movie accurately. Here's a typical Captivate HTML file:

```
<TITLE>BasicWizard</TITLE>
<meta name=keywords content="Captivate 5.0">
<HTML>
<BODY onLoad="window.document.Captivate.focus();"><center><OBJECT CLASSID=
→"clsid:D27CDB6E-AE6D-11cf-96B8-444553540000" WIDTH="578" HEIGHT="572" CODEBASE=
→"http://active.macromedia.com/flash5/cabs/swflash.cab#version=5,0,0,0" id=Captivate>
<PARAM NAME=movie VALUE="Captivate.swf">
<PARAM NAME=play VALUE=true>
<PARAM NAME=loop VALUE=0>
<PARAM NAME=quality VALUE=high>
<EMBED NAME=Captivate SRC="Captivate.swf" WIDTH=578 HEIGHT=572 loop=0 quality=high
→TYPE="application/x-shockwave-flash" PLUGINSPAGE="http://www.macromedia.com/
→shockwave/download/index.cgi?P1_Prod_Version=ShockwaveFlash" swLiveConnect=true>
</EMBED>
</OBJECT>
</center>
</BODY></HTML>
```

If you plan to place the SWF in a Web page, be sure to copy and paste this information into the HTML code. You can do this easily by opening the movie in the Edit View panel, selecting View > HTML Code, and clicking the Copy Code to Clipboard button in the HTML Required for Movie dialog box.

A Few Words About Linking *continued*

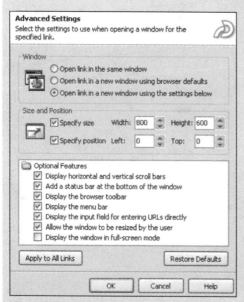

Figure 12.6 The Advanced Settings dialog box let you decide how web pages are displayed when the link is clicked.

If you create a link to a URL or other HTML file, the Advanced Settings button becomes active. Click it, and the Advanced Settings dialog box opens (**Figure 12.6**).

Essentially, the choices enable you to determine how the link will be displayed in the browser. If you choose to open the link in a new browser window, the Optional Features area at the bottom of the dialog box becomes active. You make your choices and then determine whether the choices will apply to all of the links in the MenuBuilder page (click the Apply to All Links button) or just to the link chosen (in this case, ignore the Apply to All Links button) and click OK.

You can also customize how the new browser window opens. If you select "Open link in a new window using the settings below," the Optional Features area become active.

The "Save file with project" check box enables you to save the linked files with the project file. Thus, when you export the MenuBuilder project, any linked Captivate movies will be exported at the same time.

Having said that, if the project is destined for Web playback, don't select the "Save files with project" check box. The link will reflect the path on your computer and will result in inconsistent Web playback. Instead make the link "relative," save the MenuBuilder SWF file to the same folder as the files to which you are linking.

Editing a MenuBuilder Project

After the linking information is established and the MenuBuilder project is created, you can still make changes to the document. These changes would include the following:

◆ Changing the text properties

◆ Changing and editing the text style

◆ Spell-checking the project

◆ Indenting subheadings

◆ Changing the link information

◆ Adding text to the document

◆ Adding content such as images to the document

To change the text properties:

1. Open a MenuBuilder project.

2. Double-click the text block requiring the font change, or right-click the text block and select Properties from the context menu.

   The Text Properties dialog box opens (**Figure 12.8**).

3. In the Font pop-down list, select the new font.

4. Select a point size from the pop-down list of preset sizes or enter a new size into the text input box.

5. If the text needs to be changed, select it in the Text area and enter the replacement text.

6. To change the font color, click the Color Chip in the Normal Color area and select a new color from the color picker that appears.

Figure 12.8 The text properties can be changed.

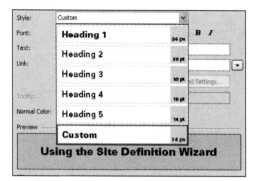

Figure 12.9 You can apply the styles from the PowerPoint template through the Styles pop down.

7. To change the hover color (the color of the text that appears when the mouse rolls over the text), click the Color Chip beside the Hover Color area and pick a new color from the color picker that appears.

8. Click OK.

✔ Tip

■ The hover color becomes active only if you add a link to the text. In the Text Properties box, roll over the text in the Preview area, and the words will change to the hover color chosen.

To change the text style:

1. Open the Text Properties dialog box.

2. In the Style pop-down list, choose a new style or select Custom to create a new style (**Figure 12.9**).

3. Click OK.

✔ Tips

■ The text styles in MenuBuilder are assigned when the PowerPoint template is created in PowerPoint. Changing the style in MenuBuilder will not result in a corresponding style change in PowerPoint.

■ If you change the font, size, and color information, click the "Apply changes to all items" button to apply the style change to all items in the project that are assigned the style.

EDITING A MENUBUILDER PROJECT

283

To edit a text style:

1. Select Tools > Format Styles.

   The Format Styles dialog box opens
   (**Figure 12.10**)

2. In the Styles area, select the style to be
   changed.

3. Select a font, style, and point size.

4. Click OK to accept the changes and
   apply them to the project.

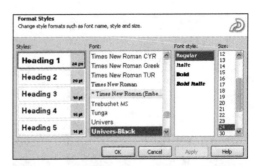

Figure 12.10 The text styles can be edited using the
Format Styles dialog box.

To spell-check a MenuBuilder project:

1. Select Tools > Spelling and Grammar or
   press the F7 key.

   MenuBuilder spellchecks the document.
   If there is an error, you will be presented
   with the Spelling dialog box (**Figure 12.11**),
   and the misspelled word will be red.

2. Select the correct word from the suggestions and click the Change button.

   The change is made, and dialog box
   informs you of this fact.

Figure 12.11 MenuBuilder
contains a Spell Check
feature.

To indent subheadings:

1. Open a MenuBuilder project and select
   the subheading to be indented.

2. Select Edit > Increase Indent.
   The selection will move to the right.

✔ Tip

- To outdent a subheading, if you select
  Edit > Decrease Indent, the selected text
  will move to the left.

To change the link information:

1. Open the Text Properties dialog box.

2. In the Link area, click the down arrow
   button.

3. Make your changes.

4. Click OK.

Figure 12.12 Text can be added to the MenuBuilder project through the New text dialog box.

To add text to a document:

1. Open a MenuBuilder project.

2. Click the text button on the Main toolbar, and press Control-T or select Insert > Text or press Control-T.

   The New text dialog box opens (**Figure 12.12**).

3. In the Style pop-down, choose a style or select Custom to create a new style.

4. In the Font area, select a font and point size.

5. Single-click the Text field and enter the text to be added to the project.

6. Assign any links to the new text.

7. Add a tool tip, if needed.

8. Assign a font and a hover color.

9. Click OK.

✔ Tip

■ Clicking OK does not lock the text in place. If you need to change a property of the text just entered, double-click the text block to open the Edit Text dialog box.

To add an image to a MenuBuilder project:

1. Open the project in which the image will be inserted.

2. Click the Image button on the Main toolbar, select Insert > Image, or press Control-I.

   The Open dialog box opens.

3. Navigate to the folder containing the image, open the folder, select the image, and click the Open button. Alternatively, double-click the desired image.

   The New image dialog box opens (**Figure 12.13**).

4. If desired, in the Link area, assign a link to the image.

5. If desired, in the "Tool tip" area, assign a tool tip.

6. Add any needed transparency options to the image.

7. Click OK.

   The image appears on the project page.

8. Resize the image and drag it into its final position (**Figure 12.14**).

9. To embed the image in the background, select the image and select Edit > Merge into Background.

✔ Tips

- Here's an interesting little trick. You don't have to use the buttons or dialog boxes to add an image to your project. Simply drag and drop the image file onto the project's interface, and the image will appear in the project. From there, all you have to do is to resize the image and set the image properties. This technique also works with other content that can be placed in a project.

Figure 12.13 Images can be added to MenuBuilder projects.

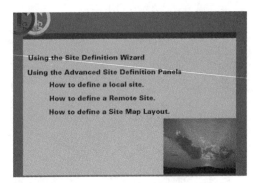

Figure 12.14 The image is resized and placed in the MenuBuilder application.

- If you make a mistake, you can correct it by simply double-clicking the image in the document to open the Image Properties dialog box.

EDITING A MENUBUILDER PROJECT

Adding Interactivity to MenuBuilder Projects

Many developers prefer to build their interfaces in applications such as Adobe Photoshop or Macromedia Fireworks MX. The great thing about this is you have full control over the look and feel of the interface. From there, the file is inevitably converted to a bitmap and is either placed into a blank project or used to replace the image in a template.

In either situation, the image contains no interactivity. You can add this feature by inserting click boxes into the MenuBuilder project. Keep in mind that the purpose of a MenuBuilder project is to construct a navigation interface to other Captivate movies, Web pages, and so on. This is why such common items as captions and text input boxes aren't available in MenuBuilder.

Click boxes are interactive boxes that don't contain images. Still, they "float" on top of everything and can be used for text and images to provide the user with a visual clue that the area is "hot."

ADDING INTERACTIVITY

To add a click box:

1. Open a MenuBuilder project and click the Clickbox button on the Main toolbar, select Insert > Clickbox, or press Control-T.
   The "New click box" dialog box opens (**Figure 12.15**).

2. In the Link pop-down list, select a value or enter the link information into the text entry box.

3. If needed, add a tool tip.

4. Click OK.
   The dialog box closes, and you are returned to the project. The click box appears on the screen.

5. If the click box is in the wrong place, single-click the click box and drag it into its final position.

6. If the click box needs to be resized, single-click it and drag a handle inward or outward to resize the click box.

7. To edit the click box's properties, double-click the click box and, in the Clickbox Properties dialog box that opens, make your change and click OK.

✔ Tips

■ A click box actually has the word "Clickbox" inside its shape. The word is there to give you, the developer, a visual clue that you have added an element to your project. It will not appear when the final project is published.

■ Click boxes in MenuBuilder don't permit the use of Success, Failure, or Hint captions.

Figure 12.15 The New clickbox dialog box is quite different from its Captivate counterpart.

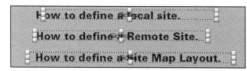

Figure 12.16 Click boxes can be aligned with each other.

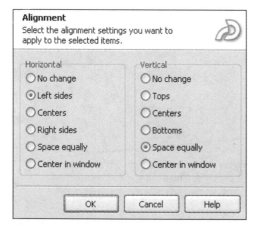

Figure 12.17 The Alignment dialog box allows you to determine how the selected objects will align with each other.

To align multiple click boxes:

1. Open a MenuBuilder project and select the click boxes to be aligned (**Figure 12.16**).

2. Select Edit > Align.

   The Alignment dialog box opens.

3. Set the horizontal alignment. Your choices, as shown in **Figure 12.17**, are:

   ▲ **No change** Select if the horizontal position of the selections will not change.

   ▲ **Left sides** Aligns boxes on their left edges.

   ▲ **Centers** Aligns boxes using their center points.

   ▲ **Right sides** Aligns boxes on their right edges.

   ▲ **Space equally** Spaces boxes equally on the horizontal plane.

   ▲ **Center in window** Aligns boxes horizontally in the Preview window.

4. Set the vertical alignment. Your choices are:

   ▲ **No change** Select if the vertical position of the selections will not change.

   ▲ **Tops** Aligns boxes on their top edges.

   ▲ **Centers** Aligns boxes using their center points.

   ▲ **Bottoms** Aligns boxes on their bottom edges.

   ▲ **Space equally** Spaces boxes equally on the vertical plane.

   ▲ **Center in window** Aligns boxes horizontally in the Preview window.

5. Click OK.

   The click boxes align according to your choices.

ADDING INTERACTIVITY

Working with the MenuBuilder Options

The MenuBuilder Project options, in many respects, can be regarded as preferences you set for the document rather than the application. The ability to change the options means you can perform such tasks as:

- Changing a project's name

- Assigning an icon to a project

- Assigning a new background image to a project

- Setting the background image transparency

- Setting the window size for the final project

You can also add audio to the project and introduce audible effects such as mouse clicks and so on to the project. Finally, you can change the MenuBuilder preferences to make global changes to the application.

To change a project's options:

1. Open a MenuBuilder project and, in the Projects Tasks area, click View Project Information or select Options > Project Options.

   The Project Options dialog box opens (**Figure 12.18**).

2. To change the project's name, select the text in the Title field and enter a new name.

   Note that renaming a project does not rename the file. The name you enter will appear as the window name when the file opens on your desktop.

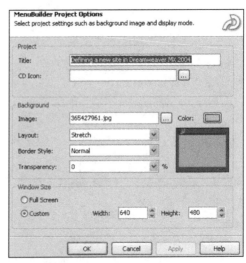

Figure 12.18 The Project Options dialog box allows you to make global changes to the project.

3. To change the project icon from the generic MenuBuilder icon to a custom icon, click the Browse button and navigate to the folder containing the icon image you want to use.

   Icons are located in the C:\Program Files\Captivate\MenuBuilder\Icons folder. You can add icons to projects destined for use as a PC EXE file only. Mac users can add icons to their projectors using the Tip presented earlier in this chapter.

   MenuBuilder does not include a set of icons. Icons must have the .ico extension and are created using PC imaging software that allows for the export of the ICO format. You can also download icons from a variety of sources on the Internet.

4. To add or change a background image, click the Browse button and navigate to the folder containing the desired image.

5. To change the background color of the project, click the Color Chip, select your color in the color picker that opens, and click OK.

   If your image fills the background, you won't see the background color. If you use a background image that is smaller than the project's dimensions or apply transparency to the background image, the background color will be visible.

   If you are finding it hard to read any text you may add to a MenuBuilder project because it is sitting on an "odd" background color, change the background color to white in the Project Options dialog box.

continues on next page

WORKING WITH THE MENUBUILDER OPTIONS

6. Use the Layout pop-down menu to determine the placement of the background image:

▲ **Stretch** Forces the image to fit the project area and, most likely, distorts the image.

▲ **Center** Places the image in the center of the project window.

▲ **Tile** Copies of the background image fill the project window.

7. To add a border to the background image, select a border style from the Border pop-down menu.

Note that selecting Normal is the same as choosing not to add a border. If you need to control the border width and style, consider creating the background image with a border in Fireworks MX 2004 using a LiveEffect (**Figure 12.19**) or apply a Photoshop filter to the image in Adobe Photoshop.

8. To add transparency to your background image, use the Transparency pop-down slider.

The values range from 0% (no transparency) to 100% (the image becomes invisible).

9. In the Window Size area, select a window size for the project.

If you want the project to fill the screen when viewed, select Full Screen. Otherwise, select Custom and enter the appropriate height and width values.

10. Click OK.

The options are applied to the project.

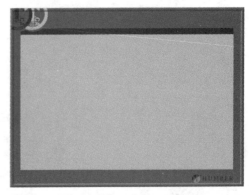

Figure 12.19 The LiveEffects in Fireworks MX 2004 contain a robust collection of special effects that can be applied to images.

✔ Tips

■ If you are using a PowerPoint template, you may be surprised to discover you actually have a background image. This file is the background image applied to the PowerPoint template when the template was created. Changing a template's background image in MenuBuilder does not affect the original PowerPoint template.

■ Selecting Full Screen may introduce distortion to your project, or the screen may appear to be fuzzy as the resolution reduces to fit the screen size. Test this option carefully on a variety of machines or screen resolutions prior to publishing the project. If you are reducing the window size using the Custom area, be sure to apply the same reduction percentage to both the width and the height values for the window. Failure to do so will distort the project.

WORKING WITH THE MENUBUILDER OPTIONS

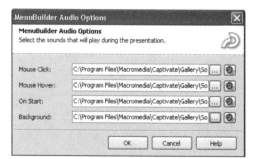

Figure 12.20 Audio can be added to MenuBuilder projects.

To add audio to a MenuBuilder project:

1. Open a MenuBuilder project and, from the Task area, select "Change audio settings." Alternatively, click the Audio button on the Main toolbar or select Options > Audio Options.

   The MenuBuilder Audio Options dialog box opens (**Figure 12.20**).

2. To add a mouse click sound, click the Browse button and navigate to the folder containing the sound to be used.

3. To add a mouse hover or rollover sound, click the Browse button and navigate to the folder containing the sound to be used.

4. To add a sound that starts playing when the project is launched, click the Browse button and navigate to the folder containing the sound to be used.

5. To add a sound that plays in the background while the project is playing, click the Browse button and navigate to the folder containing the sound to be used.

6. Click the OK button to accept the changes.

✔ Tips

- MenuBuilder accepts only WAV or MP3 files.

- If you need a couple of sound effects, use the ones found in the Captivate gallery Sound folder, located at C:\Program Files\Captivate\Gallery\Sound.

- You can preview your selected sounds by clicking the Play button—it looks like a speaker—located next to the Browse button in the Audio Options dialog box.

WORKING WITH THE MENUBUILDER OPTIONS

To set the MenuBuilder preferences:

1. Open a MenuBuilder project and select Options > Preferences.

   The Preferences dialog box opens (**Figure 12.21**).

2. Select the Preferences tab and choose the following settings:

   ▲ **Show Grid** Select to show a grid in the project window. It is ideal for aligning and spacing objects. The grid does not appear when the project is published.

   ▲ **Snap to Grid** Select to snap text and images to the grid.

   ▲ **Grid Size** Use the Up and Down arrows to change the size of the squares in the grid. The size is measured in pixels, and the sizes range from grid squares that are 2 pixels square to 100 pixels square. You can also enter your own values.

   ▲ **Project** Select to save projects automatically without being notified.

   ▲ **Desktop** Select to always open the most recent version of the project.

   ▲ Change the height and width of the new project.

   ▲ **Startup dialog** Select to have MenuBuilder ask you which file to open rather than opening the most recent project.

   ▲ **Delete confirmation** Select to have MenuBuilder open a confirmation dialog box each time you delete an object in the project.

   ▲ **Merge confirmation** Select to have MenuBuilder open a confirmation dialog box for all merge actions you may perform.

   ▲ **Link import confirmation** Select to have MenuBuilder open a confirmation dialog box for all link import actions.

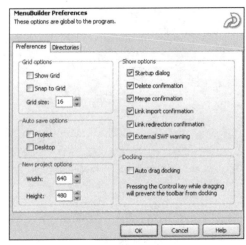

Figure 12.21 There is a lot of flexibility available to you in the MenuBuilder Preferences dialog box.

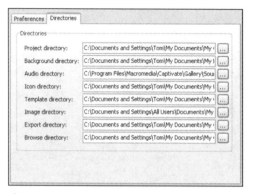

Figure 12.22 The Directories window in the MenuBuilder Preferences lets you assign the locations for many of the files used in the project.

▲ **Link redirection confirmation** Select to have MenuBuilder open a confirmation dialog box for all link changes.

▲ **External SWF warning** Select to have MenuBuilder open a confirmation dialog box for linking to a SWF file.

▲ **Auto drag docking** Select to allow the toolbar to be left-clicked and dragged to a new location. If you hold down the Control key while you drag, the toolbar will float above the project when you release the mouse.

3. Select the Directories tab (**Figure 12.22**) and set the following options:

▲ **Project Directory** Select the folder to be used to hold all MenuBuilder projects. The content of this folder is what appears in the initial MenuBuilder Projects list. The default directory is C:\Program Files\Captivate\ MenuBuilder\Projects.

▲ **Background directory** Select the folder to be used to hold all of the background images for your projects. The default directory is C:\Program Files\ Captivate\MenuBuilder\Backgrounds.

▲ **Audio directory** Select the folder to be used to hold all of the audio files for your projects. The default directory is C:\Program Files\Captivate\ MenuBuilder\Audio.

▲ **Icon directory** Select the folder to be used to hold all of the icon files (with .ico extensions) for your projects. The default directory is C:\Program Files\Captivate\MenuBuilder\Icons.

▲ **Template directory** Select the folder to be used to hold MenuBuilder templates used in your projects. The default directory is C:\Program Files\ Captivate\MenuBuilder\Templates.

continues on next page

WORKING WITH THE MENUBUILDER OPTIONS

▲ **Image directory** Select the folder to be used to hold all of the image files for your projects. The default directory is C:\Program Files\Captivate\ MenuBuilder\Images.

▲ **Export directory** Select the folder to which exported MenuBuilder projects are saved. The default directory is C:\Program Files\Captivate\ MenuBuilder\Exports.

▲ **Browse directory** Select the folder to be used to hold all your saved MenuBuilder projects. The default directory is C:\Program Files\ Captivate\Projects.

4. Click OK.

The preferences close and MenuBuilder accepts them.

✔ Tip

■ You change the default directories by clicking the Browse button and navigating to the folder to be used. Keep in mind any change made will be applied to all projects created in MenuBuilder, not only the currently open project.

Exporting MenuBuilder Projects

You can export projects in a variety of ways for quite a few different uses, ranging from browser-based presentations to running the presentation from a CD or the computer's desktop. Files can be exported in the following formats:

- **Flash** Use to create an SWF used for Web playback.

- **EXE** Use for projects destined for CD or desktop playback.

- **HTML** Use to export projects destined for the Web.

- **Word files** Use for speaker notes and handouts.

- **Mac** Use to create a Flash projector for Macintosh playback.

The interesting aspect of exporting a project is that you can export the file in the format that best meets user needs. In other words, a single project can be exported in each format. Thus, the user can view the presentation through a browser that doesn't have a Flash plug-in (HTML) or play the presentation from the desktop (EXE or Mac) and follow along using the notes (Word). Therefore, it makes sense that, prior to exporting your project, you consider how the user will access the project and that you export it using the format or formats best-suited to the user's needs.

To export a project as a Flash file:

1. Open a MenuBuilder project and click the Export button on the Main toolbar. Alternatively, click "Export this project" in the Tasks area or select File > Export.

2. If the file hasn't been saved, the Save As dialog box will open. Name the file and determine whether it will be saved as either a MenuBuilder project (.mgp file) or as a MenuBuilder Template (.mgt file). Click Save.

   The Export Options dialog box opens (**Figure 12.23**).

3. Select Flash Movie and click Next. The next panel to open will ask you to name the file and choose its location.

4. Select "Generate Autorun file for CD distribution" only if the file will be played from a CD.

5. To launch the Flash Player after the file has been exported, select "View project after export."

6. Click Finish.

   The SWF file is exported.

Figure 12.23 The Export Options allow you to export the project in a number of formats ranging from a Flash Movie to a platform-specific executable.

EXPORTING MENUBUILDER PROJECTS

Flash "Gotchas"

There are a couple of things to be aware of when planning to export a Flash SWF file.

The first is the fact the SWF file does not support font embedding. This means if the user doesn't have the font used in your project on his or her machine, the font will be substituted at runtime. The only workaround to this is to design your MenuBuilder project using the usual Web and system fonts such as Arial, Times New Roman, and so on. If fonts are critical, then create the interface, including any text, in an imaging application and export the file as a flattened JPG image. This file can then be inserted in the MenuBuilder project as a background image, and any rollovers or navigation can be done through the addition of click boxes.

The second thing to note is that all links to other Captivate movies called by the MenuBuilder SWF file should be relative links to the HTML file such as BasicWizard.html. The implication here is that all SWF and HTML files used in the project should reside in the same directory on your Web site. The only link you control is the one established when the MenuBuilder SWF file is placed into a Web page.

Finally, if you are placing the Captivate SWF files that linked to a MenuBuilder project (not the MenuBuilder SWF) in an HTML page other than the one that Captivate generated, be sure to copy and paste the header information from the Captivate HTML file into the file to be used to hold the SWF. If you don't, the file will be distorted on playback. The header information contains the sizing information the browser needs to play the SWF.

To export a project as an EXE:

1. Open a MenuBuilder project and click the Export button on the Main Toolbar to open the export options. Double-click the EXE icon to move to the next screen in the Export Options dialog box.

2. Enter a filename for the project.

3. In the Directory field, enter the path to the saved file or click the Browse button to navigate to the desired folder.

4. Select "Generate Autorun file for CD distribution" only if the file will be played from a CD.

5. To launch the EXE file after it has been exported, select "View project after export."

6. Click Finish.

   The EXE file is created.

To export a project as an HTML file:

1. Open a MenuBuilder project and click the Export button on the Main Toolbar to open the export options. Double-click the HTML icon to move to the next screen in the Export Options dialog box.

2. Enter a filename for the project.

3. In the Directory field, enter the path to the saved file or click the Browse button to navigate to the desired folder.

4. Select "Generate Autorun file for CD distribution" only if the file will be played from a CD.

5. To launch the file in a browser after the file has been exported, select "View project after export."

6. Click Finish.

   The HTML file is created.

EXPORTING MENUBUILDER PROJECTS

To export a project as a Word file:

1. Open a MenuBuilder project and click the Export button on the Main Toolbar to open the export options. Double-click the Word icon to move to the next screen in the Export Options dialog box.

2. Enter a name for the project.

3. In the Directory field, enter the path to the saved file or click the Browse button to navigate to the desired folder.

   The "Generate Autorun file for CD distribution" option will be grayed out for obvious reasons.

4. To launch the file in Word after the file has been exported, select "View project after export."

5. Click Finish.

   The DOC file is created.

To export a project for Macintosh playback:

1. Open a MenuBuilder project and click the Export button on the Main Toolbar to open the export options. Double-click the Mac icon to move to the next screen in the Export Options dialog box.

2. Enter a filename for the project.

3. In the Directory field, enter the path to the saved file or click the Browse button to navigate to the desired folder.

   The "Generate Autorun file for CD distribution" and "View project after export" options will be grayed out for obvious reasons.

4. Click Finish.

   The Mac projector file is created.

✔ **Tip**

■ A Mac projector is nothing more than a Flash EXE file that can be played only on a Macintosh desktop or from a Macintosh-formatted CD.

A Word About Word Files

When a project is exported as a Word file, MenuBuilder will create a DOC file that contains a graphic of the project and, of course, which is not interactive.

What it will contain, though, is a table showing Type, Text/Image, Link, and Tooltip Column heads (**Figure 12.24**). You can delete this table from the document and add an area for notes and so on.

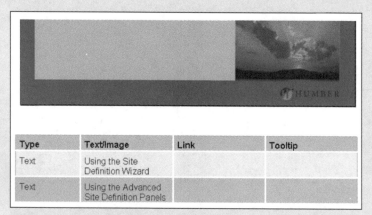

Type	Text/Image	Link	Tooltip
Text	Using the Site Definition Wizard		
Text	Using the Advanced Site Definition Panels		

Figure 12.24 The MenuBuilder project has been exported as a Microsoft Word document.

An HTML "Gotcha"

When you export a MenuBuilder project as an HTML file, there is a rather interesting "gotcha" you should keep in mind.

Everything that sits above the background image is converted to a layer. If, for example, you have a click box sitting on top of some text you added to the project, the click box and text will be incorporated into a layer on the HTML page. Keep this in mind if your site is being driven by an external Cascading Style Sheet (CSS). If you don't use CSS, be aware that certain older browsers will not render the layers properly.

The only solution is to edit the HTML or XHTML code to conform to your styles. In non-CSS sites, you might consider converting the layers to tables. This is a feature found in Dreamweaver MX 2004.

EXPORTING MOVIES TO A VARIETY OF MEDIA

Your movies can be used in a variety of media, from the Web to handheld Pocket PC devices. Captivate movies can be displayed on desktop computers, including those using the Linux operating system (OS), just as easily as they can be added to a PowerPoint presentation, and they can even be turned into stand-alone applications requiring no special software to play.

Captivate movies can be exported in a number of formats, including:

◆ Flash SWF files

◆ Email attachments

◆ PC EXE files

◆ Mac projectors

◆ Linux EXE files

◆ Flash FLA files

◆ Microsoft Word documents

You can also upload Captivate movies to the Web using FTP.

These formats permit your movies to be viewed on:

◆ PC, Mac, and Linux OS computers (desktop and kiosk)

◆ PDAs using Windows CE or Windows Mobile for Pocket PC

◆ PDAs using the Palm OS 4 and 5

Exporting Flash Files

If there is a common thread running through this book, it is the intimate relationship between Captivate and Flash MX 2004 or Flash MX Professional 2004. This isn't due to Macromedia acquiring the Captivate technology and looking to repurpose it. It is simply this: The Flash Player is one of the most ubiquitous pieces of software in the computing field.

In 2003, Macromedia released Flash Player 7, and as of the writing of this book, only eight months later, Macromedia claims that it is installed on roughly 60 percent of all computers worldwide. According to Kevin Lynch, executive vice president and chief software architect at Macromedia, that number is expected to be close to 85 percent by the time you are reading this book. Flash Player 6, which Captivate uses, is installed on just under 95 percent of all computers worldwide. It makes sense, therefore, to utilize a technology with such massive penetration into the market.

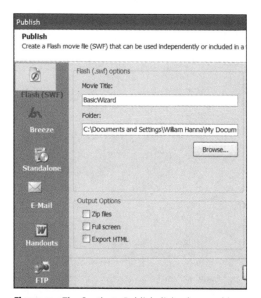

Figure 13.1 The Captivate Publish dialog box enables you to publish your movies in a variety of formats.

Figure 13.2 The SWF Publish options.

To export a movie as a Flash SWF file:

1. Open a Captivate movie, and select File > Publish or press Shift-Control-P.

   The Publish dialog box opens (**Figure 13.1**). Note that you can export your file from both the Edit View and Storyboard View panels.

2. Select Flash (SWF) from the list on the left side of the dialog box.

   The Flash (.swf) options dialog box opens (**Figure 13.2**).

3. Enter a name for the file (do not include the .swf extension at the end of the name).

4. Click the Browse button, and navigate to and open the folder to which the SWF file will be saved.

5. Select Full Screen if the file is to play in full screen mode.

6. Select Export HTML if the file is to be included in a Web page.

7. Select "View in browser after export" to open your browser and test the file locally.

8. Select "Zip files" if you will be sending the file to a colleague via email or download.

9. Click Finish.

   A "generating" progress bar appears, showing you the frame-by-frame progress of the conversion process. When it finishes, the dialog box closes and you are returned to Captivate.

✔ Tip

- If you are using Dreamweaver as your Web page editor, you don't need to select the HTML option. When a SWF file is inserted into a Dreamweaver page, the Object and Embed tags are added to the Dreamweaver document automatically.

Using Email to Deliver Your Movies

If there is an unacknowledged killer app on the Web, it has to be email. You can send your movie, as an email attachment, right out of the application. The formats that can be sent include EXE, SWF, HQX (a binary compression format recognized by the Mac), and Linux EXE.

To send a movie via email:

1. Open a movie in Captivate and select File > Publish.

   The Publish dialog box opens.

2. Click the E-Mail button.

   The "eMail options" dialog box opens (**Figure 13.3**).

3. If you want to rename the file, enter a new name in the Movie Title text entry box.

4. In the "File type" pop-down menu, select the file type to be sent:

   ▲ **Project Files** Select to send the file to another Captivate developer.

   ▲ **SWF File** Select to email the SWF file.

   ▲ **Windows executable** Select if you are sending the file to a PC user.

   ▲ **Macintosh executable file** Select if you are sending the file to a Macintosh user.

   ▲ **Linux executable file** Select if you are sending the file to a Linux user.

5. Select "Zip files" to compress the file format selected above. The user will need to have WinZip (Windows only) or StuffIt Expander (Mac and PC versions are available) to open the file.

6. Click the Publish button.

   Your email application opens. There is a message in the body of the email, and the file is attached (**Figure 13.4**). All you need to do is enter the email address.

Figure 13.3 You can email a SWF file or a stand-alone projector.

Figure 13.4 An email plus the attached movie.

✔ Tip

■ Depending upon the file type you choose in step 4, the output options will change. For example, if you select Project Files, the only output option is "ZIP files." If you choose to send a SWF, the "ZIP files," "Export HTML," and "Full screen" options are available.

Figure 13.5 Executables are stand-alone, platform-specific files.

Creating Projectors

If you are a Macromedia Director user, you are quite familiar with creating projectors. Essentially, a *projector* is a platform-specific executable file requiring nothing more than a double-click to start the movie. The term "platform-specific" is deliberate. A Mac projector can't be played on a PC or a Linux machine, a PC projector can't be played on a Mac or a Linux machine, and a Linux projector won't work on a Windows or Macintosh computer.

If you are distributing your movie on a CD, creating a projector would be the preferred option. For example, in situations requiring a cross-platform CD you can create the Mac and the PC projectors, and include them in the part of the CD read by the platform.

To create a PC EXE file:

1. Open a Captivate Movie and select File > Publish.

   The Publish dialog box opens.

2. Select Standalone from the list on the left side of the dialog box.

   The "Standalone options" dialog box opens (**Figure 13.5**).

3. Name the file and indicate where it will be located.

4. In the "File type" pop-down list, select "Windows executable."

5. In the Output Options area, indicate if the file is to be compressed as a ZIP file, whether the EXE will play using the full screen, and whether you want to have the movie autorun from a CD.

6. Click the Publish button.

   The Publish Progress dialog box appears.

continues on next page

7. When the conversion is finished, click the window's Close button (the X in the corner).

   Now you can add the EXE file (**Figure 13.6**), HTML and Autorun files to a CD or put it to other uses.

To create a Macintosh projector:

1. Open a Captivate movie and select File > Publish.

   The Publish dialog box opens.

2. Select Standalone from the list on the left side of the dialog box.

   The "Standalone options" dialog box opens.

3. Name the file and indicate where it will be located.

4. In the "File type" pop-down list, select "Macintosh executable file."

5. In the Output Options area, indicate if the file is to be compressed as a ZIP file, whether the EXE will play using the full screen, and whether you want to have the movie autorun from a CD.

6. Click the Publish button. The Publish Progress dialog box appears, showing you the progress of the conversion.

7. When the conversion is finished, click the window's Close button.

   Now you can add the EXE file (**Figure 13.7**) to a CD or put it to other uses.

✔ Tips

- The HQX file is a compressed version of the projector. Compressing it as a ZIP file is nice, but not necessary.

- You will need to open the .ZIP file on the Macintosh using an application such as StuffIt Expander before you can play it.

Figure 13.6 The icon for a PC EXE file and its autorun file.

Figure 13.7 The HQX file created for a Macintosh.

Figure 13.8 Flash MX 2004 can also create Windows and Macintosh projectors.

Figure 13.9 A Linux projector.

- Though the Mac projector displays a Flash icon, a Macintosh Flash projector can be played only on the Macintosh platform. If you are familiar with Flash, you know you can create either a Macintosh or PC projector using Flash's Publish Settings dialog box (**Figure 13.8**).

To create a Linux projector:

1. Open a Captivate Movie and select File > Publish.

   The Publish dialog box opens.

2. Select Standalone from the list on the left side of the dialog box.

   The "Standalone options" dialog box opens.

3. Name the file and indicate where it will be located.

4. In the "File type" pop-down list, select "Linux executable file."

5. In the Output Options area, indicate if the file is to be compressed as a ZIP file, whether the EXE will play using the full screen, and whether you want to have the movie autorun from a CD.

6. Click the Publish button.

   You are shown the progress of the conversion.

7. When the conversion is finished, click the window's Close button.

   Now you can add the EXE file (**Figure 13.9**) to a CD or put it to other uses.

Publishing Movies to a Web Site

Captivate movies can be uploaded directly to a Web site using the application's FTP feature. You can use this handy feature for such purposes as:

◆ Client approval through a client site

◆ Content that can change rapidly

◆ Remote testing of the page using a browser

This isn't to suggest that you should abandon such FTP applications as WS_FTP LE or WS_FTP Pro. An FTP capability is also built into Dreamweaver MX, and developers can choose whether to let Captivate do the upload or to use their third-party software.

To publish your movie via FTP:

1. Open a Captivate Movie and select File > Publish.
   The Publish dialog box opens.

2. Select FTP from the list on the left side of the dialog box.
   The "FTP options" dialog box opens (**Figure 13.10**).

3. Enter a name for the file.

4. Enter the server name. If you are unsure of this step, contact your Internet Service Provider (ISP).

5. Enter the name of the directory on the server where the files will be placed.

6. Enter your login name for the FTP site.

7. Enter the password used for access to the FTP site.

8. Enter the port number; the standard default port is 21. If you are unsure of what to enter, contact your network administrator or ISP.

Figure 13.10 You can export files to a Web server using FTP.

9. Click the Test Settings button.

Captivate attempts to connect to your server using the information you entered. You are notified if the connection was successful or not. If it wasn't successful, review your entries carefully to ensure there are no spelling errors, especially in situations where the username and password are case-sensitive. Also check with your ISP to ensure you are using the correct port number.

If you are a Dreamweaver MX 2004 user, you are familiar with this dialog box. The great thing about testing the connection is you will have to do it only once. If the connection is successful, Captivate will remember the information and use it for all subsequent uploads to that FTP site.

10. In the "File type" pop-down list, select the Captivate file type.

11. Select "Save username and password" to have Captivate remember your FTP login information for future ftp uploads.

12. To have the file treated as a download from the server, select "Zip files."

13. To have the file appear in a Web page, select Export HTML.

14. To have the movie play full screen, select "Full screen."

Note that when it comes to publishing for Web playback, "full screen" means that the SWF will fill the content area of the browser window.

15. Click the Publish button.

Two things happen. First, the SWF or EXE file is generated. When that finishes, you are shown the progress of the FTP upload. When the upload is finished, the dialog box closes and you are returned to the application.

Exporting Your Movie to Microsoft Word

Exporting a movie into Microsoft Word is one of those features that, when you first encounter it, makes you ask, "Why?" Then you discover how invaluable it is.

When a movie is exported to Word, each frame of the document is placed, if you choose, on a separate Word page. Then it occurs to you, especially if you use PowerPoint, this is a great way of generating speaker notes or handouts.

To export your movie to a Word file:

1. Open a Captivate movie and select File > Publish.

   The Publish Options dialog box opens.

2. Select Handouts from the list on the left side of the Publish Options dialog box.

   You will notice the Publish Options dialog box splits into two areas (**Figure 13.11**). The "Export range" area, on the left, is where you decide which slides will be sent to Word. The area on the right, "Layout options," determines how the Word document is formatted.

3. In the "Export range" area, select which slides of the movie are to be exported. Your choices are:
   - ▲ **All** Select to send all of the slides in the movie to Word.
   - ▲ **Current slide** Select to send only the currently open slide to Word.
   - ▲ **Selection** Select to send only the objects selected on the frame to Word.
   - ▲ **Slides** Enter a range of slides to be sent to Word. Use the form of comma-separated slide numbers (for example: 1, 2, 3, 4) and slide ranges (for example: 1-4). You can also mix them (for example: 1-4, 6, 9, 12, 21).

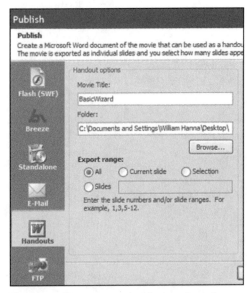

Figure 13.11 You can export handouts and speaker notes to Microsoft Word.

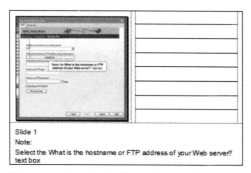

Slide 1
Note:
Select the What is the hostname or FTP address of your Web server?
text box

Figure 13.12 A handout with speaker notes in Microsoft Word.

4. In the "Layout options" area, enter the number of slides to be printed on each page of the Word document.

   The icon at the side changes to show you how the slides will be placed on the page.

5. Select "Caption text" to include any captions in the document.

   This option actually moves the captions from the frame and prints them under the frame in the Word document.

6. Select "Add blank lines for notes" if the document is to be used as a handout.

   This option adds four lines, which can be used for notes, under each frame in the document.

7. Select "Slide notes" to include notes, such as talking points, to the presenter.

   Generally, the user does not see these notes.

8. Select "Include objects (text captions, images etc)" to include all of the objects in the selected slides.

9. Select "Include hidden slides" to include any slides you may have hidden in the movie.

10. Select "Include Mouse Path" to show the mouse path in frames with mouse movement.

11. Click the Publish button.

    The Exporting Frames progress window appears.

12. When the publish process is complete, open the Word document in Microsoft Word (**Figure 13.12**).

Exporting Your Movie to Breeze

Macromedia Breeze enables you to publish your movies to a Breeze server and then make them available to participants in online meetings, presentations, and trainings. If you don't have a Breeze server, Macromedia is now making the product available on a per-use basis. You can obtain full details at https://service.breezecentral.com/cfusion/bots/purchase/index.cfm.

Captivate adds a new dimension to the Breeze experience, because you can now add software simulations and demonstrations to your Breeze meetings.

To export a Captivate Movie to Breeze:

1. Open a Captivate movie and select File > Publish.
   The Publish dialog box opens.

2. Click Breeze from the list on the left side of the dialog box (**Figure 13.13**).

3. Click the Change Server button.
   The "Breeze servers" dialog box opens (**Figure 13.14**).

4. Click the Add button.
   The "Add new service" dialog box opens (**Figure 13.15**).

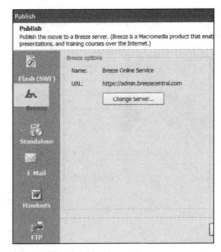

Figure 13.13 If publishing to Breeze, you must publish to your Breeze server.

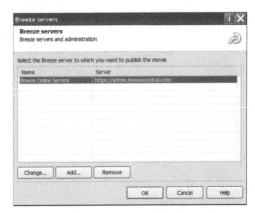

Figure 13.14 Click the Add button to add your Breeze server to the list.

Figure 13.15 Enter the URL to the Breeze server, not the address that connects you to your Breeze server's home page.

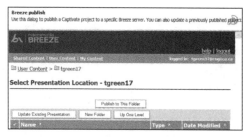

Figure 13.16 Clicking the Publish to This Folder button in Breeze will place the SWF file on the server.

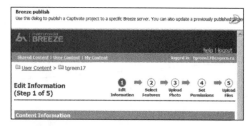

Figure 13.17 Edit the required information for the presentation to be played through Breeze.

5. Enter a name for the server and the URL that links to it.

6. Click OK.

The "Add new service" dialog box closes, and you are returned to the "Breeze servers" dialog box. Your Breeze server is added to the list.

7. Click OK.

The "Breeze servers" dialog box closes, and you are returned to the Captivate Publish dialog box. Your new server appears in the Publish area.

8. Click the Publish button.

Captivate generates the slides Then the "Breeze publish" dialog box opens, and Captivate connects with the Breeze server (providing you have an Internet connection). When the connection is made, you are taken to your Breeze server's login page.

9. Enter your username and password.

Your User Content folder on the Breeze server opens (**Figure 13.16**).

10. Click the Publish to This Folder button.

The Edit Information area opens (**Figure 13.17**).

continues on next page

EXPORTING YOUR MOVIE TO BREEZE

11. Enter the correct content and speaker information, including a title and speaker name, and click Next.

12. Indicate whether you will include an outline, if there will be a pause between slides, and how long to wait for slides without audio, and then click Next.

13. If you want to add features such as permissions, click Customize.

14. Click Next.

Your file is published to the server (**Figure 13.18**).

15. When the upload is finished, click OK.

The "Breeze publish" dialog box closes, and you are returned to the Captivate Publish dialog box.

16. Close the Publish dialog box.

You are returned to the Captivate authoring environment.

✔ Tip

■ If you discover that Captivate has a problem connecting to your Breeze server, the odds are quite good that the URL entered was the one that your Breeze administrator sent you. For example, you may have been told to link to http://breeze.mycompany.org/common/ support/course/startmain.htm. In this case, you would be unable to connect because you are going to a specific location—startmain.htm—on the server, not the server itself. Instead, enter the actual server address (which, in this case, would be http://breeze.mycompany.org).

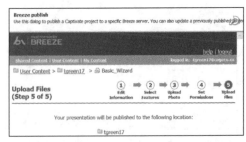

Figure 13.18 Breeze will tell where the Captivate SWF file is being published.

Creating and Exporting Movies for PDA Playback

We are rapidly moving into a media development market where our work is no longer tethered to the desktop computer. In fact, in many respects, the desktop computer is slowly changing from a development platform to a playback device as well. The rise of cell phones, handheld devices, and even tablets has expanded the reach of our development efforts.

For example, hospitals are now using tablets for drug prescriptions. A doctor can enter a prescription into the tablet, the information is checked on the hospital's patient record data base against the patient's current drug regime, and the doctor is informed almost instantly whether the drug prescribed will conflict with any others that the patient is using currently. This has reduced the drug interaction death rates dramatically.

It is only a matter of time until devices become ubiquitous in the area of manufacturing and automated-process troubleshooting. A typical scenario would be a technician walking through a Captivate movie, showing the user the steps necessary to correct a software problem for a machine on the manufacturing floor. This presentation will be delivered through the use of an iPAQ or other device that the technician who uses the machine carries.

Thanks to the popularity of text messaging, also on the horizon is content delivery to cell phones. The hottest device on the market, for obvious reasons, is the Palm Treo, which combines a cell phone and the Palm OS into one device.

You can develop movies for use on handheld devices. That is the good news. The bad news is, developing for devices is not a "one size fits all" proposition. Each device has its own unique screen size and playback requirements.

The bad news is not as bad as it may first appear. The intimate relationship between Captivate and Flash makes the development of your movies rather simple, and the fact the Flash Player (versions 5 and 6, and Lite for cell phones) is available makes delivery a rather uncomplicated process as well.

Just keep in mind that your movies simply can't be resized for Pocket PC export without a serious loss of detail. They need to be captured at the appropriate screen size for the target device.

To record a movie for a handheld device:

1. Launch Captivate and select File > "Record or create a new movie."
   The Capture window opens.

2. Click the Preset Sizes button and select either "220 × 230 with Address Bar" or "220 × 250 without Address Bar" (**Figure 13.19**).

3. Complete the recording and save the file.

✔ Tip

■ Depending on the targeted handheld model, you will be bumping up against the limitations of the Flash Player version that drives the movie. For example, handhelds that use version 4 of the Flash Player can't playback MP3 sounds. This means you should disable mouse clicks and other sounds before recording. Version 5 of the Player can't play FLV files, and Flash Player 6 doesn't understand ActionScript 2.0, which version 7 does.

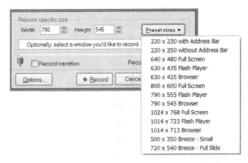

Figure 13.19 Two PDA screen sizes are preset in the Captivate Recording menu.

Picking the Right Handheld Screen Size

The most important aspect of any movie developed for handheld use is the screen size. A common size is the default size of 230 x 250 pixels. Even so, there are various devices on the market where screen size will differ.

One of the features included in Macromedia Flash MX Professional 2004 is a series of templates designed for handheld devices. These templates reflect the screen sizes of the most common handheld operating systems—Windows and Palm. As you can see in **Figure 13.20**, there is quite a difference between the screen area in a Hewlett-Packard iPAQ and that in a Sony Clié.

To use these templates for screen size purposes:

1. Open Flash MX Professional 2004.

2. In the Template area of the start screen, click the Mobile Devices button.
   A list of templates appears.

3. Double-click the template best suited to your target device.
   The white area of the device screen is the Flash stage.

4. Open the Property Inspector and note the stage size.

5. Quit Flash.

Other locations for screen size are the device manufacturer's site and the documentation that came with the device.

If you don't own the device but still wish to test the movie, emulators (except for Pocket PC) and simulators (**Figure 13.21**) are quite common. Usually you can obtain these from the device manufacturer's Web site.

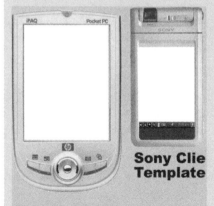

Sony Clie Template

IPaq Template

Figure 13.20 You can use the templates that are installed in Flash MX Professional 2004 to create the correct screen size.

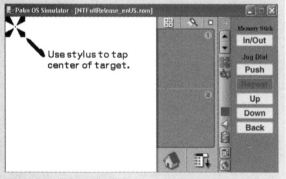

Figure 13.21 You can use simulators to test Captivate movies destined for the Palm OS.

Creating Captivate movies for a Palm handheld device

Unlike the iPAQ and other devices that use a Windows-based OS, the Palm OS, used by Palm and Sony devices, is proprietary and not exactly Windows-friendly. You can play Captivate movies on a Palm handheld device, but you will have to do a bit of extra work to create the movie for playback on a Palm device.

The reason is, though many of the Palm devices are wireless, delivery of your movies through a browser will become an issue. Though the wireless models do have the NetFront browser installed, it doesn't support the Flash Player. Therefore, the file will need to be played from the handheld.

To do this, you will need software that can convert your SWF file to a PDB file for the Palm. The PDB format enables you to install files on Palm. There are several products available that can do this conversion; the most popular are Kinoma Producer and Kinoma Player, available at www.kinoma.com.

After you have the correct software, it is easy to view Captivate SWF files on a Palm.

There are certain limitations to publishing movies for the Palm, including:

◆ Audio is converted to ACPM format.

◆ Colors are converted to the grayscale coloring of the Palm.

◆ Actions are removed, so objects such as click boxes or text entry boxes do not work properly.

✔ Tip

■ If you are recording for a Palm device, keep in mind you will be limited to a recording area of 160 × 120 pixels.

To play movies on a Palm:

1. Install a movie player (for example, Kinoma Player) on your Palm.

2. Install the PDB file that was converted from the SWF file that Captivate generated.

   After the player and movie are installed, you can view the SWF file (now in PDB format) on the Palm.

The Flash Connection with Handheld Devices

Though you can export a Captivate SWF file for use on a handheld, don't forget you can also use Flash to "finish" the file.

For example, you can do a regular recording and export the movie as a SWF file. Then you can import this file into Flash MX 2004 or Flash MX Professional 2004 and edit it accordingly. Just be cognizant of the fact that a movie recorded at 640 x 480 will have to be resized to fit into a screen area that is one-third the size of your movie.

Another approach would be to create a Flash movie that uses ActionScript 1 to load your SWF files as needed. In this instance, you could create a menu that calls the SWF files into the movie when the menu item is selected. This is a very efficient approach to the bandwidth. Instead of the user waiting for one very big SWF to open, the entire Flash movie is composed of a series of small movies that load and open rather quickly.

Also keep in mind that the Flash Player is a stand-alone application as well. This means you could create a single SWF file in Flash that isn't concerned with bandwidth. In this case, the file would be copied directly into the handheld and played from the handheld's desktop. The Sony Clié PEG-TH55 is a good example of this. It contains the Flash Player 5. To load an SWF for playback on this device, you would simply connect the Clié's memory stick to your PC, and then copy the SWF file from the PC to the memory stick. When you open the Flash Player, the list of SWF files appears, and you can choose the one you want to view.

Before developing for a handheld, you also should be very aware of the limitations of the device and the Player. For example, on the Clié, the Flash Player 5 won't play MP3 audio sounds embedded in the SWF. However, the Flash Player 5 on all other devices and desktops will play MP3 sounds. FLV files embedded in your movie will play beautifully through any device using the Flash Player 6 for Pocket PC, but that same FLV will appear as a blank area on devices using the Flash Player 5.

Here are some online and print resources for learning more about Flash Player and handheld devices:

- Macromedia's Mobile and Devices Center: www.macromedia.com/devnet/devices

- Microsoft Pocket PC: www.microsoft.com/windowsmobile/pocketpc

- Pocket PC Developer: www.microsoft.com/windowsmobile/developers

- Palm Developer: www.palmsource.com/developers

- *Flash Enabled,* by Phillip Torrone (Pearson Education, 2002): www.flashenabled.com

- *Flash: The Future,* by Jon Warren Lentz (No Starch Press, 2002): www.flashthefuture.com

INDEX

Numbers

INDEX